Focus on
College Reading and Writing

Peter Lovrick
George Brown College

Australia   Canada   Mexico   Singapore   Spain   United Kingdom   United States

THOMSON

NELSON

**Focus on College Reading and Writing,
First Edition**

by Peter Lovrick

**Associate Vice President,
Editorial Director:**
Evelyn Veitch

**Editor-in-Chief,
Higher Education:**
Anne Williams

Executive Editor:
Laura MacLeod

Marketing Manager:
Shelly Collacutt Miller

Developmental Editor:
Theresa Fitzgerald

Photo Researcher:
Daniela Glass

Permissions Coordinator:
Daniela Glass

Production Coordinator:
Susan Ure

Copy Editor:
Rodney Rawlings

Proofreader:
Liba Berry

Production Coordinator:
Ferial Suleman

Design Director:
Ken Phipps

Interior Design:
Tammy Gay

Cover Design:
Katherine Strain

Cover Image:
© Corel

Compositor:
Carol Magee

Printer:
Thomson West

COPYRIGHT © 2007, by Nelson, a division of Thomson Canada Limited.

Printed and bound in USA
1 2 3 4 10 09 08 07

For more information contact Nelson, 1120 Birchmount Road, Toronto, Ontario, M1K 5G4. Or you can visit our Internet site at http://www.nelson.com

ALL RIGHTS RESERVED. No part of this work covered by the copyright herein may be reproduced, transcribed, or used in any form or by any means—graphic, electronic, or mechanical, including photocopying, recording, taping, Web distribution, or information storage and retrieval systems—without the written permission of the publisher.

For permission to use material from this text or product, submit a request online at www.thomsonrights.com

Every effort has been made to trace ownership of all copyrighted material and to secure permission from copyright holders. In the event of any question arising as to the use of any material, we will be pleased to make the necessary corrections in future printings.

**Library and Archives Canada
Cataloguing in Publication Data**

Main entry under title:

Lovrick, Peter 1953–

    Focus on college reading and writing

ISBN-13: 978-0-17-610391-0
ISBN-10: 0-17-610391-0
1. College readers. 2. English language—Rhetoric—Textbooks.
3. Reading comprehension—Textbooks. I. Title.

PE1408.L6915 2007   808'.0427
C2007-900382-6

Focus on
College Reading and Writing

Table of **Contents**

Preface xi

Introduction   On Target   xv
    Task 1: Setting Your Goals   xvi
   Getting Started   xviii
    Task 2: Meeting the Group   xviii
   Giving Feedback   xix

Part 1   Reading and Restating   1

   Unit 1   **Reading Textbooks Effectively   2**
      Taking Stock   2
         Task 1: Assessing Your Textbook Reading   2
      Types of Reading   5
         Task 2: Identifying Different Reading
            Styles   6
      SQ3R   7
      Trying it Out   10
      SQuestion3R   15
         Task 3: Surveying and Questioning a Textbook
            Reading   15
      SQRead, Recite, Review   17
         Task 4: Reading and Marking a Textbook
            Reading   22
         Task 5: Alternative Systems for Efficient
            Textbook Reading   22
      In Summary   24

   Unit 2   **Mapping and Outlining   25**
      The Concept Map   25
         Task 1: Creating a Task Concept Map   26
         Task 2: Creating a Concept Map of a College
            Lecture   28
      The Mind Map   29

Task 3: Creating a Mind Map from a Textbook
Chapter   31
Outlining   32
Task 4: Creating an Outline from a Textbook
Chapter   36
In Summary   37

Unit 3 Restating   39
Paraphrasing   39
Task 1: Paraphrasing a Text   40
Producing a Summary   41
Task 2: Summarizing a Text   45
Abstracts   46
Task 3: Writing a Descriptive Abstract   47
The Informative Abstract   48
Task 4: Writing an Informative Abstract   49
The Evaluative Summary   50
In Summary   54

Part 2 Essay Writing   55

Unit 4 Characteristics of Essay Writing   56
Task 1: The Writing Sample   57
Task 2: Assessment   57
Some Characteristics of Academic Writing   59
In Summary   60

Unit 5 Planning   61
The Thesis Statement   61
Task 1: Focusing from Subject to Topic   63
Task 2: Differentiating Between Adequate and
Inadequate Thesis Statements   65
Task 3: Developing the Thesis Statement   67
Thinking About the Essay   68
Questioning   69
Task 4: Planning Out a Group Essay   71
Task 5: Planning Out an Individual Essay   74
In Summary   77

Unit 6 Introductions   79
Here's What to Avoid   80
The Hook   81

Task 1: Identifying the Hook   82
Task 2: Identifying Additional Strategies for Starting an Essay   85
Background Information, Purpose, Scope, and Organization   86
Placing the Thesis Statement   88
Task 3: Analysis of Introductions   88
Putting it All Together   94
Task 4: Introduction for the Group Essay   94
Task 5: Introduction for the Individual Essay   95
In Summary   98

Unit 7 Conclusions   99
Here's What to Avoid   100
Restatement of the Thesis   102
Task 1: Rewriting the Thesis Statement   102
Recapitulation   104
Closing Strategy   105
Task 2: Identifying Closing Strategies   105
Task 3: Identifying Additional Strategies for Concluding an Essay   107
Clincher   109
Task 4: Analysis of Conclusions   110
Putting it All Together   114
Task 5: Introduction for the Group Essay   115
Task 6: Conclusion for the Individual Essay   116
In Summary   118

Unit 8 Drafting, Revising, and Editing   119
Drafting   120
Task 1: Drafting   121
Revising   122
Task 2: Evaluating for Support, Unity, and Coherence   124
Task 3: Revising Your Essay   126
Editing   127
Task 4: Improving the Sentences in a Body Paragraph   129
Correcting Errors   130

Task 5: Revising and Editing Your Essay   131
In Summary   132

Part 3 Applications   133

Unit 9 Comparison and Contrast   134

Differentiating Between Comparison and Contrast Writing   134
Determining the Purpose of Comparison and Contrast Writing   135
Selecting Comparison and Contrast Criteria   136
    Task 1: Selecting Comparison and Contrast Criteria   138
Employing Different Organization Strategies   138
    Task 2: Reorganizing a Comparison and Contrast Essay   141
Outlining a Comparison and Contrast Essay   143
    Task 3: Planning a Comparison and Contrast Paper   145
In Summary   147

Unit 10 Argument   149

Defining the Characteristics of an Argument   149
The Claim   150
    Task 1: Determining Claims   151
Identifying Assumptions   152
    Task 2: Identifying Assumptions   153
Using Thesis and Antithesis   154
    Task 3: Identifying the Antithesis and Stating a Refutation   156
Recognizing Logical Fallacies   159
    Task 4: Identifying the Logical Fallacies   160
    Task 5: Identifying Additional Logical Fallacies   162
Outlining an Argument   163
    Task 6: Outlining an Argument   165
    Task 7: Writing the Argument   167
In Summary   168

Unit 11 **Classification** 169
Identifying the Principles of a Classification
    System 169
    Task 1: Principles of Classification 170
Assessing Classification Articles 172
    Task 2: Assessment of Classification
        Articles 172
Outlining a Classification Paper 176
    Task 3: Outlining a Classification Article:
        Individual Essay 177
    Task 4: Writing the Classification Paper 179
In Summary 180

Unit 12 **Cause/Effect** 181
Differentiating Between Immediate and Related
    Causes and Effects 181
Determining Probable Causes and Effects 182
Outlining a Cause / Effect Paper 183
    Task 1: Diagramming a Cause and Effect
        Article 184
    Task 2: Outlining a Cause and Effect
        Essay 185
    Task 3: Writing the Cause and Effect
        Paper 187
In Summary 188

Unit 13 **Research** 189
Identifying the Research Question 190
    Task 1: Determining the Project 190
Conducting Secondary Research 192
    Task 2: Identifying Secondary Sources 195
Reading with a Critical Eye 196
    Task 3: Evaluating Your Research
        Material 197
Conducting Primary Research 201
Determining When to Document 202
Quoting Questions and Paraphrases 203
Assembling a Bibliography 204

Task 4: Formatting a Bibliography   204
Taking Notes   205
Outlining a Research Paper   206
Task 5: Outlining the Research Essay   206
Task 6: Writing the Research Paper   207
In Summary   208

Part 4 Language Mechanics   209

Sentence Fragment   210
Run-on Sentence   213
Pronoun Shifts   217
Modifier Problems   221
Improper Comma Use   224
Article Problems   228
Faulty Parallel Structure   231

Answer Key   235

Sentence Fragment Exercise   235
Run-on Sentence Exercise   236
Pronoun Shifts Exercise   237
Modifier Problems Exercise   239
Comma Problems Exercise   239
Article Problems Exercise   240
Faulty Parallel Structure Exercise   241

Closing Notes   243

Task 1: Assessing the Assignments   243
Task 2: Personal Objectives for This Book   244
Task 3: Preparing a Refection on Your Writing   245

Preface

Postsecondary study requires you to read textbooks and write academic essays. This book gives you two goals to work toward. The first is to develop your academic reading and writing skills so that you get the most out of your textbooks and write effective papers. The second is to help your classmates develop their skills, too. To reach these goals, you will work through a series of tasks that ask you to discover for yourself the strategies and techniques of efficient textbook reading and effective academic essay writing. The tasks ask you to work with other people, investigate different resources, and try out specific techniques in focused assignments. As you help other people hone their reading and writing skills, you will develop your own. In addition, as others help you, they will also learn valuable lessons.

The approach in *Focus on College Reading and Writing* is for you to take charge of your own learning. That means you need to take the initiative—to find out rather than wait to be told. It also means that you share what you discover. Finally, you need to be a creative problem solver. Apply that problem solving to the issues around working with others for common goals and to finding the information you need to successfully complete the assignments.

Here's what to expect.

You will work in small groups. The cooperative learning approach in this book asks you to work with other people and pool your knowledge. It isn't necessary to agree with everything you hear. It is necessary, though, to be a good listener, to give everyone a chance to contribute, and to critically evaluate how helpful the discussion is to your own writing. Each unit presents you with a series of problems or tasks designed for four people, but you can still carry them out with a different number. That's where your problem solving comes in. You have many options. If you have fewer than four people, you might decide to split up the work of the fourth person, or visit another group for the missing piece. If you have more than four, you can have two people work on one task, or work out a rotation so that a different person is an observer each time. Your group is in charge of how you manage the issues and challenges. Be creative.

You will keep a group portfolio. Your group will keep a common portfolio. Your professor will give it to your group at the beginning of class and collect it at the end. It is your communication tool with the professor. Use it to submit assignments, outlines, and forms. Your professor will use it to give you feedback, evaluations, announcements, and other material.

You will present individual work. You will meet in groups, but your writing is your own. Keep in mind that as you prepare your essays, the help and advice of other people will give you the tools you need to refine your work so that it becomes the best it can possibly be.

You will work with textbooks in your field. After working with examples from various textbooks presented throughout the units on reading and writing, you will work with the textbooks you are currently using in your other courses. You will integrate the reading and writing tasks throughout this book with the material that you are studying in your program.

You will uncover the information you need as you need it. This book does not lay out all the information that the author has decided you should have. Instead, your group will look at the different tasks, decide what it needs, and go get it. Your answers may be very different from those of other groups working on the same projects. Far from anything being wrong with that, it will be a wonderful opportunity to see different perspectives in action.

You have several resources to work with to accomplish the tasks set out for you.

The Internet

The Internet offers a wide variety of websites that you can consult for this course. You will find helpful addresses at different points in the book, but look beyond these sites to find whatever information you need to complete the writing tasks. Be creative in your search and use alternative search terms. "Textbook reading," "academic reading," "essay writing," and "college writing" are just some of the terms that will take you to sites offering advice and tips that you can bring to your group discussions. Look at the educational sites first. You can identify them by the extensions ".ca" or ".edu."

Libraries

Several excellent texts on essay writing are on the market. Two wonderful books are Clifford Werier, Sandra Scarry, and John Scarry's *The Essay Workplace*, and Joanne Buckley's *Fit to Print*. Check them out and see what else is on the shelves of your public or college library. Some of the tasks ahead will ask you to do some research into specific components of academic reading and writing. Look at the literature available and bring the results to your group.

Your Professor or Teacher

Your professor or teacher has expertise in academic reading and writing. Consult him or her as a special resource. Test ideas, ask questions, and invite comments on the ideas your group develops. Find out what special requirements your professor might have regarding style and form.

Your Own Experience

Many of the tasks in the units of this book ask you to reflect on your work as well as on the work of your group members. The book will give you different tools to do just that. You will assess the work of your group partners and think critically about what you have done. Use this experience to discover what works or doesn't work. Analyze that experience in the tasks ahead and share what you learn from that analysis with your group members.

This book sets up a series of experiences for you. Work through the experiences and be prepared to grow.

About the Author

Peter Lovrick has been a professor at George Brown College since 1987. He teaches college English, presentation skills, technical/business writing, report and thesis writing, and communications for internationally trained professionals. His CV includes teaching philosophical writing, philosophical reading, and homiletics. He has also taught the History of Chinese Performing Arts at the University of Toronto for over 10 years and writing, modern drama, and Shakespeare at Soochow University in Taiwan.

Peter has also authored *Focus on Presentations* (2006) published by Thomson Press and *Chinese Opera: Images and Stories* (1997), published by the University of British Columbia Press, which was shortlisted for the 1997 Kiriyama Book Prize.

He and his wife, Theresa, have three beautiful children: Adrian, Katrina, and Anthony. Ordained as a Permanent Deacon for the Archdiocese of Toronto, Peter is also currently working on a doctorate in preaching.

Introduction

Here's what you'll work on in the introduction.

- Setting individual objectives
- Writing a goal statement
- Creating a work group
- Interviewing a team member
- Writing a draft paragraph
- Reviewing a draft paragraph
- Writing a final paragraph

You are faced with a number of academic tasks in postsecondary studies. One of those tasks is giving presentations. Another book in this series, *Focus on Presentations*, provides a series of collaborative learning exercises to help you hone your presentation skills. This book, *Focus on College Reading and Writing*, focuses on two other academic tasks, reading textbooks and writing essays.

Many people approach these tasks directly without reflecting on the task or refining a strategy. In that way, they miss an opportunity to get the most out of what they read and put the most in what they write. Academic reading is different from other kinds, just as academic writing is different from other kinds of writing. Thinking about the differences will help you develop and employ specific and effective strategies. *Focus on College Reading and Writing* takes you through a process that helps you learn and apply them to focused work in your field.

You will use the textbooks for your other courses in this one as a source for your reading and writing tasks. That way, you will integrate the techniques developed here with your field of study. You will get the perspectives of team members that will help you refine and polish your work until it is the best it can possibly be. At the same time, you will have the opportunity to develop your own academic skills by helping team members who are working on the same task. You will also share your experience and learn from the experience of others. Some of the insights your classmates have discovered will work for you while others won't.

Improving your academic reading and writing skills is not a matter of listening to lectures, but of doing and reflecting on the doing. That is what you will do in this book.

On Target

The first thing to do before working on the units in this book is to establish your goals. When you do that right at the beginning, you ensure that you will be focused on all the benefits that the book's tasks and instruction can bring. In the end, it helps you set the tone for a positive learning experience. Take a few moments and think about it. When you get to the end of this book, you will work on a task that asks you to evaluate whether you have reached some or all of the targets you set for yourself.

TASK ONE Setting Your Goals

Here's what to do. First, in the box entitled "Personal Objectives" below write down as many specific objectives as you want. Here are some questions to help you with this task.

- What specific aspects of reading textbooks would you like to work on?
- What specific aspects of writing essays would you like to work on?
- What kinds of skills would you like to learn?
- What is it that you would like for yourself, when you have finished this book?
- Imagine yourself writing the final essay in this course or in some other course. What skills would you like to be able to demonstrate then?

Hint

Keep your answers very specific and focused on particular skills, so that at the end of the book you will be able to say whether you have developed them.

PERSONAL OBJECTIVES

```
┌─────────────────────────────────────────────────┐
│                                                 │
│                                                 │
│                                                 │
│                                                 │
└─────────────────────────────────────────────────┘
```

Now, look over the different individual objectives you wrote in the box above. Do some of them connect? Do some specific objectives belong to larger goals? Do one or two main goals stand out? Spend a little time reconsidering your points and then work out a general goal statement in full sentences. If you have only one or two sentences, or a full paragraph, that's okay. Think about how you would answer the following question: What would you like to achieve here?

Hint

While an objective is a specific skill you would like to develop, a goal is the larger destination to which the objectives point. Think of it this way: Why do you want to accomplish the specific objectives? Why is it important to reach each one of those targets?

GENERAL GOAL STATEMENT

As you go through this book, you will likely discover other skills that you will want to work on. Just write them in the "Additional Objectives" box below as they come up. Refer back to this page at various times as you move through this book to see how you're doing. Are you making progress? Are you mastering the skills and reaching the goals you set for yourself?

ADDITIONAL OBJECTIVES

Getting Started

To move ahead with the projects in this text, you need to get into a work group. The tasks work best if your group is small and has an even number of people. Four works well. If that isn't possible for your group, divide the instructions for each of the tasks as evenly as possible among the group members. Each person needs to take a number that identifies him or her as 1, 2, 3, or 4. The group members will help you accomplish your goal statement and meet your specific objectives, just as you will help them do the same. This means pooling ideas, contributing to the completion of tasks, and critiquing each other's work.

The place to start, then, is to get to know each other a little better.

TASK TWO   Meeting the Group

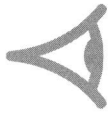

Person 1: Please read the instructions below and facilitate this activity.

Person 2: Please keep track of the time and inform the group for each of the parts.

Part One: 20 minutes

1. The group manager (Person 1) makes sure everyone in the group has a partner. Each person is designated A or B.
2. A interviews B for 10 minutes. A takes notes to find out whatever B is willing to share about likes, dislikes, background, personality, hopes, goals, or anything that comes to mind. B also reads out the goal statement from Task One.
3. B interviews A for 10 minutes and takes notes. A, too, reads out the goal statement from Task One and answers questions on whatever he or she is willing to share.

Part Two: 15 minutes

Everyone takes 15 minutes to organize the notes from the interview and write a paragraph that introduces the person to the team.

Hint

Rearrange the information from the interview. Rather than reciting questions and answers in the order asked, put all the information together to create a total picture of a person. Finally, work out a beginning, middle, and end.

Part Three: 15 minutes

1. Give your draft paragraph to the person you interviewed.
2. When you get a paragraph, read it and write any comments you care to at the bottom. Here is what you can write on the draft:
    - Correct any mistaken or incomplete information.
    - Add information that would clarify things.
    - Circle any parts of the sentences that you think might have a spelling, grammar, or punctuation problem.
    - Make any suggestion that you think would help the writer put together an even better paragraph.
3. Return the paragraph to the writer.
4. When you get your paragraph back, read the comments.
5. Rewrite the paragraph, taking the comments into account.

Part Four

Starting with person number 1, each person reads his or her paragraph to the group. Sign the paragraph and place it in the portfolio.

This task summarized what you will do throughout this book and in your academic studies. You

- collected information,
- organized it,
- wrote a draft,
- obtained some feedback, and
- made changes based on the feedback, and after reading the work of your group members. This process is the foundation for what you will do throughout the book.

Giving Feedback

As you look at the specific techniques in the various units, you will be able to give more and more concrete suggestions. Each of the units ahead will give you some specific questions to ask before you read the work of your group members. For now, ask yourself if the material is clear, complete enough for the task, and readable. That is:

- Do you understand it?
- Does the writing provide what it needs to accomplish its task?
- Is it a smooth read?

Don't worry about correcting any mistakes in language mechanics for the writer. Simply circle anything you know or suspect might be wrong. That will draw the sentence to the attention of the writer, who will then check it out. Part 4 of this book lists some of the most common language mechanics errors in student writing. As you become familiar with them throughout the course, you might write the section number of the problem beside the error. For example, if you notice that an article is missing, you might circle the word and write "4.6" beside it. Part 4 also provides useful website addresses for you to use when checking out grammar problems. Finally, ask your group members and your professor for help in solving language mechanics problems.

Part 1

Reading and Restating

Unit 1: Reading Textbooks Effectively
Unit 2: Mapping and Outlining
Unit 3: Restating

Advanced postsecondary work involves reading academic texts and writing academic essays. Part 1 of this book focuses on reading, the first main task you will encounter in postsecondary education. Reading a textbook requires a specific method to help you get the most out of what you read and to retain it. Unit 1 introduces you to that strategy. One of the best ways to ensure that you have fully understood your texts and to fully integrate the material is to recast it in different ways. Units 2 and 3 present different methods for representing the material in your texts. Together, these techniques form a strategy for you to use with the textbooks that you will read throughout your program.

UNIT 1

Reading Textbooks Effectively

Here's what you'll work on in this unit.

- Assessing your reading ability
- Identifying different types of reading
- Applying the SQ3R reading strategy
- Researching alternative reading methods

Your postsecondary work starts with reading. You will have to read a large variety of academic material for the different courses you take. Your main reading is likely to focus on your textbooks. In some cases, you may have very little time to get through a great deal of material. As the semester goes by and the work piles up, it sometimes can seem all too overwhelming. That's where effective reading strategies come in. For many people, the difference between doing passable work and doing well is using a reading technique that gets the most out of a text in an efficient way.

Taking Stock

The first thing to do is take stock of what you're good at and where you could improve.

TASK ONE   Assessing Your Textbook Reading

One of your professors has given you a reading assignment to prepare for a class discussion. Take 10 minutes and read the following passage from Beckman and Rigby's college text *Foundations of Marketing*.

The Brand Name Should Be Legally Protectable

S. C. Johnson and Son, makers of Off, lost a court case against Bug Off since it was held that OFF was an improper trademark because it was not unusual enough to distinguish it from other, similar products.

When all offerings in a class of products become generally known by the brand name of the first or leading brand in that product class, the brand name may be ruled a descriptive or **generic name**, after which the original owner loses all right to the exclusive use of it. Generic names like nylon, zipper, kerosene, linoleum, escalator, and shredded wheat were once brand names.

Bayer's Aspirin is the only ASA tablet permitted to carry that protected trademark in Canada. All other acetylsalicylic acid tablets are called ASA. In the United States, because Bayer did not protect its trade name, the generic name "aspirin" is given to all acetylsalicylic acid tablets. Most drug purchasers there would not know what an ASA tablet is.

There is a difference between brand names that are legally generic and those that could be perceived to be generic in the eyes of many consumers. Jell-O is a brand name owned exclusively by General Foods. But to most grocery purchasers the name Jell-O is the descriptive generic name for gelatine dessert. Legal brand names—such as Formica, Xerox, Frigidaire, Kodak, Frisbee, Styrofoam, Kleenex, Scotch Tape, Fiberglas, Band-Aid, and Jeep—are often used by consumers in a descriptive manner. Xerox is such a well-known brand name that it is frequently used as a verb. British and Australian consumers often use the brand name Hoover as a verb for vacuuming.

To prevent their brand names from being ruled descriptive and available for general use, companies must take deliberate steps to inform the public of their exclusive ownership of brand names. They may resort to legal action in cases of infringement. The Eastman Kodak Company developed a series of advertisements around the theme "If it isn't Eastman, it isn't a Kodak." The Coca-Cola Company and many other companies use the ® symbol for registration immediately after their brand names. Coca-Cola sends letters to newspapers and novelists and other writers who use the name Coke® with a lowercase first letter, informing them that the trademark is owned by Coca-Cola. Walt Disney Co. actively protects its brand names and is prepared to sue if necessary. West Edmonton Mall learned this the hard way when it lost a ten-year court battle with Disney over its indoor amusement park named Fantasyland. It lost an estimated $5 million in replacing all the Fantasyland signs and paraphernalia associated with the name. Thus, companies may fact the ironic dilemma of attempting to retain the exclusive rights to a brand name that, chiefly due to the success of their own marketing efforts, could become generic to a large market segment if they do not take appropriate steps to protect their trademark.

Since any dictionary word may eventually be ruled to be a generic name, some companies create new words to use for brand names. Such brand names as Keds, Rinso, Kodak have obviously been created by their owners.

For the marketing manager, the brand serves as the cornerstone around which the product's image is developed. Once consumers have been made aware of a particular brand, its appearance becomes further advertising for the firm. The Shell Oil Company symbol is instant advertising to motorists who view it while driving. Well-known brands also allow the firm to escape some of the rigours of price competition. Although any chemist will confirm that all ASA tablets contain the same amount of the chemical acetylsalicylic acid, Bayer has developed so strong a reputation that it can successfully market its Aspirin at a higher price than competitive products. Similarly, McDonald's "golden arches" attract customers to its outlets.

The "attractiveness" of Bayer, McDonald's, and hundreds of other respected brands is called **brand equity**. Brand equity really represents the value customers (and the stock

> markets) place on the sum of the history the customer has had with a brand. If a brand has consistently been associated with high quality and resulted in high customer satisfaction, the equity of that brand will be high. Sony is a valuable brand, with high brand equity, because the company has delivered high-quality electronic products for decades. On the other hand, the Russian car manufacturer Lada has struggled for years to overcome an initial public perception of poor quality. Lada is not considered a particularly valuable brand in North America.
>
> We shall see that many brand-related decisions—from initially choosing a name, to protecting the name in court if necessary, to brand extension strategies—are driven by a company's desire to create, preserve, and exploit brand equity.
>
> Brand equity has four components. *Brand awareness* is a measure of how well and widely a brand is known. *Perceived quality* reflects customers' assessments of the quality of the product that carries a particular brand. *Brand associations* are the connections customers make between the brand and other aspects of their experience and understanding. For example, Nike tends to be associated with high performance as well as individualism. Brand loyalty is the single most important aspect of brand equity. *Brand loyalty* reflects the level of commitment a customer has to a particular brand. This aspect of brand equity is so important that we need to discuss it in more detail.
>
> **Source:** From Foundations of Marketing, Eight Canadian Edition by BECKMAN. 2003. Reprinted with Permission of Nelson, a division of Thomson Learning: www.thomsonrights.com. Fax 800-730-2215.

Part One

Answer the following questions for yourself. You do not need to share your answers with anyone else in your group.

Did you read the passage as quickly as you would have liked?

Yes ❏   No ❏

Did you at any point skip back to reread for understanding?

Yes ❏   No ❏

Did you hesitate over any new vocabulary?

Yes ❏   No ❏

Do you remember all the main points without looking back at what you have just read?

Yes ❏   No ❏

Are you able to clearly explain the passage in your own words to someone who has not read it?

Yes ❏   No ❏

What is the main message of the section?

What are the main points made?

Part Two: 15 minutes

Work together to prepare group answers to the last two questions of Part One.

Person 2: Facilitate a discussion on the textbook reading without looking at the text itself. Give everyone an opportunity to contribute to a final group answer for these questions:
- What is the main message of the section?
- What are the main points made?

Person 3: Take notes and write down the group consensus.

Person 4: Keep track of the time and give the group a three-minute warning.

Person 1: Be prepared to give your answers to the class.

Hint

Listen carefully and keep track of how the different groups report the main message. What words did they choose to use or emphasize? Does your group's message statement need to change?

Types of Reading

You read different material in different ways depending on what it is and what purpose you might have in picking it up. Newspaper editors, for example, know that most people read across a newspaper looking at the first paragraph of many stories. The number of people who read the second paragraph of each story drops significantly. Most readers will select a story and read as long as it holds their interest or until they get the information they need. They then move to something else. The percentage of people who actually read an entire story from beginning to end is the lowest. Consequently, news article structure matches the way people read. Newspaper articles don't use an essay-style introduction leading up to main points in the body. Instead, the first paragraphs present the most important information up front—usually answering the question "What happened?" The rest of the article fills in the details, usually going from most important to least important information on the assumption that fewer people are reading the later paragraphs.

You wouldn't read a newspaper, a telephone book, or a novel in the same way. Improving reading skills depends on tailoring your method to the kind of reading material and the reason you are reading it in the first place.

TASK TWO   Identifying Different Reading Styles: 15 minutes

Discuss the following reading tasks. Determine the purpose and the reading methods that best fit each. The first one is done for you.

Person 3: Facilitate this task. Give everyone an opportunity to contribute.

Person 4: Record the results as you go for the group portfolio.

Person 1: Keep track of the time and give everyone a three-minute warning.

Person 2: Report on your group answers in a class discussion to follow.

Type of Reading	Purpose	Method
Newspaper	To obtain information on a wide variety of current events	• Moving across the titles • Reading the first paragraph of several stories • Reading parts of some stories • Reading all of only those stories of particular interest
Engrossing novel		
Telephone book, catalogue, or TV magazine		
Equipment manual		
Canada Tax Guide		

Type of Reading	Purpose	Method
Popular magazine		
Encyclopedia article		
Video game manual		

Your work on Task Two demonstrates a variety of purposes and reading styles. It also shows that you just don't read everything the same way. Sometimes you read carefully word for word. At other times you skim though to get the gist of things. Yet at other times you don't want the gist of the whole document, but rather only a piece of information, and so you just scan the page. Or you may use a combination of close reading, skimming, and scanning.

Textbooks also require a targeted reading strategy. There is a big difference between reading something you choose to read on your own and reading something assigned to you. The least productive thing to do when assigned a chapter in a textbook is just to sit down and start reading. It won't be long before distractions creep in, and if the reading is not particularly interesting you might find yourself getting lost. Getting the most out of a textbook means applying particular reading techniques.

SQ3R

Francis P. Robinson, a psychologist at Ohio State University, began work in the 1940s on a model for reading textbooks that has helped many students. SQ3R is a process for methodically reading academic texts to get the most of out them for your studies. It is called SQ3R because the process is **S**urvey, **Q**uestion, **R**ead, **R**ecite, and **R**eview. Many variations of SQ3R are available, but are firmly based on Robinson's work. Here is one way you can apply it.

SurveyQ3R

Surveying the text chapter or article that you are assigned means getting the lay of the land before you plough in. You get an overall picture of what the article is about, where it is heading, and how it is organized. That means when you do start reading you already have some reference points and context so that the ideas hang together and make sense.

Here's how you survey.

Read the Title

First, take a good look at the title and then the subheadings if there are any. The title gives you clarity about the topic. A careful look at the title can also give you insight into what is coming. For example, the title of an article that appeared in Newsweek, "What TV Does to Kids," tells you a number of things:

- The subject is television.
- The topic is television and children.
- Finally, one word in the title gives you an indication of what the overall message is. The title indicates that the article is what television does "to" rather than "for" children. That means that the article is likely focused on negative effects rather than positive ones. In fact, that is what actually happens in the article.

Read the Subheadings

Second, browse through the reading looking for subheadings. The subheadings give you an indication of how the article is going to achieve its purpose by showing you how the material is organized. Section III of Rosalie Chappell's text *Social Welfare in Canadian Society* is titled "Ideological Influences on Social Welfare." The subheadings show you just what those influences are before you read a single line.

>Political Ideology
>
>Conservatism
>
>Liberalism
>
>Socialism and Social Democracy
>
>Religious Ideology
>
>Judeo-Christian Views of Charity
>
>Social Welfare and the Roman Catholic Church
>
>Protestant Influences on Social Welfare
>
>Religious Ideologies and the Shaping of Social Welfare

Looking at the subheadings shows you that all the material in the chapter breaks down into two main sections: political and religious influences. You can expect that the article will provide information on political ideologies like conservatism, and that the discussion involving religion will focus on Judeo-Christian influence.

Read the Opening and Closing Sections

Third, pay close attention to the opening and closing sections. The first sections are usually introductions that give essential background or define a key term. You can also determine the purpose and main message of the chapters, usually in a thesis statement. Closing sections are often conclusions that summarize or emphasize main points. In other cases, they are a bridge making important connections to the next section of the text. Closing sections can also draw out implications. By reading the first and the last paragraphs you will get a sense of where the article or chapter is going and what its main concerns are. Put that together with what you have learned from looking at the title and subheadings and you already are beginning to grasp material before even having read it.

Here is the opening of Chappell's "Ideological Influences on Social Welfare."

> There are diverse opinions about how people should behave as individuals with others; however, when widely shared opinions converge, they sometimes create ideologies. An **ideology** is a paradigm or belief system that shapes our perception of the world and guides the ways we interact with that world. Since all ideologies are subjective, they cannot be proven right or wrong by objective measures. Ideologies nevertheless have the power to influence the types of formal institutions we develop in our society, including social welfare. Indeed, our opinions about people in need and the giving of "charity" are largely the result of prevailing ideas, values and attitudes in society.
>
> Canada's social welfare system is not the product of any one ideology; rather, that system reflects a number of ideologies that have arisen in our history in response to various social, economic, and political developments. This section explores some of the ideologies that have shaped social welfare in Canada.
>
> ***Source:*** From Social Welfare in Canadian Society, Third Edition, by CHAPPELL. 2005. Reprinted with permission of Nelson, a division of Thomson Learning: www.thomsonrights.com. Fax 800-730-2215.

This introduction
- gives a clear working definition needed to understand the chapter
- provides background on the relationship between ideologies and formal institutions
- states the purpose of the section

Hint

Introductions can run from a single paragraph to several paragraphs long. If the text has subheadings throughout, the introduction is likely all the text up until the first subheading.

The last subheading in the section is "Religious Ideologies and the Shaping of Social Welfare." It makes the point that although social welfare is secular, it has been formed by religious influences. The section ends this way:

> We can expect that as Canada becomes more culturally diverse, social welfare programs and services will evolve to reflect a rich blend of Christian and non-Christian ideologies.

Looking at the title, subheading, opening, and closing gives you a strong foundation for understanding and remembering what you read.

Read the Supporting Material

Fourth, look over the material that is not part of the actual text. Textbooks often have column notes, boxes with highlighted information, and visuals with captions. These are usually examples which will help make the ideas more concrete.

Skim the Text

Fifth, skim through the chapter by reading the first one or two lines of each paragraph. In many cases, that first line will be the topic sentence giving the main point of the paragraph. In other cases, it will at least indicate what the topic is going to be.

The important thing to keep in mind is that surveying should only take a few minutes. You are not reading the article, but just getting ready to read it. On the other hand, those few minutes are well worth the investment. Students who preview generally read faster and retain more. That is because the survey work provides them with a map of where they are going. When they actually read, they encounter familiar markers and can link the information not only with what came before but with topics and ideas that are coming up. In this way, the writing makes more sense and the points are etched deeper in their memory. In fact, Robinson reports that students in his study who used SQ3R moved up 22 percentiles from 34 to 56 in average rate. Not only did the reading rate rise, but the comprehension rate rose as well (see Francis Pleasant Robinson, *Effective Study*, 4th ed. [New York: Harper & Row, 1970]).

Trying It Out

Take a look at the following section from the textbook *Developmental Psychology: Childhood and Adolescence* by David Shaffer, Eileen Wood, and Teena Willoughby. Do not read the article; just take three minutes to survey it by

1. reading the title and subheadings
2. looking at supplemental material like visuals or highlighted words
3. reading the opening and closing paragraphs and
4. skimming the beginning of each paragraph.

Child Development in the Computer Age

Like television, computer technology has the potential to influence children's learning and lifestyles. But in what ways? Most educators today believe that computer technology is an effective supplement to classroom instruction that helps children to learn more and to have more fun doing so. By 1999, there was one computer for every nine elementary-school students, one for every eight lower-secondary students, and one for every upper-secondary students (Statistics Canada, 2000a). Eighty-eight percent of elementary-school and 97 percent of secondary-school students attend a school that has access to the Internet for instruction. In fact, Canada ranks among the highest in the world in terms of computer access at school and at home. In 2000, close to 90 percent of young Canadians reported having a computer at home and 70 percent had access to the Internet. So computers are now widely accessible, but do they really help children to learn, think, or create? Is there a danger that young "hackers" will become so enamoured of computer technology and so reclusive or socially unskilled that they risk being ostracized by their peers?

Computer Technology in the Classroom

Studies reveal that classroom use of computers produces many benefits. For example, elementary-school students do learn more and report that they enjoy school more when they receive at least some **computer-assisted instruction (CAI)** (Clements & Natasi, 1992; Collis et al., 1996; Lepper & Gurtner, 1989). Many CAI programs are simply drills that start at a student's current level of mastery and present increasingly difficult problems, often intervening with hints or clues when progress breaks down. Other, more elaborate forms of CAI are guided tutorials that rely less on drill and more on the discovery of important concepts and principles in the context of highly motivating, thought-provoking games. Regular use of drill programs during the early grades does seem to improve children's basic reading and math skills, particularly for disadvantaged students and other low achievers (Clements & Natasi, 1992; Fletcher-Flinn & Gravatt, 1995; Lepper & Gurtner, 1989). However, the benefits of CAI are greatest when children receive at least some exposure to highly involving guided tutorials as well as simple drills. In addition, having access to computers does not necessarily mean that they are being used effectively. One study of Canadian

15-year-olds revealed that only 39 percent of students reported that they used a computer at school almost every day or a few times a week (Statistics Canada, 2002d).

Word Processing. Aside from their drill function, computers are also *tools* that can further children's basic writing and communications skills (Clements, 1995). Once children can read and write, using word-processing programs eliminates much of the drudgery of handwriting and increases the likelihood that children will revise, edit, and polish their writing (Clements & Natasi, 1992). Furthermore, computer-prompted metacognitive strategies help students think about what they want to say and organize their thoughts into more coherent essays.

Internet Use. In a study of Internet use in the classroom, about one-third of elementary-school and over half of secondary-school students had used e-mail, and two-thirds had used the World Wide Web for educational purposes (Statistics Canada, 2000a). An increasing number of high-school teachers and university/college professors offer courses and content on-line, giving students the flexibility to learn at their convenience. These instructors often stimulate discussion of course material on-line, a strategy they believe will reduce concerns about speaking in public while inducing students to ponder course materials more deeply and critically (Hara, Bonk, & Angeli, 2000; Murray, 2000). ... [E]ducators and students report many benefits of the Internet for ease of access to information and for communication purposes[;] research on its benefits, however, is still in its infancy.

Learning by computer is an effective complement to classroom instruction and an experience that can teach young children to collaborate.

Computer Programming and Cognitive Growth. Finally, it seems that teaching students to *program* (and thus *control*) a computer can have important benefits such as fostering mastery motivation and self-efficacy as well as promoting novel modes of thinking that are unlikely to emerge from computer-assisted academic drills. In his own research, Douglas Clements (1991, 1995) trained first- and third-graders in Logo, a computer language that allows children to translate their drawings into input statements so that they can reproduce their creations on the computer monitor. Although Clements's "Logo children" performed no better on achievement tests than age-mates who participated in the more usual kinds of computer-assisted academic exercises, Logo users scored higher on tests of Piagetian concrete-operational abilities, mathematical problem-solving strategies, and creativity (Clements, 1995; Natasi & Clements, 1994). And because children must learn to detect errors and debug their Logo programs to get them to work, programming fosters thinking about one's own thinking and is associated with gains in metacognitive knowledge (Clements, 1990).

Clearly, these findings are important because they suggest that computers are useful not only for teaching children academic lessons but also for helping them to think in new ways.

Social Impacts. Are young computer users at risk of becoming reclusive, socially unskilled misfits as some people have feared? Hardly! Children often use home computers as a toy to *attract* playmates (Crook, 1992; Kee, 1986). And research conducted in classrooms reveals that students who are learning to program or solve problems with a computer are (1) likely to *seek* collaborative solutions to the challenges they face and (2) more inclined to persist after experiencing problems when they are collaborating with a peer (Natasi & Clements, 1993, 1994; Weinstein, 1991). Conflicts may arise should collaborators disagree about how to approach a problem; yet the strong interest that collaborators frequently display when facing a programming challenge often supersedes their differences and encourages amiable methods of resolving conflicts (Natasi & Clements, 1993). So computer technology seems to promote (rather than impede) peer interactions—contacts that are often lively and challenging and that appear to foster the growth of socially skilled behaviours.

Concerns About Computer Technology

What are the danger signs of exposing children to computer technology? Three concerns are raised most often.

Concerns About Video Games. The results of one recent survey in British Columbia revealed that more than 80 percent of adolescents in that province play video games at least occasionally (Media Analysis Laboratory, 1998). Fifty percent of the sample spent less that three hours a week on video games, but 25 percent spent between three and seven hours a week and the remainder over seven hours a week. It is not that this activity necessarily diverts children from schoolwork and peer activities, as many parents have assumed; time spent playing at the computer is usually a substitute for other leisure activities, most notably TV viewing. Nevertheless, critics have feared (and early evidence suggests) that heavy exposure to such popular and incredibly violent video games as *Alien Intruder* and *Mortal Kombat* can instigate aggression and cultivate aggressive habits in the same ways that televised violence does (Fling et al., 1992; Williams, 1998).

The critics' concerns are valid ones. At least three surveys of fourth- to twelfth-graders found moderate positive correlations between the amount of time spent playing video games and real-world aggressive behaviours (Dill & Dill, 1998). The experimental evidence is even more revealing: one study of third- and fourth- graders (Kirsch, 1998) and another study of college students (Anderson & Dill, 2000) found that participants randomly assigned to play violent video games displayed a strong hostile attributional bias toward later ambiguous provocations and significantly more aggressive behaviour than their counterparts who had played nonviolent video games. And because violent game players are *actively* involved in planning and performing aggressive acts and *reinforced* for their successful symbolic violence, it has been argued that the aggression-instigating effects of violent video games is probably far greater than that of violent television programming, in which children are only passively exposed to aggression and violence (Anderson & Dill, 2000; Larson, 2001). Clearly, these early findings suggest that parents should be at least as concerned about what their children are playing on-screen as they are about what their children watch.

Concerns About Social Inequalities. Other critics are concerned that the computer revolution may leave some groups of children behind, lacking in skills that are required in our increasingly computer-dependent society—commonly referred to as the "digital divide." For example, children from economically disadvantaged families may be exposed to computers at school but are unlikely to have them at home (Rocheleau, 1995). Also, boys are far more likely than girls to take an interest in computers and to sign up for computer camps. Why? Probably because computers are often viewed as involving mathematics, a traditionally masculine subject, and many available computer games are designed to appeal to boys (Lepper, 1985; Ogletree & Williams, 1990). Yet this gender gap is narrowing, largely due to the increasing use of computers to foster *cooperative* classroom learning activities that girls typically enjoy (Collis et al., 1996; Rocheleau, 1995).

Concerns About Internet Exposure. The proliferation on home computers and on-line services means that literally millions of children and adolescents around the world may now have unsupervised access to the Internet and the World Wide Web. Clearly, exposure to information available on the Web can be a boon to students researching topics pertinent to their school assignments. Nevertheless, many parents and teachers are alarmed about potentially unsavoury Web influences. For example, children and adolescents chatting with acquaintances on-line have been drawn into cybersexual relationships and, occasionally, to meetings with and exploitation by their adult chat-mates (Curry, 2000; Donnerstein & Smith, 2001; Williams, 1998). Furthermore, the Web is (or has been) a primary recruiting tool for such dangerous cults as Heaven's Gate and hate organizations such as the Ku Klux Klan (Downing, 2001). So there are reasons to suspect that unrestricted Web access could prove harmful to some children and adolescents, and additional research aimed at estimating those risks is sorely needed.

Like television, then, computer technology may prove to be either a positive or a negative force on development, depending on how it is used. Outcomes may be less than positive if a young person's primary uses of the computer are to fritter away study time chatting about undesirable topics on-line, or to hole up alone, zapping mutant aliens from space. But the news may be positive for youngsters who use computer technology to learn, create, and collaborate amicably with siblings and peers.

Source: From Developmental Psychology: Childhood and Adolescence, Second Edition by SHAFFER. 2005. Reprinted with permission of Nelson, a division of Thomson Learning wwwthomsonrights.com. Fax 800-730-2215.

Here is what can be learned from surveying this text.

Title	The subject is child development.
	The focus is on the effects of computers.
Subheadings	The section is organized into two main parts. The first focuses on the classroom; the second focuses on concerns.
Visuals and highlights	The only visual is in the classroom section with a caption stating that computers are effective in the classroom.
	Highlighted words in the classroom section indicate how computers are helpful to children: word processing, Internet, computer programming and cognitive growth, social impact. Highlighted words in the second section note specific concerns: video games, social inequalities, Internet exposure.
Opening paragraph	The opening section links this discussion to an earlier one on the effects of television on children. It provides background material that indicates a huge percentage of Canadian children have frequent access to computers. Finally, the purpose of the article is to consider whether this exposure is beneficial or harmful.
Closing paragraph	The closing paragraph refers to the earlier section on television mentioned in the opening. It concludes that computers are beneficial when educational, but not so when used in unproductive ways.

Skimming	1. Studies reveal that classroom use of computers produces many benefits.
2. Aside from their drill function, computers are also tools that further children's basic writing and communication skills.
3. In a study of Internet use in the classroom, about one-third of elementary-school and over half of secondary-school students had used email, and two-thirds had used the World Wide Web for educational purposes.
4. Finally, it seems that teaching students to program (and thus control) a computer can have such important benefits as fostering mastery motivations and self-efficacy as well as promoting novel modes of thinking that are unlikely to emerge from computer-assisted academic drills.
5. Clearly these findings are important, because they suggest that computers are useful not only for teaching children academic lesions but also for helping them to think in new ways.
6. Are young computer users at risk of becoming reclusive, socially unskilled misfits as some people have feared? Hardly!
7. What are the danger signs of exposing children to computer technology? Three concerns are raised most often.
8. The results of one survey in British Columbia revealed that more than 80 percent of adolescents in that province play video games at least occasionally.
9. The critics' concerns are valid ones.
10. Other critics are convinced that the computer revolution may leave some groups of children behind, lacking in skills that are required in our increasingly computer-dependent society—a situation commonly referred to as the "digital divide."
11. The proliferation of home computers and online services means that literally millions of children and adolescents around the world may now have unsupervised access to the Internet and the World Wide Web.

It takes only a few minutes to get this information, but you can already draw some conclusions. The article looks at both the benefits and the problems of children using computers as part of a larger discussion that includes the effects of television. The background material in the opening paragraph establishes that this is an important topic because of the extensive exposure of Canadian children to computers and the Internet. The article groups three concerns in the second half. The first half is actually titled "Computer Technology in the Classroom," leading readers to expect that the article will show that the benefits of computers for children lie with education. The writers conclude that, like television, computers can be a positive or negative influence depending on whether they are used for productive and educational purposes or as time wasters

Surveying does not replace a close reading of the text, but it sets the stage for effective reading, better comprehension, and longer retention. You have created a mental map of the article. When you read it more closely, you already know what is coming up, how the ideas fit together, and what conclusion the writers will draw from them.

SQuestion3R

Simply beginning at the first line of a textbook selection and going to the end, letting the words wash over you, is passive reading. You can get a great deal more out of the section if you read actively. That means getting involved. One way to do this is to devise questions to give you a focus. That way, reading the text is also a process of looking for answers to specific questions. By determining to get the answers to specific questions, you engage the text more fully and will grab on to the content more securely. Here's how you question:

- **First**, look at the title and subheadings to see what questions grow out of them. *The Criminal Event: An Introduction to Criminology in Canada* is a college text by Vincent Sacco and Leslie Kennedy. The section titles in Chapter 10 of the book include "Crime, Employment, and Unemployment"; "Victimization and Work"; "Crime and Legitimate Work"; and "Enterprise Versus Organized Crime." These titles suggest questions like:

    What is the relationship of employment rates to crime?

    What has work to do with victims?

    How is crime connected to legitimate work?

    What do the writers have to say about business and organized crime?

- **Second**, consider if you have questions that come from class sessions, other reading, or your own experience that the reading might answer.
- **Third**, ask yourself what you need to find in the reading that will likely be needed in a course assignment or on an exam.

You can formulate these questions automatically as you survey. One variation of SQ3R asks students to make a note of the questions so that they can go back to them later. Whatever you choose to do, the act of asking questions with the purpose of searching for the answers means you are already entering the text in much more than a superficial way.

Questioning while surveying "Child Development in the Computer Age" might give you questions like these:

- What kind of computer technology is used in the classroom?
- Is there a social impact of computers on children?
- Why do critics have concerns about video games?
- How can computers be connected to inequality?

Whether or not you agree with the answers to the questions in the Sacco and Kennedy text, finding them helps you pay closer attention to the writing and will help you summarize the selection later on.

Surveying and Questioning a Textbook Reading — TASK THREE

Select a chapter or section of a chapter from one of your textbooks common to everyone in the group and that relates to your field of study. Work together as a group to fill out the form below. Resist reading the article. Just use the techniques discussed so far.

Person 3: Facilitate the task. Be sure everyone has an opportunity to contribute to the task.

Person 4: Record the group's answers in the form below.
Person 1: Keep track of the time and keep your group posted.
Person 2: Represent your group in a class discussion of the task afterwards.

Textbook:	Selection Title:

Survey results

Title	
Subheadings	
Visuals and highlights	
Opening paragraph	
Closing paragraph	
Skimming	

Conclusions and inferences before reading

```
┌─────────────────────────────────────────────────────────────┐
│                                                             │
│                                                             │
│                                                             │
│                                                             │
└─────────────────────────────────────────────────────────────┘
```

Questions developed during surveying

```
┌─────────────────────────────────────────────────────────────┐
│                                                             │
│                                                             │
│                                                             │
│                                                             │
└─────────────────────────────────────────────────────────────┘
```

SQRead, Recite, Review

After investing some time in surveying and questioning, you can now begin reading from the beginning. Keep the questions you have in mind and look for the answers. Questioning was one of the ways to help you read actively. Now it is time to use some other methods as well. These methods will help you recite and review the selection later on.

Marking

One of the most helpful reading techniques is to mark up the text. You will develop your own system of marking as you go, but you have a large number of options.

You can

- underline topic sentences,
- circle important ideas or numbers,
- put stars beside important facts,
- enumerate points that you want to remember, or
- put an exclamation point beside something you disagree with.

If you don't understand something, put a question mark beside it. You will be able to find that passage easily later to ask a question in class or of other students. Many students like to use highlighters. They can help the text stand out, but they are not as versatile as a coloured pen or pencil, which you can use to write notes as well as highlight.

Marking the text involves a number of actions:

First, you read information.

Second, you identify that information as particularly important or useful.

Third, you decide to make that information stand out in some way.

Fourth, you physically interact with the text in a way that is particularly useful to you.

That whole process of deliberation, decision, and action that ends with a sign that is useful for recalling memory is a powerful way to deepen the impression of the reading in your mind. Be careful not to over-mark, however. If your page ends up full of highlights and notes, it isn't helpful for quick recall. The key to good marking technique is to be selective.

Summary Words

Another valuable reading technique is to select summary words for each paragraph. After you read a paragraph, decide what it is that you want to remember about it. Try to come up with a word or short phrase rather than a full sentence. One way to do that is to look at the marks you have made in the text. Check to see if you can mentally summarize what you have just read. Write those words in the column directly beside the paragraph. After you have done that, move to the next section. When you have finished the article, review the questions you formulated while surveying. Note down any unanswered questions so that you can pursue them later.

Reviewing

Later, when you review your text, simply look down at all the column words. If you can recall what you need, move on to the next one; if you cannot fully recall what you want, then look into the text to refresh your memory. It is possible to go through a long text in a short time if you have provided yourself with these summary words. They act as keys that unlock your experience with the text. You will find that they are helpful long after you have finished reading. One way to verify whether you have understood the reading is to explain it in your own words without referring to the book. If you do that with a study group of students who have read the same selection, you will quickly find out whether you got it. Periodically review the reading by looking at the way you have marked up the text. This will keep the information fresh.

Here is how "Child Development in the Computer Age" might look after completing SQ3R:

Child Development in the Computer Age

question—computers are helpful or harmful?

Like television, computer technology has the potential to influence children's learning and lifestyles. But in what ways? Most educators today believe that computer technology is an effective supplement to classroom instruction that helps children to learn more and to have more fun doing so. By 1999, there was one computer for every nine elementary-school students, one for every eight lower-secondary students, and one for every seven upper-secondary students (Statistics Canada, 2000a). Eighty-eight percent of elementary-school and 97 percent of secondary-school students attend a school that has access to the Internet for instruction. In fact, Canada ranks among the highest in the world in terms of computer access at school and at home. In 2000, close to 90 percent of young Canadians reported having a computer at home and 70 percent had access to the Internet (Statistics Canada, 2002d). <u>So computers are now</u>

widely accessible, but do they really help children to learn, think, or create? Is there a danger that young "hackers" will become so enamoured of computer technology and so reclusive or socially unskilled that they risk being ostracized by their peers?

Computer Technology in the Classroom

Studies reveal that classroom use of computers produces many benefits. For example, elementary-school students do learn more and report that they enjoy school more when they receive at least some **computer-assisted instruction (CAI)** (Clements & Nastasi, 1992; Collis et al., 1996; Lepper & Gurtner, 1989). Many CAI programs are simply drills that start at a student's current level of mastery and present increasingly difficult problems, often intervening with hints or clues when progress breaks down. Other, more elaborate forms of CAI are guided tutorials that rely less on drill and more on the discovery of important concepts and principles in the context of highly motivating, thought-provoking games. Regular use of drill programs during the early grades does seem to improve children's basic reading and math skills, particularly for disadvantaged students and other low achievers (Clements & Nastasi, 1992; Fletcher-Flinn & Gravatt, 1995; Lepper & Gurtner, 1989). However, the benefits of CAI are greatest when children receive at least some exposure to highly involving guided tutorials as well as simple drills. In addition, having access to computers does not necessarily mean that they are being used effectively. One study of Canadian 15-year-olds revealed that only 39 percent of students reported that they used a computer at school almost every day or a few times a week (Statistics Canada, 2002d).

WORD PROCESSING. Aside from their drill function, computers are also *tools* that can further children's basic writing and communication skills (Clements, 1995). Once children can read and write, using word-processing programs eliminates much of the drudgery of handwriting and increases the likelihood that children will revise, edit, and polish their writing (Clements & Nastasi, 1992). Furthermore, computer-prompted metacognitive strategies help students think about what they want to say and organize their thoughts into more coherent essays (Lepper & Gurtner, 1989).

INTERNET USE. In a study of Internet use in the classroom, about one-third of elementary-school and over half of secondary-school students had used e-mail, and two-thirds had used the World Wide Web for educational purposes (Statistics Canada, 2000a). An increasing number of high-school teachers and university/college professors offer courses and course content on-line, giving students the flexibility to learn at their convenience. These instructors often stimulate discussion of course material on-line, a strategy they believe will reduce concerns about speaking in public while inducing students to ponder course materials more deeply and critically (Hara, Bonk, & Angeli, 2000; Murray, 2000). Although educators and students report many benefits of the Internet for ease of access to information and for communication purposes, research on its benefits, however, is still in its infancy.

COMPUTER PROGRAMMING AND COGNITIVE GROWTH. Finally, it seems that teaching students to *program* (and thus *control*) a computer can have such important benefits as fostering mastery motivation and self-efficacy as well as promoting novel modes of thinking that are unlikely to emerge from computer-assisted academic drills. In his own research, Douglas Clements (1991, 1995) trained first- and third-graders in Logo, a computer language that allows children to translate their drawings into input statements so that they can reproduce their creations on the computer monitor. Although

computer-assisted instruction (CAI)
use of computers to teach new concepts and give students practice in academic skills.

Logo case study ↓ *Innovative thinking*

Clements's "Logo children" performed no better on achievement tests than age-mates who participated in the more usual kinds of computer-assisted academic exercises, Logo users scored higher on tests of Piagetian concrete-operational abilities, mathematical problem-solving strategies, and creativity (Clements, 1995; Nastasi & Clements, 1994). And because children must learn to detect errors and debug their Logo programs to get them to work, programming fosters thinking about one's own thinking and is associated with gains in metacognitive knowledge (Clements, 1990).

Clearly, these findings are important because they suggest that computers are useful not only for teaching children academic lessons but also for helping them to think in new ways.

peer interaction

SOCIAL IMPACTS. Are young computer users at risk of becoming reclusive, socially unskilled misfits as some people have feared? Hardly! Children often use home computers as a toy to attract playmates (Crook, 1992; Kee, 1986). And research conducted in classrooms reveals that students who are learning to program or solve problems with a computer are (1) likely to seek collaborative solutions to the challenges they face and (2) more inclined to persist after experiencing problems when they are collaborating with a peer (Nastasi & Clements, 1993, 1994; Weinstein, 1991). Conflicts may arise should collaborators disagree about how to approach a problem; yet the strong interest that collaborators frequently display when facing a programming challenge often supersedes their differences and encourages amiable methods of resolving conflicts (Nastasi & Clements, 1993). So computer technology seems to promote (rather than impede) peer interactions—contacts that are often lively and challenging and that appear to foster the growth of socially skilled behaviours.

Concerns about Computer Technology

What are the danger signs of exposing children to computer technology? Three concerns are raised most often.

1

CONCERNS ABOUT VIDEO GAMES. The results of one recent survey in British Columbia revealed that more than 80 percent of adolescents in that province play video games at least occasionally (Media Analysis Laboratory, 1998). Fifty percent of the sample spent less than three hours a week on video games, but 25 percent spent between three and seven hours a week and the remainder over seven hours a week. It is not that this activity necessarily diverts children from schoolwork and peer activities, as many parents have assumed; time spent playing at the computer is usually a substitute for other leisure activities, most notably TV viewing. Nevertheless, critics have feared (and early evidence suggests) that heavy exposure to such popular and incredibly violent video games as *Alien Intruder* and *Mortal Kombat* can instigate aggression and cultivate aggressive habits in the same ways that televised violence does (Fling et al., 1992; Williams, 1998).

violence & video games

The critics' concerns are valid ones. At least three surveys of fourth- to twelfth-graders found moderate positive correlations between the amount of time spent playing video games and real-world aggressive behaviours (Dill & Dill, 1998). The experimental evidence is even more revealing: One study of third- and fourth-graders

link validated

(Kirsch, 1998) and another study of college students (Anderson & Dill, 2000) found that participants randomly assigned to play violent video games displayed a strong hostile attributional bias toward later ambiguous provocations and significantly more aggressive behaviour than their counterparts who had played nonviolent video games. And because violent game players are actively involved in planning and performing aggressive acts and *reinforced* for their successful symbolic violence, it has been argued that the aggression-instigating effects of violent video games is probably far greater than that of violent television programming, in which children are only passively exposed to aggression and violence (Anderson & Dill, 2000; Larson, 2001). Clearly, these early findings suggest that parents should be at least as concerned about what their children are playing on-screen as they are about what their children watch.

CONCERNS ABOUT SOCIAL INEQUALITIES. Other critics are convinced that the computer revolution may leave some groups of children behind, lacking in skills that are required in our increasingly computer-dependent society—commonly referred to as the "digital divide." For example, children from economically disadvantaged families may be exposed to computers at school but are unlikely to have them at home (Rocheleau, 1995). Also, boys are far more likely than girls to take an interest in computers and to sign up for computer camps. Why? Probably because computers are often viewed as involving mathematics, a traditionally masculine subject, and many available computer games are designed to appeal to boys (Lepper, 1985; Ogletree & Williams, 1990). Yet this gender gap is narrowing, largely due to the increasing use of computers to foster *cooperative* classroom learning activities that girls typically enjoy (Collis et al., 1996; Rocheleau, 1995).

CONCERNS ABOUT INTERNET EXPOSURE. The proliferation of home computers and on-line services means that literally millions of children and adolescents around the world may now have unsupervised access to the Internet and the World Wide Web. Clearly, exposure to information available on the Web can be a boon to students researching topics pertinent to their school assignments. Nevertheless, many parents and teachers are alarmed about potentially unsavoury Web influences. For example, children and adolescents chatting with acquaintances on-line have been drawn into cybersexual relationships and, occasionally, to meetings with and exploitation by their adult chat-mates (Curry, 2000; Donnerstein & Smith, 2001; Williams, 1998). Furthermore, the Web is (or has been) a primary recruiting tool for such dangerous cults as Heaven's Gate and hate organizations such as the Ku Klux Klan (Downing, 2001). So there are reasons to suspect that unrestricted Web access could prove harmful to some children and adolescents, and additional research aimed at estimating those risks is sorely needed.

Like television, then, computer technology may prove to be either a positive or a negative force on development, depending on how it is used. Outcomes may be less than positive if a young person's primary uses of the computer are to fritter away study time chatting about undesirable topics on-line, or to hole up alone, zapping mutant aliens from space. But the news may be positive for youngsters who use computer technology to learn, create, and collaborate amicably with siblings and peers.

TASK FOUR Reading and Marking a Textbook Reading

Return to the textbook selection that you surveyed in Task Three. This time read and mark the text as you go. When you finish, exchange your marked-up text with your group members. Look at the different ways that people have marked up the reading and the column summary words that they have chosen.

Alternative Strategies

The more you use SQ3R, the faster and more efficient you will be. You will find that your comprehension and retention has improved. SQ3R is not the only technique, however. Since Francis P. Robinson developed his system, many variations have appeared, such as SQ4R, SQ5R, and PORPE. It is useful to look at them so that you can begin to develop a method that works well for you. The important thing is to end up with a technique that will help you get the most out of your reading before you work with your texts.

TASK FIVE Alternative Systems for Efficient Textbook Reading

Give your group members at least three more tips for efficient textbook reading apart from the ones we have considered. Your group will put these methods together for everyone else in the class.

Part One: Research

Explore the Net and the library to see what really useful methods you can discover. One place for you to start to look is http://www.chemistrycoach.com/lbe5.htm#Reading. It has collected Web pages on skills for reading textbooks from universities and colleges all across North America. You will find the information organized under "Reading," "Reading SQ3R," "Reading Textbooks," and "Highlighting."

Part Two: Group Meeting

Person 2: Facilitate the task. Be sure everyone has an opportunity to present the different reading tips in turn.

Person 1: Record the different tips and methods discovered.

Person 3: Prepare a word-processed version of the different tips for your group portfolio.

Person 4: Be prepared to present the results to the class.

Good reading technique will help you in all your postsecondary studies. Not only will it help you improve comprehension, but it will help you improve retention as well. The graph in the following box, based on research originally presented in the *Journal of Educational Psychology*, shows how dramatic a difference a reading strategy can make.

You're Right! Your Memory Is Like a Sieve!

The Memory Loss Curve

- Review immediately after learning and 24 hours later
- Review immediately after learning and one week later
- Review 24 hours later
- Review a week later
- Review 2 weeks later
- No review

(x-axis: 1, 7, 14, 21, 28)

> If there is just one "magic bullet" study habit that could change your grades, this is it! **Review immediately after learning new material!** List all the major terms, concepts, processes, and formulas in tonight's reading, and quiz yourself on them all immediately after the reading. As you can see from this chart, you will remember a heck of a lot more than if you wait even 24 hours. When in doubt, review now.

The Memory Loss Curve shows how you can retain memory by reviewing immediately after you learn something new (dotted lines at the top.). It also shows how your memory falls off a steep cliff without review. Within 24 hours, you lose nearly 50% of new learning. In three weeks, the loss stabilizes, and you retain about 20% of what you originally learned.

Many students have the mistaken notion that when they finish reading an assignment, they should move on to the next assignment. Not true! **Review, review, review,** while you've still got the material in your head, and it will stay in your head much longer.

Source: Adapted from: "Studies in Retention", by Herbert F Spitzer. (*The Journal of Educational Psychology*). Vol. XXX, No.9, December 1939, pages 641-656.

In Summary

Take three minutes to write a summary of what you have learned participating in the tasks of Unit 1.

UNIT 2
Mapping and Outlining

Here's what you'll work on in this unit.

- Developing concept maps
- Producing a mind map from a text
- Applying outlining techniques to textbook selections
- Researching alternative visual outlining methods

Developing and applying a reading strategy like SQ3R to your college reading is the first major step to improving comprehension and long-term retention of the material. Finding ways to re-present that material is the next one. Many people have the experience of learning best when they have to teach. That is because teaching involves not only understanding the original material, but repackaging it in a different way for a particular situation. The process of repackaging and expressing the material in a different way is a powerful technique for learning. Whether it be a lecture or a text reading, the material becomes your own. You can do this in several ways.

The Concept Map

Cognitive psychologist David Ausubel developed *subsumption theory* in the 1960s. Essentially, Ausubel's idea is that people learn by relating new material to an existing framework of concepts. One of the key helps to learning is a diagram. A diagram of ideas can be an invaluable tool for seeing how concepts connect. Professor J. Novak working at Cornell University in the 1970s developed the *concept map* on the basis of Ausubel's work. The concept map is a visual that makes relationships clear. It can be used as a problem-solving tool, as a method for developing a team project, or as an effective way to re-present text as a diagram.

One of the reasons why the concept map is so effective is that it makes use of the brain's powerful ability to think in images. In addition, a map makes connections explicit. Reading a textbook presents you ideas one by one in order. Our minds, however, are capable of free association—in other words, of switching from one concept to another. The difference is somewhat like reading a book as opposed to surfing the Net with various windows open and moving from link to link. That's what happens with a concept map.

Concept maps use lines to relate concepts in boxes or squares to other ones. The kind of relationship is written on the line. For example, if you were producing a concept map on the subject of rising tuition fees for students, you might start if off like this:

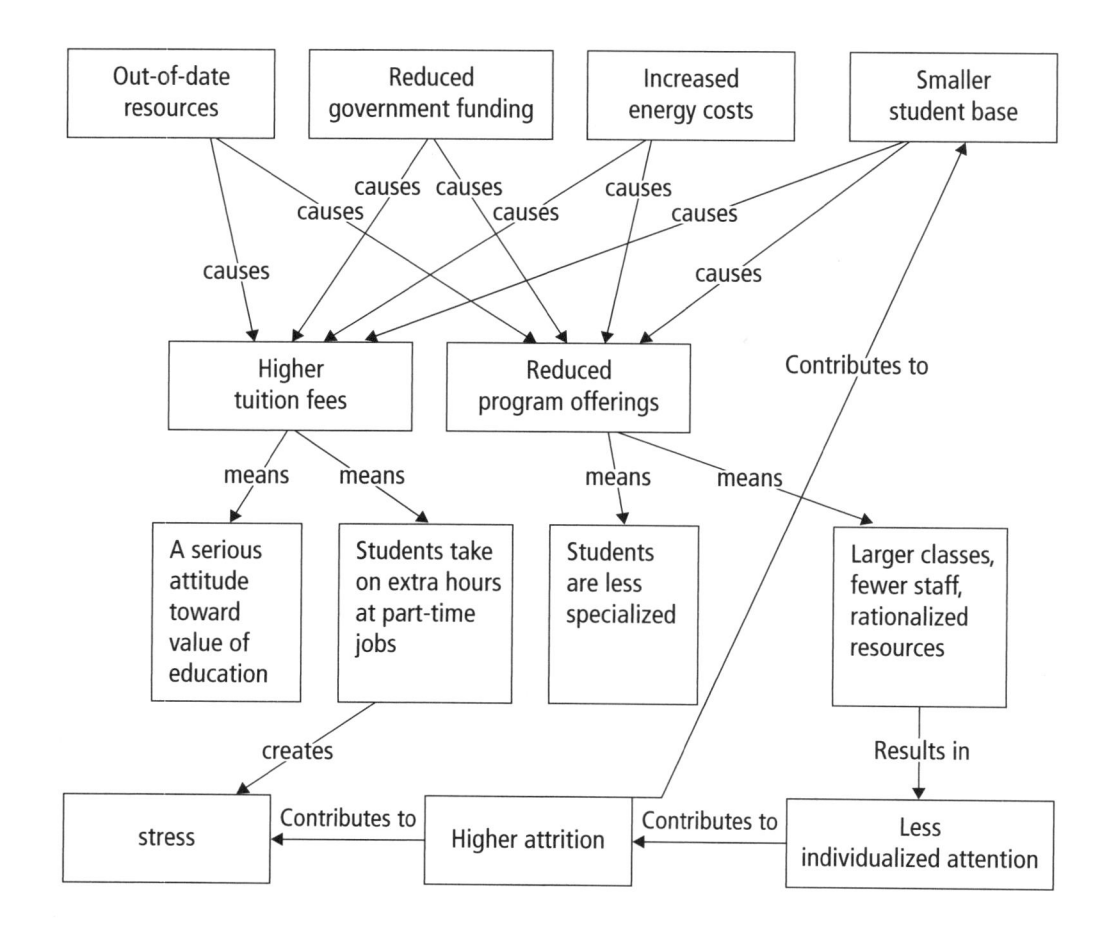

```
┌─────────────┐  ┌─────────────┐  ┌─────────────┐  ┌─────────────┐
│ Out-of-date │  │   Reduced   │  │  Increased  │  │   Smaller   │
│  resources  │  │ government  │  │ energy costs│  │student base │
│             │  │   funding   │  │             │  │             │
└─────────────┘  └─────────────┘  └─────────────┘  └─────────────┘
```

    causes   causes causes   causes
  causes   causes   causes
        causes   causes

```
        ┌─────────────┐        ┌─────────────┐           Contributes to
        │   Higher    │        │   Reduced   │
        │ tuition fees│        │program      │
        │             │        │offerings    │
        └─────────────┘        └─────────────┘
```
      means   means   means   means

```
┌─────────┐ ┌──────────┐  ┌──────────┐   ┌────────────┐
│A serious│ │Students  │  │ Students │   │Larger      │
│attitude │ │take on   │  │ are less │   │classes,    │
│toward   │ │extra     │  │specialized│  │fewer staff,│
│value of │ │hours at  │  │          │   │rationalized│
│education│ │part-time │  │          │   │resources   │
│         │ │jobs      │  │          │   │            │
└─────────┘ └──────────┘  └──────────┘   └────────────┘
```
                creates   Results in

```
┌────────┐  Contributes to  ┌──────────────┐  Contributes to  ┌────────────────┐
│ stress │ ←──────────────  │Higher        │ ←──────────────  │     Less       │
│        │                  │attrition     │                  │individualized  │
│        │                  │              │                  │   attention    │
└────────┘                  └──────────────┘                  └────────────────┘
```

This map is just the beginning of a brainstorming session around the issue of rising tuition fees. It might be used to think through a problem, probe for insights, plan out a report or essay, or even do some problem solving. Concept maps allow for more than one main concept and show complex relationships. The labelled lines can go in any direction, even relating back to a previous idea.

Hint

Concept maps often begin at the top of a page and work down. The arrows allow you to make changes in direction at any time.

TASK ONE   Creating a Group Concept Map

An assignment in one of your classes asks for a group presentation on a contemporary Canadian issue. Your group has selected immigration. Take 30 minutes and use concept mapping to develop a visual that shows interconnected concepts.

Person 4: Please facilitate the discussion. Keep everyone on track.

Person 3: Write down any concepts or ideas that come up during the conversation on slips of paper or sticky notes. Display them in front of the group. Use additional notes to indicate the relationships between the concepts.

Person 2: When the group has finished working out the concept map, copy it onto a single sheet of flip chart paper, directly onto a whiteboard, or onto a computer file that can be projected for the entire class to see.

Person 1: Present and explain your concept map to the entire class.

You have worked together as a team thinking through an issue. You also have seen how the concept maps of other teams on the same issue as yours approach the subject from different perspectives providing different insights. Concept mapping can also be used to translate lecture material into a visual format to make a more striking, long-lasting impression and clarify how information relates to other information. A lecture in a construction management class on ventilation systems for houses, for example, might be mapped out like this:

Lecture on ventilation in housing

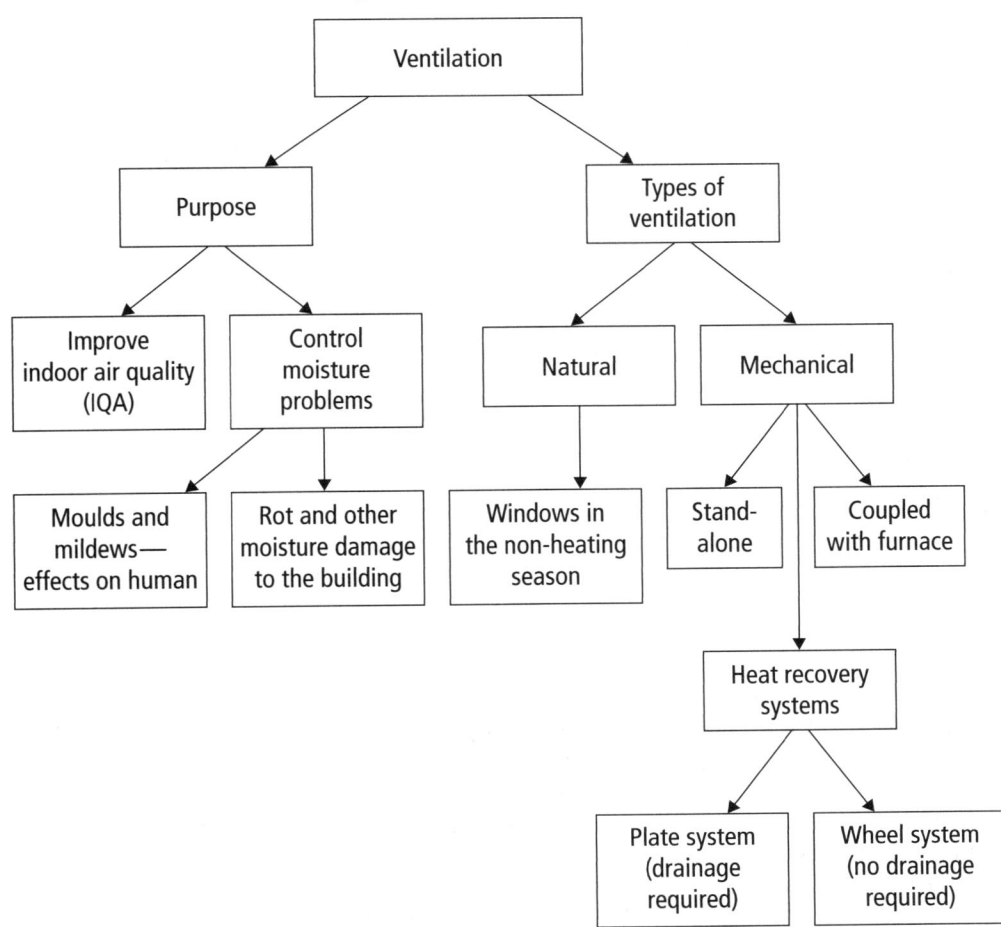

```
                        Ventilation
                       /           \
                  Purpose          Types of
                  /    \          ventilation
                 /      \          /      \
           Improve    Control   Natural   Mechanical
        indoor air   moisture    |        /      \
        quality      problems    |    Stand-   Coupled
        (IQA)        /    \      |    alone   with furnace
          \         /      \     |              |
       Moulds and  Rot and other Windows in     |
       mildews—    moisture damage the non-heating
       effects on  to the building season
       human                                    |
                                          Heat recovery
                                            systems
                                           /       \
                                    Plate system  Wheel system
                                    (drainage    (no drainage
                                    required)    required)
```

Transferring lecture notes in this way into a diagram makes the ideas readily accessible and makes review later on easier.

TASK TWO   Creating a Concept Map of a College Lecture

Part One

Meet as a group to select an upcoming class in any subject common to everyone. Each person in the group will take notes in the class and then produce a concept map of the ideas and learning that happened. Make copies for each person in your group.

Part Two

Person 3: Please manage this part of the task. Give every person in the group three minutes to describe the concept map. Ask for feedback from the group after each person's presentation. After the presentations are completed, facilitate a 10-minute discussion that highlights the differences and similarities in the maps. What are the advantages and disadvantages of concept mapping applied to lectures?

Person 2: Please fill in the following form with the results of your group discussion.

Advantages of Concept Mapping for Lecture Material	Disadvantages or Challenges in Using Concept Mapping

The Mind Map

You have applied concept mapping both as a team exercise and individually to academic material. A similar system of diagramming ideas, called mind mapping, was developed by Dr. Allan Collins in the 1960s, and then promoted and copyrighted in the 1970s by Tony Buzan. Mind mapping is a simpler way of producing a visual of ideas and can be applied, as can concept mapping, to taking notes of lectures, sketching out ideas or plans for a project, or diagramming a textbook reading. Variations of this system are called bubble diagrams, because they tend to use circles rather than rectangles.

To produce a mind map, start with a central idea circled in the centre of the page. Extend branches from that circle to subtopics. Each of those subtopics can branch out as well. You can continue this approach as long as you want. When used as a brainstorming technique, the best thing is to keep on going without pausing to think too much or make judgments on what you have diagrammed. Simply keep the process going. It may be that later on you want to use the whole picture for a particular project, essay, or solution to a problem, or you may want to focus on some corner of the larger visual that you have just created. The following mind map is the result of brainstorming on the subject of the Internet:

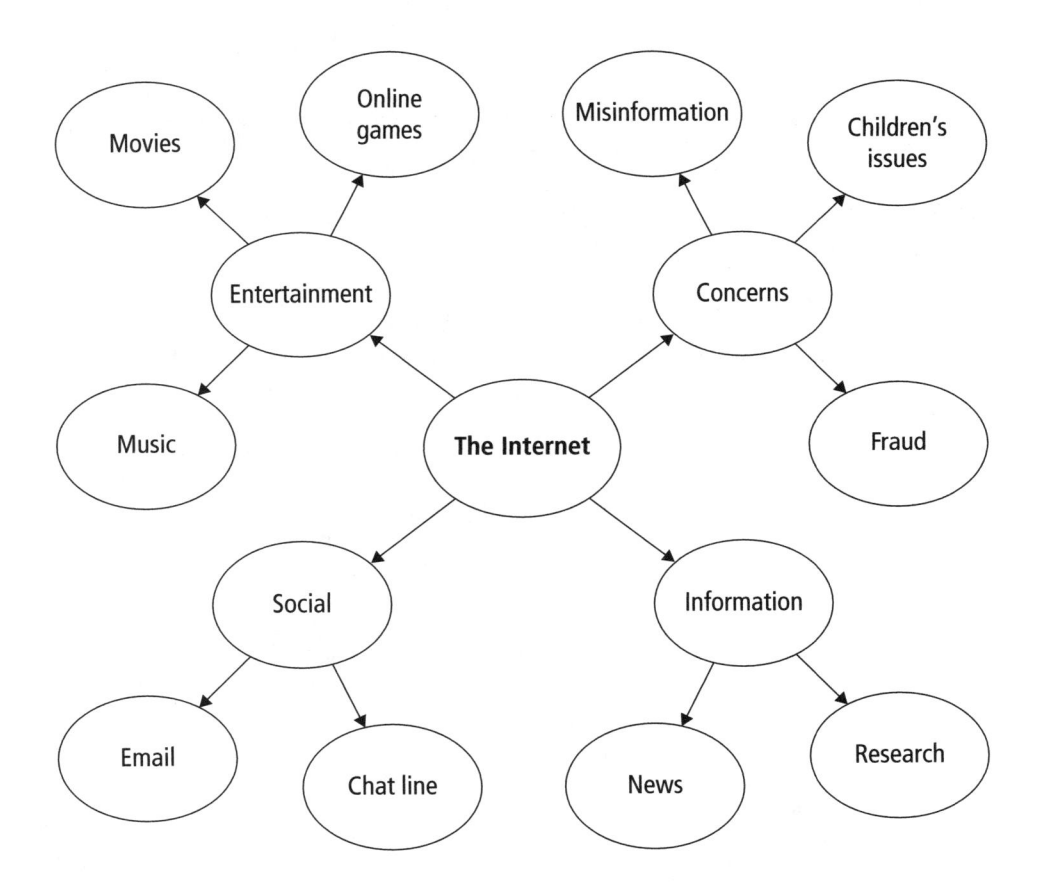

This map gives both a larger picture of the Internet and ideas about its value and challenges. It also provides a different focus in different sections of the page. Its centre hub spokes outward as different considerations make themselves apparent. The map might continue to add branches to any one of the subgroups.

One excellent application of mind mapping is preparing textbook reading assignments. Textbooks are normally arranged with various levels of subheadings which make it easy to put a map together. Look for the central idea of a section or chapter. Put it in the centre of the page and then add spokes to the various subsections. Use as many branches for each subsection as necessary to fully cover the information. When you are finished, you will have a picture of the chapter that will be invaluable in both preparing for the upcoming class and studying for an exam.

You can do the same thing for articles, no matter how long or short, without subtitles. The following article is taken from a college criminology textbook, *The Criminal Event: An Introduction to Criminology in Canada* by Vincent F. Sacco and Leslie W. Kennedy. Read through the article and then compare it to the mind map that follows.

The Sources of Crime News

Studies of news production practices emphasize how judgments of "newsworthiness" come to be applied to categories of events (Chibnall, 1977; Fishman, 1978). These judgments reflect how journalists perceive their society, the work they are engaged in, and the audiences they serve. For several reasons, criminal events—especially violent ones—conform closely to the professional values of journalists (Ericson, Baranek, and Chan, 1987).

First, such incidents have spatial and temporal characteristics that lend themselves easily to news production routines. Murders, thefts, and sexual assaults are discrete events. They are also "short term"—that is, they happen between one newspaper edition and the next, or one newscast and the next. *Second,* reports of criminal events are easily understood by audiences and so require little in the way of background information. Also, because there is an almost limitless supply of crime news, the number of crime-related stories can be expanded or reduced depending on the needs of media decision makers and on the amount of space or time that must be filled on any given day (Warr, 1991). *Third,* many crimes lend themselves to a dramatic narrative form that features the exploits of clearly defined "good guys" and "bad guys" (Ericson, 1991).

News organizations rely heavily on a continuous flow of crime news. As a result, they have developed well-defined relationships with those they perceive as reliable and credible suppliers of that news (Gordon and Heath, 1981). The police are the main source of crime news; the "police wire," the press release, the news conference, and the beat reporter provide the link between the world of crime and the news media (Ericson, Baranek, and Chan, 1987). Because the police can supply a steady stream of stories that are "entertaining, dramatic, amusing and titillating" (Ericson, 1991:207), journalists implicitly adopt a police perspective on the problem of crime (Fishman, 1981).

The relationship between police and journalists is mutually beneficial (Katz, 1987). Journalists are allowed regular access to a valued news commodity; also, they gain credibility, authority, and objectivity when they refer to the police as the official spokespeople on crime. At the same time, the police are able to present themselves as experts on crime and as "owners" of the problem of crime.

All of this helps explain why interpersonal violent crimes such as homicide and robbery receive greater coverage than crimes by or against businesses (Ericson, 1991). The established source–journalist relationships that exist with respect to "common" crimes generally do not exist in the case of business crime. Furthermore, stories about business crime are often judged as less noteworthy because they tend to be more complex, less dramatic, and more difficult to personalize (Randall, Lee-Sammons, and Hagner, 1988).

Source: From The Criminal Event 3rd Edition by Sacco/Kennedy, 2002. Reprinted with permission of Nelson, a division of Thomson Learning: www.thomsonrights.com. Fax 800-730-2215.

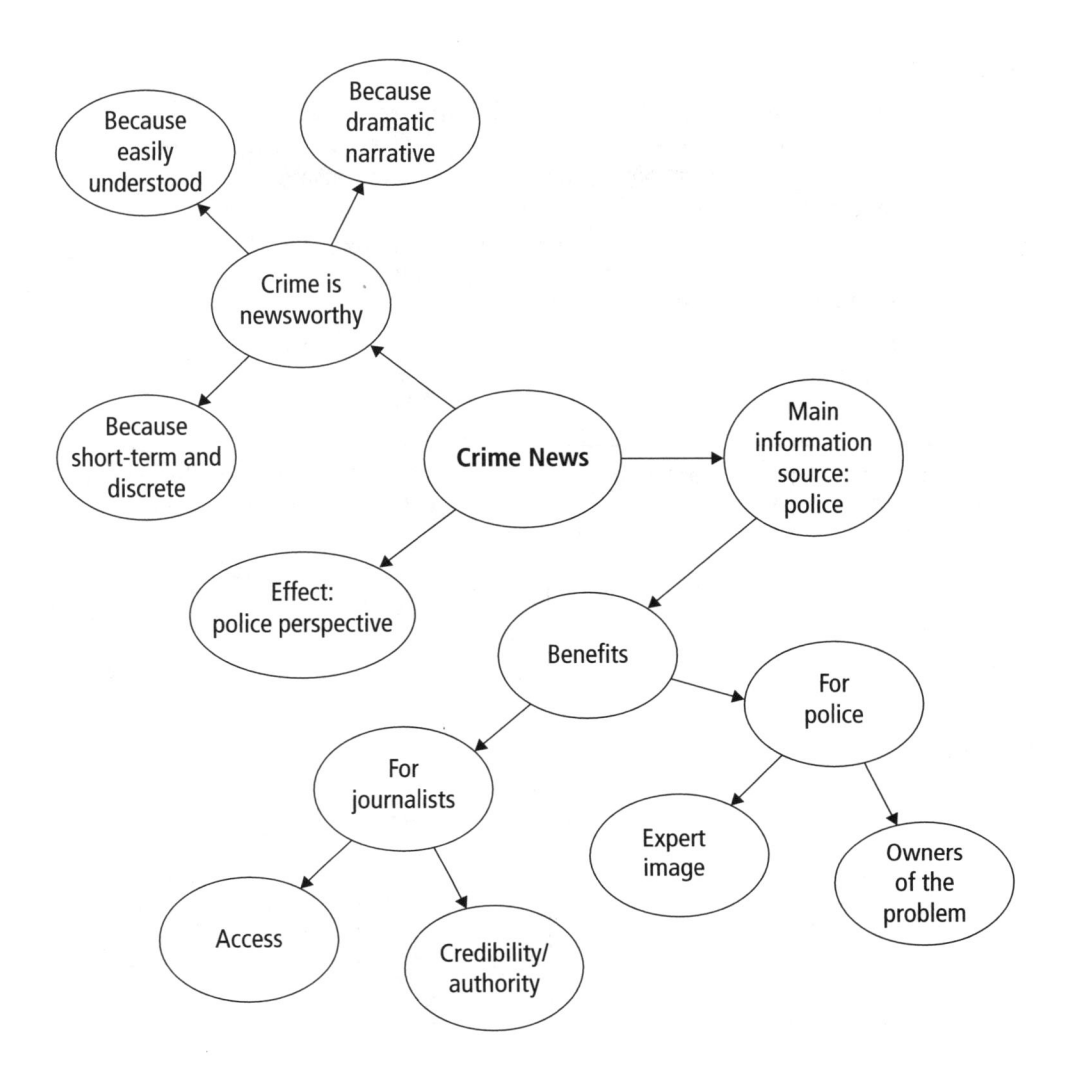

```
                Because
  Because       dramatic
   easily       narrative
 understood
      ↑            ↑
       \          /
        Crime is
       newsworthy
        /     ↑                          Main
       ↓       \                      information
  Because       \                       source:
short-term and   Crime News  ─────→     police
   discrete
                   │  ↘                    │
                   ↓    ↘                  ↓
                 Effect:   Benefits
             police perspective    ↘
                         /           For
                        ↓           police
                       For          /    \
                    journalists    ↓      ↓
                      /    \     Expert   Owners
                     ↓      ↓    image    of the
                  Access  Credibility/             problem
                          authority
```

Creating a Mind Map from a Textbook Chapter

TASK THREE

This task gives you the opportunity to apply the mind map strategy to academic reading in your field.

Part One

Meet as a group to select a chapter in any of your textbooks common to everyone. Each person in the group will take notes on the chapter and then produce a mind map. Make copies for every person in your group.

Part Two

Person 4: Please manage this part of the task. Give every person in the group three minutes to describe the mind map. Ask for feedback from the group after each person's presentation. After the presentations are completed, facilitate a 10-minute discussion that highlights the differences and similarities in the maps. What are the advantages and disadvantages of mind mapping applied to textbook readings?

Person 2: Please fill in the following form with the results of your group discussion.

Advantages of Mind Mapping for Lecture Material	Disadvantages or Challenges in Using Mind Mapping

Outlining

Turning your chapters or units in a textbook into visuals that fit on one sheet of paper is a way to engage the different capabilities in your brain to ensure learning. You have had to read a text, make decisions on what you have read, and transfer the information onto paper in a different format. In addition to comprehending, you have had to get involved physically by drawing and writing to produce a picture that will evoke what you have read any time you return to it.

The visuals work like spiderwebs. Another, more linear way of transferring text is the outline. Just as mapping uses a series of circles or squares and interconnecting lines, so outlining uses numbers, titling and subtitling, and indentation. It begins with creating a skeleton or what looks like a table of contents for the section.

For example, a skeleton outline of this unit so far could look like this:

Mapping and Outlining

1.0 Introduction
2.0 The Concept Map
    2.1 Background
    2.2 Task One
    2.3 Application to lecture material
    2.4 Task Two
3.0 The Mind Map
    3.1 Background
    3.2 Application to textbook reading
    3.3 Task Three
4.0 Outlining

To be an effective tool for understanding a reading and later recalling its content, outlining needs to go a step further and hang specific main points on the skeleton. The following selection is taken from a college-level textbook used in business programs. Read the article and look at how it has been converted into an outline below.

Three Types of Business Orientation

Most companies have an orientation that fits one of the following three categories: product-oriented, sales-oriented, or market-oriented.[1] That is, most companies act as if organizational success is achieved either through their product design, through intensive sales efforts, or through integrated marketing activities. Marketers argue that the surest route to organizational success is by following the marketing concept. Let's look at each orientation in turn.

Product or Production Orientation
In firms with a **product orientation**, the emphasis is on the product itself rather than on the consumer's needs. For the production-oriented firm, the dominant considerations in product design are those of ease or cheapness of production. In either case, market considerations are ignored or de-emphasized. Firms stress production of goods or services,[2] then look for people to purchase them. The prevailing attitude of this type of firm is that a good product will sell itself. Beginning entrepreneurs often take this approach, convinced that their product idea is a sure-fire winner. Such a strategy is very limiting, for it assumes that the producer's tastes and values are the same as those of the market. Often a firm does not consider changing from this narrow approach until it runs into trouble.

Sales Orientation
A **sales orientation** is an improvement on a product orientation. This firm is still quite product-oriented, but it recognizes that the world will not beat a path to its door to purchase its products. Therefore, the firm focuses its marketing efforts on developing a strong sales force to convince consumers to buy. "Get the customer to fit the company's offerings" could be a motto of such a sales-oriented strategy. From this perspective, to be successful, what you really need is an aggressive, high-powered sales organization and advertising program.

As you are watching TV some evening (with your marketing text in your lap), try to identify some ads with a pure sales orientation. For some reason, furniture retailers often use this approach.

Clearly, good, persuasive communication is an important part of a marketing plan. However, selling is only one component of marketing. As marketing expert Theodore Levitt has pointed out, "Marketing is as different from selling as chemistry is from alchemy, astronomy from astrology, chess from checkers."[3]

Market Orientation

Many firms have discovered that the product and sales orientations are quite limiting. They have found that it makes a great deal of sense to pay careful attention to understanding customer needs and objectives and then make the business serve the interests of the customer rather than trying to make the customer buy what the business wants to produce. A primary task under a **market orientation**, then, is to develop ways to research and understand various aspects of the market.

A market-oriented strategy can produce any of the benefits of the other two orientations, but it avoids their drawbacks. In addition, it can identify new opportunities and avoid nasty surprises as changes occur in the market.

In a market-oriented firm, the marketing function is not tagged on at the end of the process. It takes a primary role right from the beginning of the planning process. A marketing orientation represents a set of processes that touch on all aspects of the company. It involves much more than just understanding the customer. Three characteristics make a company market-driven:

- *Intelligence generation.* The market-oriented firm generates intelligence in three major areas: customers' current needs, customers' emerging needs, and competitive activity. Understanding the current needs of customers is a relatively straightforward matter that involves formal and informal dialogue with target customers. The formal dialogue can take the form of customer surveys and other types of marketing research. The market-oriented firm is not satisfied with simply trying to understand customers' present situation and needs—it also looks to the future to anticipate customers' unfolding needs. Such anticipation usually involves monitoring the environment for legal, technical, or other developments that might influence customers' requirements. Market-oriented computer manufacturers, for example, are monitoring the development and refinement of voice-recognition software, because it represents a potentially superior method of inputting computer data for their customers. The third area of intelligence generation focuses on competitive activity. Companies must have an accurate understanding of what competitors are doing to ensure that their own products or services are not left behind, and to evaluate the attractiveness of different markets.

- *Intelligence dissemination.* Market-oriented firms not only gather intelligence, they make it available throughout the organization. Customer information must reach all areas of the organization, including research and development, engineering, manufacturing, and accounting.

- *Responsiveness.* Up-to-the-minute information that is widely available within the organization serves no purpose unless the organization actually adjusts its products or processes based on that information. A remarkable number of organizations are fully aware that customers are unhappy with some aspect of their product or service delivery—long waits at an automotive service desk, for example—but make no attempt to address the problem. The market-oriented firm does not just understand its customer and its environment, it acts on that understanding.[4]

Notes:

1. Many discussions of this topic have suggested that marketing passed through a series of "eras": product, sales, and market orientations. However Ronald A. Fullerton shows that there is little historical support for the concept of progression through various eras in his article "How Modern Is Modern Marketing? Marketing's Evolution and the Myth of the 'Production Era,'" *Journal of Marketing* (January 1988), pp. 108–25.

> 2. Henceforth, the term "product" will apply to both goods and services, except as otherwise noted. The marketing principles that apply to products normally apply to services as well.
> 3. Theodore Levitt, *Innovations in Marketing* (New York: McGraw-Hill, 1962), p. 7.
> 4. Ajay K. Kohli and Bernard J. Jaworski, "Market Orientation: The Construct, Research Propositions, and Managerial Implications," *Journal of Marketing* (April 1990), pp. 1–18; Bernard J. Jaworski and Ajay K. Kohli, "Marketing Orientation: Antecedents and Consequences," *Journal of Marketing* (July 1993), pp. 53–70.
>
> ***Source:*** From Foundations of Marketing, Eight Canadian Edition by BECKMAN. 2003. Reprinted with Permission of Nelson, a division of Thomson Learning: www.thomsonrights.com. Fax 800-730-2215.

Three Types of Business Orientation

1.0 Introduction: Most companies operate in one of three modes or types
2.0 Type 1: Product or production orientation
    2.1 Focus is on the product that sells itself
    2.2 Limited approach based on assumption of common taste and value
3.0 Type 2: Sales orientation
    3.1 Focus is on selling strategies
    3.2 Persuasive communication is key
4.0 Type 3: Market orientation
    4.1 Focus is on customer research
    4.2 Advantages over Types 1 and 2
        4.2.1 Identifies new opportunities
        4.2.2 Flags dangers or problems in advance
    4.3 Primary role in marketing with three characteristics
        4.3.1 Intelligence generation:
            4.3.1.1 Customer's current needs
            4.3.1.2 Customer's emerging needs
            4.3.1.3 Competitive activity
        4.3.2 Intelligence dissemination: Customer information goes to all company departments
        4.3.3 Responsiveness: Changes made on the basis of customer information

This outline uses a decimal system. The different sections of the reading are identified, pulled to the left and indicated by ".0." Main points under each section are indented, grouped using the section number, and differentiated by a decimal place division. This kind of subdivision can go on as far as necessary. In this case, there is a fourth-level subdivision under Section 4. Each subdivision is indented one place over so that it lines up with the same-level information in other sections. This arrangement makes it easy to identify the number of sections, and the weight of that section in the whole article. Such outlines of articles or text chapters bring clarity, and they are particularly useful if you have to write a response or use them in writing for other purposes.

Hint

Although you do need to capture every main point, avoid trying to fit in all the details. An outline generally only needs to go down a few levels.

TASK FOUR Creating an Outline from a Textbook Chapter

This task gives you the opportunity to apply outlining using headings, sub-headings, indentation, and decimal system numbering to academic reading in your field.

Part One

Meet as a group to select a chapter in any of your textbooks common to everyone. Each person in the group will take notes on the chapter and then produce an outline. Make copies for each person in your group.

Part Two

Person 4: Please manage this part of the task. Give every person in the group three minutes to describe the mind map. Ask for feedback from the group after each person's presentation. After the presentations are completed, facilitate a 10-minute discussion that highlights the differences and similarities in the maps. What are the advantages and disadvantages of outlining applied to text readings?

Person 2: Please fill in the following form with the results of your group discussion.

Advantages of Outlining for Textbook Material	Disadvantages or Challenges in Outlining

In Summary

Take three minutes to write a summary of what you have learned participating in the tasks of Unit 2.

UNIT 3
Restating

Here's what you'll work on in this unit.

- Paraphrasing academic material
- Producing a summary
- Differentiating between a descriptive and an informative abstract
- Preparing a double-entry journal
- Writing an evaluative summary

Mapping and outlining texts are excellent ways to grasp academic material. On occasion, you will also need to summarize that material. Summary writing is an essential part of professional communications. Most business and technical reports, for example, begin with a section titled "Summary" or sometimes "Executive Summary." It is also a critical part of postsecondary writing. Advanced academic writing around special research projects usually begin with an abstract. Both summaries and abstracts boil down the original, lengthier writing and recast it in tighter form. The reader has an opportunity to get the gist of the whole report before digging in for the details. Writing summaries is also a useful method to check just well how you have really understood an article and to review texts for upcoming testing.

Paraphrasing

Summary writing depends on developing an ability to paraphrase. Writing a summary is not an exercise in cutting and pasting sentences from the original into a new paragraph. Instead, it is a new presentation of the original material in digest form. Think of summarizing a text as translating someone else's words into your own. Look for a fresh way to recast the information even if you are summarizing your own writing. Not only does this help make the original even more accessible to a reader, it also means that you have fully mastered the original text. Think of when you had to explain something you read or saw to someone else who had not read or seen it. If you could cover all the main points easily and clearly without having to refer to the original, you have demonstrated that you fully grasped the text.

Paraphrasing is a tool used in summary writing, but is not summary writing in itself. All that paraphrasing aims at is re-presenting the information and concepts in different words. It is not necessarily shorter, as a summary is, and in fact might even be longer. For example, paraphrasing a taut, technical document might actually require a higher word count than the original, as certain terms or concepts may require several words to replace them.

Hint

One of the best ways to develop paraphrasing skills is to resist the temptation to look at the original. Give yourself all the time you need to understand the original including mapping it or outlining it, but try putting the original away when it comes time to paraphrase.

The following paragraph from Shaffer, Wood, and Willoughby's *Developmental Psychology: Childhood and Adolescence* introduces a section subtitled "Theories of Language Development":

> As psycholinguists began to chart the course of language development, they were amazed that children could learn such a complex symbol system at such a breathtaking pace. After all, many infants are using arbitrary and abstract signifiers (words) to refer to objects and activities before they can walk. And by age 5, children already seem to know and use more of the syntactical structures of their native tongue, even though they have yet to receive their first formal lesson in grammar. How do they do it?

From Developmental Psychology: Childhood and Adolescence, Second Edition by SHAFFER. 2005. Reprinted with permission of Nelson, a division of Thomson Learning: www.thomsonrights.com. Fax 800-730-2215.

Here is one way this paragraph might be paraphrased.

> Psychologists who study how children learn language have been surprised at just how quickly infants pick up words and learn how to associate them with things or even concepts. Without any formal instruction in grammar, most children have already got the main sentence structure of their language down before they are five years old. The question is: How?

This paraphrase was written without the original at hand. That permitted the writer to think about what the paragraph actually said, and reflect on how well he understood it. It also reduced the chances of copying phrases from the original. In some cases, the paraphrase was longer than the original. For example, "psycholinguists" became "psychologists who study how children learn language." The writer can compare the completed paraphrase with the original to verify that it is a faithful representation.

TASK ONE Paraphrasing a Text

This task gives you the opportunity to employ and assess your paraphrasing skills.

Person 1: Please facilitate this task. Keep the group focused on each part of the task and move them on to the next part when ready.

Person 2: Please keep time, and give everyone a one-minute warning.

Part One: 5 minutes

Meet as a group to select a paragraph in any of your textbooks common to everyone.

Part Two: 5 minutes

Each person in the group will read and mark the paragraph.

Part Three: 5 minutes

Each person closes the text and writes a paraphrase of the paragraph.

Part Four: 15 minutes

Pass your paraphrase to someone else in the group. Read the paraphrase you receive. Circle any language error you see or suspect. Write a brief note to the writer at the end about the paraphrase. Here are some questions you can consider:

- Was it in the writer's own words?
- How well does the paraphrase capture the information from the original?
- Is it clear?

When you have finished, exchange the paraphrase you have just read for another one. Continue this until everyone in the group has seen everyone's paraphrase.

Part Five: 5 minutes

Get your paraphrase back and read the assessments at the bottom. Look at the circles which indicate possible language problems. Repair the ones you can now. Ask about the ones you are unsure of either now or later.

Producing a Summary

Summary writing uses your paraphrasing skills along with all the skills developed in using SQ3R, mapping and outlining. The aim is to distil the original text and rewrite it in your own words in significantly shortened format. Some forms of summary writing, like the abstract, have specific guidelines around length and content. General summary writing is looser. Aim at clarity, brevity, and the use of your own words, and you will be on the right track.

Here is a way to approach the job:

1. Read the article, mark it, and produce either a map or an outline.
2. Identify the title and the writer of the article for the title or first line of your summary.
3. Determine the purpose or thesis of the article. That purpose or thesis will appear early on in your summary.
4. Locate the topic sentences throughout the article. Each of these is an idea or move in the article that must appear in the summary.
5. Differentiate between the most significant points of support and detail for each of the topic sentences. You will likely use many, but not all, of the significant support points, and none of the detail.
6. Put the original text aside and write a summary in your own words.

Here's how it can be applied. Read through the following article from Beckman and Rigby's text *Foundations of Marketing*.

The Case for Complaining in a Restaurant

Many friends, colleagues and acquaintances who are assertive, articulate and outspoken turn into wimps when we dine out. When the chicken is dry or the service is inadequate, they can't seem to muster the courage to complain. I don't understand why they find this so difficult.

All the professionals I've spoken with in the restaurant industry swear they want to know the truth when they wander over to ask, "How is everything this evening?" But they know people lie to them—and they told me how they spot the liars. They say they'd prefer to be given a chance to fix a problem than to see a customer leave the restaurant unhappy. Unfortunately, they're seldom given that chance.

Some people have told me they say everything is okay when it's not because they don't believe the waiter really wants to know when something goes wrong. I don't think that's a reason to clam up. If you're paying a lot of money for dinner, you have every right to expect a good experience and you certainly shouldn't return to a restaurant that doesn't handle your complaint properly. My own experience is that the vast majority of foodservice professionals do care what you think.

So why are people afraid to complain? Sometimes they're intimidated—by the menu, by the posh surroundings or by the uniformed servers—and sometimes they're afraid of a confrontation. Will the chef be insulted if the plate goes back to the kitchen? However, when I've questioned people more closely, what inevitably comes out is that they're afraid of being branded as a "troublemaker" or a "complainer." Some people see that as a negative thing, but the irony is that a good restaurateur loves complainers.

I prefer to think of a complaint as a gift to the restaurant, and the professionals I spoke with agree. What's critical is that you do it in the right way. There's no need to raise your voice or to be angry. Be polite, stay calm and explain the problem as clearly as you can. If you're unhappy with the food, speak up right away. It's bad form to say you didn't enjoy your meal after you've licked your plate clean.

You may not want to spoil the mood of the evening. In that case, excuse yourself from the table and discreetly seek out the waiter or maitre d'. And if it's a very special occasion or a business meeting, you may not want to focus any attention on your unhappiness with the meal.

Try this: as you're leaving the restaurant, inform the maitre d' that you'll be calling the next day because you were unhappy about something. Before you phone, think about what kind of recourse you want. For example, would you like to give the restaurant a second chance or do you want some money back because you were overcharged?

> I don't believe in leaving a small tip for bad service. That only sends a message that you're a cheapskate. Again, it's important to speak up early and give the restaurant a chance to fix the problem; but if that doesn't work, my own policy is to leave no tip at all and write the words "service unacceptable" across the bill.
>
> In the eyes of restaurateurs, some customers fall into the category called "impossible to please." If you have a complaint, be prepared to accept a reasonable solution. And watch out for minefields. It might be wise to order something else if you request the venison steak well-done and the waiter says it might not be tender if it's cooked that way.
>
> Ultimately, it's important to have courage. If something isn't right with your restaurant experience and you say nothing, you're guaranteed to be unhappy as you leave. If you speak up, you may salvage your meal and your evening—and you'll be giving the restaurant a chance to turn a negative experience into a positive one.
>
> Just try it.
>
> **Source:** Adapted from "The Case for Complaining in a Restaurant", by Talin Vartanian (Broadcasted on *Marketplace*, February 27, 2002). http://www.cbc.ca/consumers/citizentalin/tips_restaurant.html.
> © Copyright Canadian Broadcasting Corporation. Reprinted with Permission.

Step One: Producing an outline after reading and marking the text.

1.0 Introduction: Outspoken people often lose their nerve in restaurants. Why?
2.0 Restaurant professionals really want to know customer concerns
    2.1 Most people lie
    2.2 Restaurant professionals are not given a chance to help customer leave contented
3.0 Customers believe waiters do not care
    3.1 If true, no reason to keep quiet
    3.2 Right to expect a good experience
4.0 Customers are often intimidated
    4.1 By menu, environment, staff, chef
    4.2 Afraid of being branded a troublemaker
5.0 Complaints are a gift to the industry
    5.1 Must be done well
    5.1.1 Calm voice, without anger
    5.1.2 Immediate rather than delayed criticism
6.0 Method 1 for discreet handling during a special event: Leave the table and seek out staff
7.0 Method 2 for discreet handling during a special event: Inform the restaurant you will call the next day
    7.1 Have a clear plan (money back or second chance)
8.0 Don't leave small tips
    8.1 Give professionals a chance to fix the problem
    8.2 Leave no tip if problem is not fixed, and write why on the bill
9.0 Avoid being an impossible customer
9.1 Accept reasonable solutions
9.2 Pay attention to waiter's cautions or advice
10.0 Conclusion: Courage is important to turn around a bad situation

Step Two: Identify the title and writer of the article for the first line of your summary

The notes at the end of the article indicate that this article was actually a broadcast script for CBC's *Marketplace*. It was prepared by Talin Vartanian for a February 2002 broadcast.

Step Three: Determine the purpose or thesis of the article.

The article states that the writer does not understand why so few people are willing to complain in restaurants. The purpose of the article is to make a case for the benefits of speaking up about unacceptable dining experiences.

Step Four: Locate the topic sentences.

- All the professionals I've spoken with in the restaurant industry swear they want to know the truth when they wander over to ask, "How is everything this evening?"
- Sometimes they're (customers) intimidated.
- I prefer to think of a complaint as a gift to the restaurant, and the professionals I spoke with agree.
- You may not want to spoil the mood of the evening. In that case, excuse yourself from the table and discreetly seek out the maître d'.
- Try this: as you're leaving the restaurant, inform the maître d' that you'll be calling the next day because you were unhappy about something.
- I don't believe in leaving a small tip for bad service.
- In the eyes of restaurateurs, some customers fall into the category called "impossible to please."

Step Five: Differentiate between the most significant points of support and detail for each of the topic sentences

Unimportant detail to omit:
- "Will the chef be insulted if the plate goes back to the kitchen?"
- "It's bad form to say you didn't enjoy your meal after you've licked your plate clean."
- Venison steak example.

Step Six: Put the original text aside and write a summary in your own words.

A Summary of Talin Vartanian's "The Case for Complaining in a Restaurant" from CBC Television's *Marketplace*

Otherwise outspoken people often hesitate to complain in restaurants. Possibly intimidated by the atmosphere or just unconvinced that restaurant staff actually want to improve their service, many customers do not make it clear when or why they are unhappy. The truth is that most industry professionals want to know how they can improve the dining experience. Customers do need to make their complaints politely and reasonably. They can step away from the table to talk with staff, or at special events let the restaurant manager know they will call the next day. Not tipping at all and writing why on the bill is better than leaving a small tip if the problem could not be settled during the meal. In any case, courage is important to turning a bad experience into a good one.

Summarizing a Text

TASK TWO

Everyone in your group prepared maps and outlines of two different chapters in a textbook common to all of you. This task asks you to select one of these for summary writing work.

Part One: 20 minutes

The group selects one of the chapters that it worked on for the tasks in Unit 2.

Review the chapter by looking at the marks you put on the text, and the map or outline your prepared. Now quickly skim the chapter once again. Discuss any points that you need to with anyone in the group.

Part Two: 30 minutes

Put the original aside and write a short summary. You can refer to your map or outline.

Part Three: 30 minutes

Pass your summary to someone else in the group. Read the summary you receive. Circle any language error you see or suspect. Write a brief note to the writer at the end about the summary.

Here are some questions you can consider:

- Did the summary announce that it was a summary?
- Did the summary provide the title and the author of the original?
- Did the summary clearly indicate the purpose and/or thesis of the original?
- Did the summary provide all the main points?
- Did the summary avoid including unnecessary detail that would make it more like an article than a summary of one?
- Was it in the writer's own words?
- Was the summary clear?
- Were there any language errors that need fixing?

When you have finished, exchange the summary for another one. Continue this process until everyone in the group has seen everyone else's summary.

Abstracts

You may be asked to write summaries in various courses to show that you have read and mastered some material. You may also be asked to write abstracts for advanced research assignments. Abstracts are formal summaries. They have a tighter structure than the general summary. If you search a library or the Internet you will come across two different kinds: the descriptive and the informative abstract.

The Descriptive Abstract

A descriptive abstract tells the reader what the original article is about without giving specific details. You will find descriptive abstracts when you research databases or Internet sources. It is a tool for researchers to decide whether the article is on target for their purposes. Consequently, they are short, single paragraphs even for long dissertations.

You can find examples of informative abstracts for dissertations at University Microfilms accessed through ProQuest Information and Learning at wwwlib.umi.com/dissertations. Type in any subject that interests you, and Proquest will search out dissertations from over 1,000 North American and European graduate schools. Click on the citation and abstract connection to read the abstract. That information gives you a good idea of whether you would find the original document useful.

Here's what to put in a descriptive abstract:

- Subject and topic area
- Context in which the original was written
- Purpose
- Indication of what general areas the article will cover
- Comments as to the scope and any particular method used to write the article

Here's what a descriptive abstract for "The Case for Complaining in a Restaurant" might look like:

> Talin Vartanian's broadcast piece for CBC Television's *Marketplace* examines why customers do not complain in restaurants and makes a case for why they should when service is unacceptable. The article is based on discussions with both customers and hospitality professionals. It also provides specific methods and guidelines for effective complaining.

This abstract provides:

Subject:	Customers in restaurants
Topic:	Complaints
Context:	A broadcast text for a CBC television program
Purpose:	To convince people they should complain in restaurants if service is unacceptable
Areas covered:	1. Reasons why people do not complain
	2. Reasons why they should complain
	3. Specific methods and guidelines for effective complaining
Method:	Discussions with customers and hospitality professionals

Writing a Descriptive Abstract

TASK THREE

Everyone in your group prepared a summary of one of your textbook chapters. Now write a descriptive abstract suitable for posting in a database.

Part One: 10 minutes

Write a descriptive abstract of the chapter on which you wrote a summary. Use the guidelines above.

Hint

Rely on the summary you wrote of the chapter rather than looking at the chapter itself.

Part Two: 15 minutes

Pass your descriptive abstract to someone else in the group. Read the descriptive abstract you receive. Circle any language error you see or suspect. Write a brief note to the writer at the end. Here are some questions you can consider:

- Does the abstract clearly identify the subject, topic and context?
- Does the abstract indicate the main areas covered in the original?
- Does the abstract keep out specific detail about the main areas covered?
- Is the abstract written in the writer's own words?

When you have finished, exchange the descriptive abstract you have just read for another one. Continue this until everyone in the group has seen everyone else's work.

Part Three: 5 minutes

Get your descriptive abstract back and read the assessments at the bottom. Look at the circles which indicate possible language problems. Repair the ones you can now. Ask about the ones you are unsure of now or later.

The Informative Abstract

An informative abstract is usually the last thing you write when preparing a formal academic report, but it is the first thing that gets read. This kind of summary is essentially a report of a report. Unlike the descriptive abstract, the informative abstract provides specific content from the original. The idea is that a busy reader could read the informative abstract and get all the main points or arguments made in the original document. Some readers might decide they do not need to read further. Others might decide that one or two points are intriguing and that they want the full details that a complete reading of those sections would give them. Finally, others might decide at some point to give the whole text a careful reading. Consequently, an informative abstract aims at being faithful to the original in terms of both content and how that content was organized.

Features of an Informative Abstract
- Subject and topic area
- Context in which the original was written
- Purpose
  — The first three points above are common to both descriptive and informative abstracts.
- All the main points made in the original presented in the same order with the same emphasis
  — The shift in the informative abstract is away from answering the question "What is the article about?" to answering the question "What does the article say?"
  — A general summary can rearrange the material to make ideas connect or hang together more smoothly. An abstract, however, reproduces the organization of the original. Consequently, the points appear in the same order. In addition, if the original devotes more space to one particular point than another, the abstract needs to reflect that weighting as well. By keeping the emphasis the same, the abstract becomes a faithful miniature of the original.
- 1/10th the length of the original
  — This length is a general rule of thumb. Anything longer likely includes too much detail. Anything shorter means the article likely leaves out some of the main points or arguments.

Hint

One of the temptations in abstract writing is to forget about paraphrasing and simply lift from the original. Be faithful to the content and organization of the original, but still rewrite it in fresh words.

Here's what an informative abstract for "The Case for Complaining in a Restaurant" might look like:

> Talin Vartanian's broadcast piece for CBC Television's *Marketplace* wonders why otherwise outspoken people are timid about making complaints in restaurants. It reports that hospitality professionals have told Vartanian that they want their guests to be honest with them, but that too many are not. Restaurant professionals do care, however, about finding ways to improve their service and gain satisfied customers.

Customers are not convinced of this commitment. But even so, that is no reason not to complain, as they have a right to good service. Intimidation is one possible cause of this timidity. Upscale environments and the fear of being labelled a complainer tend to inhibit people. Yet complaints are valuable help for the hospitality industry when done well. That means raising problems whenever they occur in a polite way, and being open to reasonable solutions.

If customers are worried about introducing a sour note, they can leave the table to talk to restaurant staff quietly. If the event is a very special one, customers can indicate there is a problem, but will call or visit the next day to discuss it with some kind of plan of action in mind.

The article advises against leaving small tips to indicate dissatisfaction, as it simply looks cheap. If the problem was raised and not settled, it is better to leave no tip at all and write why on the bill.

Essentially, customers need to be reasonable and pay attention to warnings or advice from restaurant staff, particularly when ordering.

Courage in speaking up is essential to transforming a poor experience into a good one.

This informative abstract contains the subject, topic, purpose, context, and methodology notes that the descriptive abstract does, but introduces all the main points as well, so that the reader can get a firm grasp on the content. It is shorter than the original, but longer than the general summary earlier in this unit. In that summary, some ideas were put together. For example, the need for customers to be reasonable was connected to the earlier point urging customers to be polite when complaining. The informative abstract, however, keeps the ideas separate, striving to reproduce not just the content, but the structure and organization of the original broadcast piece.

Writing an Informative Abstract — TASK FOUR

You have written a summary and a descriptive abstract of one of the chapters in a textbook common to everyone in the group. This time, write an informative abstract of either that same chapter, or of the other chapter on which you worked in Unit 2.

Person 3: Please facilitate this task. Keep the group focused on each part of the task and move them on to next part when ready.

Person 4: Please keep the time and give everyone a one-minute warning.

Part One: 30 minutes

Meet as a group to decide on which chapter to use.

Each person writes an informative abstract of the chapter. Use the guidelines above.

Hint

Rely on the map or outline you prepared for the chapter rather than looking at the chapter itself.

Part Two: 30 minutes

Pass your informative abstract to someone else in the group. Read the informative abstract you receive. Circle any language error you see or suspect. Write a brief note to the writer at the end. Here are some questions you can consider:

- Does the abstract present all the main ideas?
- Are the ideas presented in the same order with the same emphasis?
- Is the abstract about 1/10th the length of the original?
- Is the abstract written in the writer's own words?

When you have finished, exchange the informative abstract you have just read for another one. Continue this until everyone in the group has seen everyone else's work.

Part Three: 10 minutes

Get your informative abstract back and read the assessments at the bottom. Look at the circles which indicate possible language problems. Repair the ones you can now. Ask about the ones you are unsure of now or later.

The Evaluative Summary

The main job of summary writing is to provide a faithful retelling of an original text. Just how extensive that retelling is depends on the kind of summary and the situation for which it is meant. So far, you have worked on the general summary, the descriptive abstract, and the informative abstract, all of which are used for academic work.

Another kind of summary common to postsecondary work is the evaluative summary. In addition to a paraphrase of the original in an abbreviated form, the evaluative summary also provides commentary. That commentary might be a critique of the content as in a movie or book review, or an analysis of the usefulness of the original for some particular purpose. One example of the latter is the annotated bibliography which you will work on in Unit 13, "Research."

One way to approach an evaluative summary if you are asked to write one is to start with the **double-entry journal** technique. The double-entry journal uses two columns. If you are working in Microsoft Word, you can set this up by creating a two-column table. The left-hand column is for specific content from the original. You might write particular quotes or points from the text. An alternative to that is to paste in an outline of the original. The right-hand column is for your comments, observations, questions, or connections. You do not need to put in an entry for every point in the left column. Simply put in anything that occurs to you at any time directly beside the original point that suggested it to you. Like brainstorming, entering these comments should be a spontaneous activity. Avoid second-guessing yourself, or filtering out ideas before you write them down because you are not sure about them. The important thing is to get everything down and then consider it more fully in the context of all your thoughts in the journal later.

This unit has used the reading "The Case for Complaining in a Restaurant" as an example for developing a general summary, a descriptive abstract, and an informative abstract. If a professor asked you to write an evaluative summary of that article, you might start by creating a double-entry journal for the article.

Double-Entry Journal for Talin Vartanian's "The Informed Consumer" in Beckman and Rigby's *Foundations of Marketing*

Content	Commentary
1.0 Introduction Outspoken people often lose their nerve in restaurants. Why?	How accurate is this? The article depends on this assumption. It seems reasonable that normally timid people would not complain, but on what does he base the assertion that normally assertive people lose their assertiveness in restaurants? Is this article much ado about nothing?
2.0 Restaurant professionals really want to know customer concerns 2.1 Most people lie 2.2 Restaurant professionals not given a chance to help customer leave contented	This sounds like another big assumption. The term "restaurant professionals" covers a lot of different people in a lot of different settings. Vartanian suggests that they are really interested in the customer's well-being, but he skips the whole motive of self-interest. Are waiters really concerned to give the customer a good experience, or are they concerned about getting a tip? Is the concern for the customer really a sham for self-interest purposes so that the professionals complain about the customers among themselves? Vartanian claims to have checked out his assumptions. How thorough was that? Is there a difference in attitude from one kind of restaurant, a posh one for instance, and a fast food restaurant?
3.0 Customers believe waiters do not care 3.1 If true, no reason to keep quiet 3.2 Right to expect a good experience	If it is true that many or most customers believe that waiters do not care, where does this belief come from? Does that mean that many have had the experience of waiters who do not care? Another possibility—is it that waiters do not care, or is it possible that the perception they do not care comes from overwork? Busy waiters handling too many tables in peak hours may be struggling to get the basics done and so do not seem attentive. There is a parallel here to airline attendants.

Content	Commentary
	I agree that you have the right to expect your money's worth. This idea means that you can expect more in an expensive restaurant but shouldn't expect as much or complain as much in a cheap restaurant. In that case, the customer made the choice to accept lower quality and service.
4.0 Customers are often intimidated 4.1 By menu, environment, staff, chef 4.2 Afraid of being branded a troublemaker	The article never clearly states if the writer means the whole industry or just part of it. This point, however, suggests that what he really has in mind is expensive, fancy restaurants.
5.0 Complaints are a gift to the industry 5.1 Must be done well 5.1.1 Calm voice, without anger 5.1.2 Immediate rather than delayed criticism	I have trouble believing this one. Many restaurant professionals may do their best to resolve problems, but I doubt they are happy to get complaints in the same way they would be to receive a gift. This part of the article is a useful corrective to the impression of complaining as being nasty and accusatory.
6.0 Method 1 for discreet handling during a special event: Leave the table and seek out staff	This practical advice is the most useful part of the whole piece.
7.0 Method 2 for discreet handling during a special event: Inform the restaurant you will call the next day Have a clear plan (money back or second chance)	This is a good idea for dealing with any kind of service problem anywhere.
8.0 Don't leave small tips: 8.1 Give professionals a chance to fix 8.2 Leave no tip if problem is not fixed and write why on the bill	This really makes sense. I have never heard of writing explanatory notes on the bill. It is a good idea because it creates a record that service staff and management will see. I think I might add an email address so the manager could follow up.
9.0 Avoid being an impossible customer 9.1 Accept reasonable solutions 9.2 Pay attention to waiter's cautions or advice	Good general advice. It seems out of place, though. Shouldn't it go with 5.0?
10.0 Conclusion: Courage is important to turn around a bad situation	Good principle of living in any situation.

After you finish your double-entry journal, you need to decide how much of your commentary you are actually going to use. That will depend on the assignment. Double-check about length requirements and how thorough an evaluation is needed.

You also need to decide how you will put the evaluative summary together. One way is to simply write it in two parts. The first part presents an objective presentation of the material without your own voice. The second part presents your evaluation. If you write it this way, the evaluative summary might look like this:

A Summary of Talin Vartanian's "The Case for Complaining in a Restaurant" from CBC Television's *Marketplace*

Vartanian observes that otherwise outspoken people often hesitate to complain in restaurants. Possibly intimidated by the atmosphere or just unconvinced that restaurant staff actually want to improve their service, many customers do not make it clear when or why they are unhappy. The article insists that the truth is that most industry professionals want to know how they can improve the dining experience. Customers do need to make their complaints politely and reasonably. They can step away from the table to talk with staff, or at special events let the restaurant manager know they will call the next day. Not tipping at all is better than leaving a small tip if the problem could not be settled during the meal. In any case, courage is important to turning a bad experience into a good one.

The article's advice on how to complain in a reasonable way is a useful corrective to the impression that complaining is negative because it is just angry or accusatory. Vartanian makes an unfounded stretch, however, when he says that restaurant professionals actually welcome complaints as gifts. The article is at its best when it deals with specifics like tipping. On the other hand, much of the article seems based on assumptions or generalizations, possibly because of limited broadcast time.

A second way to put your evaluative summary together is to incorporate your comments all the way through. That approach might produce an evaluative summary like this:

A Summary of Talin Vartanian's "The Case for Complaining in a Restaurant" from CBC Television's *Marketplace*

Vartanian's broadcast piece is based on two assumptions. The first is that otherwise outspoken people are unwilling to complain in restaurants. The second is that restaurant professionals are eager to make things right and see complaints as gifts. Neither of these assumptions is well supported in the article. Vartanian simply comments that he has spoken to some people. The article does not clearly distinguish between one kind of restaurant environment and another, although it seems that Vartanian has expensive places in mind. Despite the questionable premises, the article does provide practical advice on how to register complaints, including stepping away from the table; telling management that you will call the next day with a clear plan; and couching complaints in polite terms, showing that you are always open to reasonable solutions. He makes the excellent point that even if customers are intimidated by the restaurant environment or are convinced that restaurant staff do not really want to hear complaints, they have a right to expect a good experience. Vartanian's discussion on not using small tips as a means to register dissatisfaction is particularly valuable. He suggests the interesting idea of writing clearly on the bill why you are not leaving a tip. In the end, he advocates that customers should have the courage to speak up when not satisfied in order to change bad experiences into good ones. This principle is a good one for life in general.

In Summary

Take three minutes to write a summary of what you have learned participating in the tasks of Unit 3.

Part 2

Essay Writing

Unit 4: Characteristics of Essay Writing
Unit 5: Planning
Unit 6: Introductions
Unit 7: Conclusions
Unit 8: Drafting, Revising, and Editing

Part 1 looked at academic reading. Part 2 focuses on academic writing. The two activities are closely linked. Much of your writing will either be in response to a reading or involve bringing together information from various readings for you to make your point. In both cases, the writing process requires reflection on what other writers have to say. Writing an academic essay is a process that, like reading, also requires a strategy. The units in Part 2 suggest a strategy for thinking through, planning, and writing a complete paper. They also present alternatives for putting together the basic building blocks of an essay. This section asks you to examine the characteristics of an academic in Unit 4. You will try out the questioning system in Unit 5, alternative approaches to crafting introductions and conclusions in Units 6 and 7, and a method for drafting, revising, and editing your papers through a peer review process in Unit 8. Part 2 asks you to apply all of these techniques to a particular writing task that will end in a complete academic paper.

UNIT 4

Characteristics of Essay Writing

Here's what you'll work on in this unit.

- Producing a writing sample
- Assessing your work
- Identifying main characteristics of academic essay writing

The Writing Sample — TASK ONE

WRITING SAMPLE

Purpose	The purpose of the writing sample assignment is to give you an opportunity to produce a piece of writing with a specific purpose for a particular audience. It will also give you a first piece of writing to use during a self-assessment process.
Assignment	The chair of your department is interested in learning about the students and why they have chosen to study their programs. The department will use this information to familiarize faculty with the students and devise ways to enhance their learning experience. Your first writing task is to put together a complete first draft of a short essay addressed to your department chair.
Method	1. List your ideas (5 minutes). 2. Organize them into a rough outline (5 minutes). 3. Add to or delete from that outline as necessary (5 minutes). 4. Write out a draft (20–30 minutes).

Assessment — TASK TWO

Exchange drafts with another person in your group and work through the following assessment process. Read through the paper given to you before you use the assessment tool below. Circle any errors in language mechanics—including grammar, spelling, and punctuation—that you see or suspect as you read.

Assessment of the writing sample

Your Name _____ Writer's Name _____

1. Did the writer produce a short essay with recognizable paragraph divisions?

   Yes ❑

   No ❑

2. Is the writing clearly aimed at the chair of your department?

   Yes ❑ I know this because _____

   No ❑

3. Does the writing begin with an opening paragraph that establishes some kind of background to the essay?

   Yes ❑

   No ❑

   Somewhat, but more is needed. For example, _____

   _____

4. Does the opening paragraph make a clear statement of purpose?

   Yes ❑ If yes, which sentence? _____

   No ❑

   Somewhat. It needs improvement. For example, _____

   _____

5. Does each of the paragraphs expand upon an idea that is connected with the purpose in the opening paragraph?

   Yes ❑

   No ❑

   Generally, except for _____

6. Does each of the paragraphs provide specific concrete examples or detail so that the reader can clearly understand what is meant?

   Yes ❑

   No ❑

   Generally, except for _____

7. Does the essay clearly demonstrate in an understandable way why the writer has entered his or her field?

   Yes ❑

   No ❑

   Somewhat, but more is needed. For example, _____

8. Does the essay have a closing paragraph that ties things up instead of just ending abruptly making a main point?

   Yes ❑

   No ❑

   Somewhat, but it needs improvement. For example, _____

9. Is the writing free from errors in language mechanics?

   Yes ❑

   No ❑ I have circled words, punctuation, and sentence parts that I think might have problems.

10. Write a short message in three to five sentences that tells the writer what you think works well and what could be made to work even better.

This assessment helped you identify some of the characteristics of academic essay writing which are the exit goals for a course in writing like this one.

Some Characteristics of Academic Writing

Question 1: Paragraph Divisions
Essay writing is divided into paragraphs to mark off separate ideas. When readers move from one paragraph, they expect to move from one main point to another one. On one hand, these sections are separate, distinct blocks that each present a different facet of the topic. On the other hand, they fit together to make a unified whole around the central message of the essay. For the purposes of the essay writing in this text, each paragraph should have at least five sentences. Paragraphs that have fewer than five sentences have likely not fully explained or developed the point you want to make.

Question 2: Readership
Never pick up a pen or start typing on a computer without a clear sense of who your readership is. The way you write to one kind of reader will be different from the way you write to another. Your choice of words, your style, and even the points you want to make differ from one context to another. The academic essay writing you do at college will usually be aimed at a professor who wants an essay in Standard English using a formal or semi-formal style that demonstrates you have researched and understand a topic. There may well be situations, however, in which you write in case-study situations aimed at a different readership that requires alternative strategies.

Question 3: Opening
Academic essay writing begins with an *introduction*. One of the purposes of such a section is to provide essential background to the topic. It sets the context, defines any terms, or briefly outlines any necessary information that a reader would need to understand the main message.

Question 4: Purpose and Thesis
The introduction also presents the main purpose and message of the essay in a *thesis statement*. That statement clearly identifies the topic and what your essay wants to say about it.

Question 5: Relevant Paragraphs
Each of the paragraphs in the body of the essay announces a single main point in a topic sentence that in turn is directly connected to the message statement or thesis in the introduction. A paragraph that has an idea not directly connected to that idea is out of place, even if the material is true and valuable.

Question 6: Concrete Examples or Detail
One of the reasons paragraphs in academic writing should be a minimum of five sentences long is that, after they present their main point in a topic sentence, they also present specific details about that point. This material is called *support*, and it can take many forms: several examples; an expanded example, also called an *illustration*; explanation; facts; and other possibilities.

Question 7: Demonstrates in an Understandable Way
The essay is meant to accomplish a purpose announced in the introduction. It does not simply state a message, but also demonstrates that the message is valid. That is why an essay needs to extend itself through body paragraphs with concrete points. The writer's job is to write a piece so that the reader can see what is meant from the reading alone.

Question 8: Closing Paragraph
Academic writing uses a "bookends" approach. The introduction marks one side of the essay while a *conclusion* marks the other side. Many people opt for using a conclusion to summarize what has already been written, but that is not the only, or even always the best, choice. The conclusion mostly functions to end the essay neatly, to avoid an abrupt stop.

The conclusion to an essay can do many things, but it should not, in academic writing at least, suddenly announce a new point. In that case, it would not be a conclusion at all, but another body paragraph.

Question 9: Free from Language Mechanics Errors
College academic writing should be polished. It is meant to demonstrate care not only in the thinking and the organizing of ideas, but in the presentation of those ideas through Standard English. That is where a peer assessment model comes in. It is valuable to get someone else to proofread, as you often cannot see your own errors and glitches.

The above list includes only some of the characteristics of academic writing. Others include research, proper documentation, and format. You will work on these characteristics as you put together essays in the tasks ahead.

In Summary
Take three minutes to write a summary of what you have learned participating in the tasks of Unit 4.

UNIT 5
Planning

Here's what you'll work on in this unit.

- Writing focused thesis statements
- Applying questioning to plan an essay
- Developing an essay with a box outline
- Differentiating different kinds of support

Part 1 asked you to produce summaries and abstracts as your first type of academic writing. That kind of writing is primarily a re-presentation of other work. Part 2 of this text focuses on the main kind of academic writing expected of students in post-secondary programs—essay writing. You will likely be asked to write many different kinds of essays for specific purposes and situations. Those different types share common elements. Planning these elements in advance of writing will help you write more effectively.

The Thesis Statement

Planning and writing an essay depend on a well-crafted central message. That message, or *thesis statement*, is the reason for the essay, and is the measure of whether the essay was successful. In other words, a good thesis statement is critical to two important questions in the essay writing process:

- What does the essay want to say?
- Does the essay accomplish what it set out to do in a convincing manner?

Paying attention to the thesis statement at the beginning helps make the whole process smooth. It gives clarity to what you hope to achieve and helps you focus your work.

From Subject to Topic

Putting together a clear thesis statement begins with moving from subject to topic. In many cases, you will work with an assigned topic. In others, however, you have a general subject that needs narrowing. If you were a student in a fitness and recreation program, for example, you might be working on the subject of dieting. Going to a search engine and entering the term "dieting" yields millions of results. You could not possibly sift through all of them. The problem is that you have a subject, not a topic. The next step is to narrow the subject down so that it is manageable. You might work on the effects of dieting, the causes of dieting, a particular type of dieting, the psychology of dieting, or some other specific focus. The idea is to keep refining the focus so that in the end you have something about which you can craft a meaningful message. This continuing refinement from subject to topic might look like this:

Dieting

Effects of Dieting

Effects of Dieting on Women

Physical Effects of Dieting on Women

Physical Effects of Dieting on Pregnant Women

Physical Effects of High-Protein, Low-Carbohydrate Dieting on Pregnant Women

The Primary Physical Effect of High-Protein, Low-Carbohydrate Dieting on Pregnant Women

Two things happen when you focus in this way. The first is that each line is a little longer than the one above it. If you have only one or two words, you likely do not have a *topic*, but a *subject*. Generally, the more words it takes to express what you are writing about, the more likely it is that you have a focused topic. The second thing that happens is that you make it clear for yourself what you don't need to put in the essay. Essentially, focusing in this way rules out a great deal of the material connected with the subject. It is like continually refining your search terms for a database or on a search engine. You make it more and more clear what you do not need so that you are left with a narrower, manageable pool of information.

How far you go down with the focus depends on the parameters of the project. The farther down you go, the more targeted your writing. Here's one way of assessing the kind of writing suitable for the dieting project:

Dieting	This is an unfocused subject about which you could write endlessly.
Effects of Dieting	Although there is the beginning of a focus here, covering all the effects of all kinds of dieting adequately would mean a major project covering several volumes.
Effects of Dieting on Women	Covering all the effects, including physical and psychological considerations, would require at least a book-length treatment.
Physical Effects of Dieting on Women	The subject is still enormous. It might be best treated in a lengthy dissertation.
Physical Effects of Dieting on Pregnant Women	Although the target group is narrow, considering dieting and its effects in general would require a great deal of space, perhaps in a lengthy formal report.

Physical Effects of High-Protein, Low-Carbohydrate Dieting on Pregnant Women	This topic has narrowed down the dieting to one particular kind. It still intends to discuss a number of physical effects, so this likely will also require a report, but shorter than the one above.
The Primary Physical Effect of High-Protein, Low-Carbohydrate Dieting on Pregnant Women	Since the focus is one physical effect, this topic is suitable for a short article.

Focusing from Subject to Topic

TASK ONE

15 minutes

Your group will begin planning an academic essay on a subject in your field of study. Work together to select a subject. It can be from class lectures or from your text. It should only be one or two words. Focus that subject down through at least five levels. Identify what sort of writing for which the different levels would be suitable.

Person 2: Please facilitate Task One. Be sure that everyone has a chance to speak while keeping the discussion focused on the task.

Person 3: Please write down the results of the group discussion in the form below.

Person 4: Please keep track of the time and remind your group of how much time is left.

Person 1: Be ready to the present the results to the class at the end.

Subject to Topic	Type of Writing

Subject to Topic	Type of Writing

The Message

Once you have a focused topic, the next step in writing the thesis statement is to develop a clear message. In some cases, that message will occur to you right away. In other cases, you will need to do some research first to learn more about the topic before you form an opinion or identify what you want to say about it. In any case, keep in mind the following considerations about what a thesis is and isn't.

1. The thesis statement is not a simple fact, such as:

    Immigration is up.

    To say that immigration numbers are up in a particular year is a fact not a thesis statement. It does not convey a message but only information. Information is used in support of a message or thesis statement, but does not replace the thesis statement itself.

2. The thesis statement conveys an idea that will need support, such as:

    Canada needs to increase immigration.

    One message about the subject immigration might be that Canada needs to drastically open up its immigration policy to allow in larger numbers in a broader range of categories. That message is not a fact but an idea that will be supported by some, but certainly not by everyone who might read the essay. Such a message is a thesis because it immediately makes many people ask why. In other words, it requires argument and information to back it up.

3. The thesis statement requires a complete sentence, unlike the following:

   Challenges to Canadian immigration policy.

   Effects of increased immigration.

Sentence fragments like this do not convey a clear message in a complete sentence. They might be good titles, but they are not good thesis statements. What *about* the challenges to Canadian immigration policy? Are they easily managed or are they serious obstacles? What *about* the effects of increased immigration? Are they positive or negative?

4. The statement should not be expressed as a question:

   Should Canada open its doors to more immigrants?

The above expresses a problem or a course of inquiry, but does not convey a message. The *answer* to that question would be the thesis statement.

Differentiating Between Adequate and Inadequate Thesis Statements

TASK TWO

Read through the following thesis statements. Identify which ones are adequate on the basis of the criteria above. Determine the reasons why any of the following statements are inadequate thesis statements. Suggest ways that the inadequate statements could be improved.

Person 3: Please facilitate this task.
Person 4: Please record the group's answers in the chart below.
Person 1: Please keep track of the time.
Person 2: Please be spokesperson for your group in the class discussion.

Ottawa is the capital city of Canada.	
Ottawa and cultural activities.	
Is Canada's military really underfunded?	

Unit 5 Planning

Canada's military has been increasingly called upon for peacekeeping in more and more countries in the world.	
Canadian multiculturalism is a better approach than the American melting pot.	
Illegal immigrants in Ontario and British Columbia.	
The severe problem of illegal immigration in Canada.	
Canada and the United States would benefit from adopting a common currency.	
The differences between postsecondary education at colleges and post-secondary education at universities in Canada.	
Do private schools offer a better education than public ones?	

Developing the Thesis Statement

TASK THREE

15 minutes

Your group focused a subject in your field in Task One. Work with the focus suitable for a short essay and develop an appropriate thesis statement for an academic paper to be submitted to a professor who teaches that subject.

Part One

Person 4: Please facilitate the task and be sure that everyone has a chance to make suggestions.

Person 1: Please takes notes of the discussion and enter the final version of the thesis statement in the box below.

Person 2: Please keep track of the time.

Person 4: Please present the thesis statement to the rest of the class.

Thesis statement

Part Two

Listen to the thesis statements prepared by the different groups in the class. Be prepared to make comments on whether or not they are adequate, and how they could be improved.

Person 1: Please note down any comments that people from other groups make about your group's thesis statement.

Thesis statement critique

Thinking About the Essay

The essay expands the thesis statement. It makes the statement clear, makes arguments around it, and provides support for what you write. That is done through a series of paragraphs. The opening or introduction and the closing or conclusion use specific strategies that you will consider in upcoming units. Body paragraphs, the meat of the essay, are organizing devices that help you arrange your material and also help the reader make sense out of your discussion. Here are some general guidelines to keep in mind as you think about expanding the thesis statement.

Guidelines

1. *The rule of thumb is that each body paragraph includes only one main point.* A ten-paragraph essay that includes one paragraph as an introduction and one as a conclusion has eight body paragraphs. That is a signal to the reader to look for eight main points. If any one paragraph has more than one point, it likely means that the points have not been fully explained or adequately supported.

2. *Write a clear topic sentence for each paragraph.* Just as a thesis statement is a message that governs the entire essay, the topic sentence is a message that governs a paragraph. The topic sentence announces a point that relates directly to the message or controlling idea of the thesis statement. Remove any point that does not fit that message. Take a look at the following outline for an essay.

   ### THESIS: JUNK FOOD IS UNHEALTHY.
Topic sentence 1.	Deep-fried junk food is responsible for increased cases of heart problems.
Topic sentence 2.	Sweet junk food causes early cases of diabetes.
Topic sentence 3.	Junk food is expensive.
Topic sentence 4.	Empty carbs cause obesity.

   The message of this essay has to do with dangers to health. Whereas topic sentences 1, 2, and 4 are on target and help explain that message, topic sentence 3 does not. The idea may be true, but it is not connected to the controlling idea of the essay. Consequently, topic sentence 3 might go in a different essay on junk food, but not in this one.

3. *Put the topic sentence at the beginning of each body paragraph.* You will read text by experienced writers that put the topic sentence at the end or middle of a paragraph. In some cases, you will not find a topic sentence at all because it is implied. For the essay work in this book, however, put your topic sentences right at the beginning of each paragraph. That will help you plan and write more efficiently. Readers will appreciate the clarity because they will be able to find your points quickly.

4. *Expand each topic sentence with specific support.* Each topic sentence needs support. That support can come in a number of ways:
   - Full explanation of an idea
   - Several examples
   - One extended example, sometimes referred to as an illustration
   - Details, facts, statistics

5. *Plan for about five to eight sentences for each paragraph.* Paragraphs with only two or three sentences likely are not supporting the topic sentence as well as they might.

Paragraphs that go much beyond eight sentences may be getting off track, providing more detail than necessary, or providing material best presented in a separate paragraph.

Questioning

Once you have developed a strong thesis statement, you are ready to develop a plan for your essay. One useful way to do that is to use questioning. Questioning starts with a clear thesis statement, turns it into a question, and then answers the questions in as many ways possible.

Take, for example, the following thesis statement:

> Canada needs to broaden its immigration policy to admit more people in more categories.

Step one in the questioning process is to turn the thesis statement into a question. The question that comes out of that statement is:

> Why does Canada need to admit more people in more categories?

Step two in the questioning process is to list out as many answers to the question as possible. Do not stop at the obvious answers but keep going even if they seem a little farfetched at the time until you run out of ideas. Some of the answers to the question might be:

- We need replacement workers.
- We need people to contribute to our social services.
- We need to increase our population.
- We need to stimulate economic growth.
- We need different perspectives.
- We need enriched cultural contributions.
- We need to increase international contacts.
- We need more highly trained professionals

Step three is to select the type and number of answers that best fit the parameters of the assignment. For example, if you were asked to write a five-paragraph essay, you would choose three points. Each point would require one body paragraph that along with the introduction and conclusion would fulfill the requirements. If you were writing a significantly longer paper, you would be able to include more of the points on your list.

You also need to select those points that best fit the purpose and readership of your essay. In some cases, you might be writing for specific readerships like students, older people, managers, or labour. Those groups will have specific interests. Certain points will be of more interest to them than others. Here's one way of making that decision around the paper on immigration for different readers:

Readership	Discussion to Include
Labour (e.g. union publication)	Replacing workers Taking jobs
Older adults (e.g. seniors' publications)	Demographics and retirement Supporting social services
Management (e.g. business magazine or newspaper)	Stimulating economic growth Highly trained professionals as employees
Cultural and social special interest groups	Expanding cultural perspectives Increasing international contacts

Thus, how many points you choose and which of them you end up working with depends on what you want to accomplish for a particular target audience in a particular format. For academic writing, however, your target reader is usually your professor, unless you have been assigned to write for someone else. Consequently, you are writing to an academic who is looking to see that you can demonstrate an ability to use well-reasoned and well-supported arguments. In that case, you need to choose your strongest points that show you have a clear grasp of the issue.

Step four is to turn each of the answers you have selected for your essay into a topic sentence. Here is how that might look:

1. Immigration can help Canada solve a looming labour shortage problem.
2. Another advantage of increased immigration is that it provides increased support for social programs.
3. Finally, more immigration means greater economic activity.

Step five is to put the thesis statement and topic sentences into a box outline. A box outline provides a separate box for each paragraph of the essay. It helps you see each paragraph as both self-contained and as part of a larger whole, in much the same way that every car in a train is a unit with its own content but still part of the larger train. Put the thesis statement at the bottom of the introduction box. Put each of the topic sentences at the beginning of the body paragraph boxes. Here is how that would look:

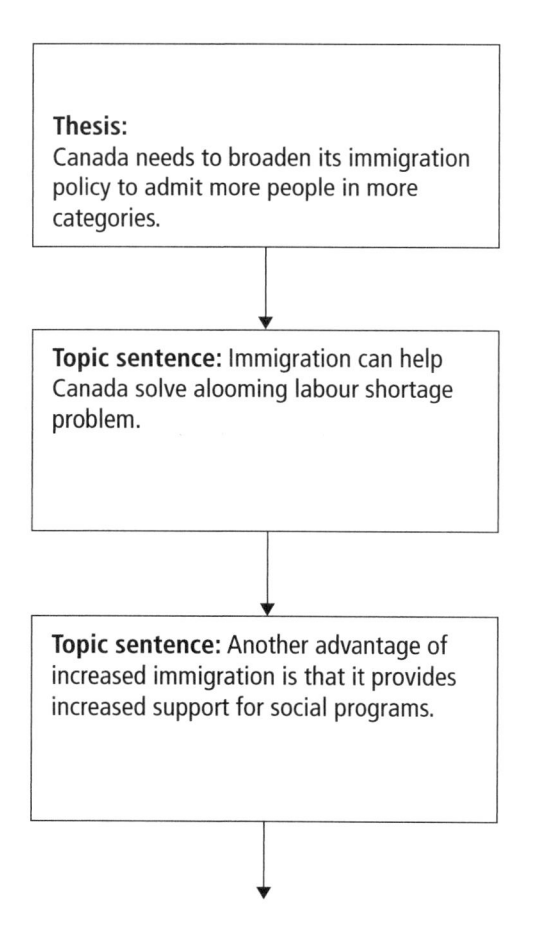

Thesis:
Canada needs to broaden its immigration policy to admit more people in more categories.

↓

Topic sentence: Immigration can help Canada solve a looming labour shortage problem.

↓

Topic sentence: Another advantage of increased immigration is that it provides increased support for social programs.

↓

> **Topic sentence:** Finally, more immigration means greater economic activity.

> **Conclusion**

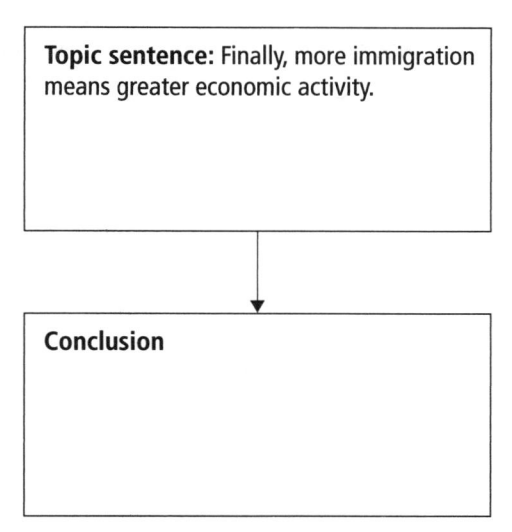

Step six is to fill in the boxes with bulleted points that indicate the kind of support you plan to use. For example, you might fill in the first body paragraph box this way:

Immigration can help Canada solve a looming labour shortage problem.

- Baby boomers who currently make up 1/3 of Ontario's workforce have already begun retiring.
- Some professions have a retirement rate of over 50%. (Ontario Job Futures).
- Affects construction and other industries, as there are not enough people to do the work.
- Baby boomers have begun retiring in large numbers.
- Canada is forecast to have a shortage of 1.2 million workers by 2020 (Consultancy Watson Wyatt)
- Trained immigrants are eager to find positions and use their skills to build up Canada.

You now have a valuable outline that you can turn into a rough draft. This kind of arrangement helps you see how well your ideas fit together. It also helps you verify that all of your ideas match the thesis, and that all of the support in each box matches the controlling idea of the topic sentence.

Planning Out a Group Essay TASK FOUR

Your group developed a thesis statement in Task Three. This task gives you an opportunity to work together to apply the questioning technique and develop a box outline.

Plan a short paper with two or three body paragraphs around the thesis statement developed in Task Three.

Part One

Person 1: Please facilitate this task.
Person 2: Please keep track of the time for your group.
Person 3: Please record the outline in the blank outline below.
Person 4: Be ready to explain your outline to another group.

Thesis

Topic sentence 1:

Support

Topic sentence 2:

Support

Topic sentence 3:

Support

Closing paragraph

Part Two

Person 4: Please leave your group and visit another one. Explain your box outline to the group. Note down any comments or suggestions that they give you.

Preparing a box outline in this way takes a little time, but it is well worth the investment. You will be able to write more efficiently, keep on track, and stay focused on a clear message. This technique is also extremely helpful for essay exams. Simply plowing into an essay on an exam can be dangerous. You might write yourself into a corner, get off track, forget to put information only to remember it later, and so on. Organize the time you have available so that you provide time for checking, writing, and especially planning. Ten minutes or so up front for an hour-long writing task can actually save you time. Another advantage of using the box outline on an essay exam is that you have a planning document that you can hand in along with your work. If you run out of time on an exam, that document shows what you were planning to say and how you were planning to say it.

TASK FIVE   Planning Out an Individual Essay

This task gives you the opportunity to individually apply questioning and the box outline method to an academic topic in your field.

A professor in one of your courses has asked for a five-paragraph essay on a subject in your field. The purpose of the assignment is to demonstrate that you understand the subject and can explain a particular aspect of it in your own words.

Part One

Select a subject in your field that interests you and which you already know something about. It might be something discussed in your texts or on the curriculum. Everyone in the group can work on something different. It is all right, too, if more than one person is working on the same subject. Narrow the subject to a specific focus and develop a topic sentence.

Apply the five steps in the questioning process to produce a box outline. Use the blank boxes below.

Thesis

Topic sentence 1:

Support

Topic sentence 2:

Support

Topic sentence 3:

Support

Closing paragraph

Part Two

Exchange your box outline with each person in your group. Read through each of the box outlines that they give you. Write a brief assessment for each one using the following guidelines:

- Does the outline show a focused topic?
- Does the thesis statement have a clear message?
- Does each of the topic sentences serve the message in the thesis sentence?
- Does each of the support points in the different boxes support the topic sentence to which it is connected?
- How might the writer improve this outline?

In Summary

Take three minutes to write a summary of what you have learned participating in the tasks of Unit 5.

UNIT 6
Introductions

Here's what you'll work on in this unit.

- Crafting leading sentences
- Determining necessary background information
- Identifying scope
- Clarifying the principle of organization
- Placing thesis statements
- Writing introductions for an essay plan

Unit 4 asked you to work out an outline for the body of the essay before you begin the first draft. The next step in the process is to outline an introduction. Introductions or openings are critical to the success of an essay. They are the first contact the reader has with your essay and your writing style. The first impression made by the introduction will predispose the reader's reactions to your essay. Whether a professor who is grading the paper or a general reader who has picked up your work out of interest, the reader's attitude depends a great deal on what happens in that first paragraph. Introductions hook the reader, provide necessary orientation to background and purpose, and provide the thesis statement.

Think of the introduction as an inverted pyramid. It begins with broad statements that gradually lead the reader to a tight focus and then to a specific message about that focus. You can diagram your introductions in the following way:

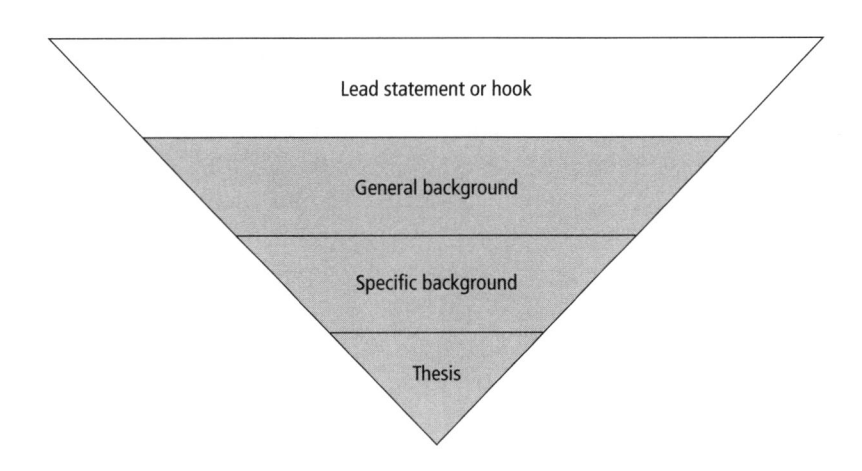

Lead statement or hook

General background

Specific background

Thesis

One way to get started with the introduction is to ask yourself what you would find useful if you were reading it. The answer depends on putting yourself in the shoes of the reader. Just how familiar is the reader with that subject? Some readers will need to be filled in more than others. What would the reader expect out of your treatment? Your professor might expect evidence that you have carefully read the material, thought about the topic, and made connections to other information or ideas. Answering a few basic questions that your specific readership may have will help you orient that reader in your opening.

Hint

Write your introduction after you have planned out your paper in detail so that you have a clear idea of what you are introducing the reader to.

Here's What to Avoid

You have many options for putting your introduction together, but there are a few things to stay away from. Take a look at the following introduction for an essay in the social sciences:

> This report is about Canadian demographics. It will discuss the increasing number of seniors and birth rates. Demographic change also relates to BPI. It will also discuss the Canadian family in terms of percentages of marriages and divorce cases.

This introductory paragraph is neither engaging nor particularly helpful, for a number of reasons.

Absence of an Opening Strategy

The lead sentence does not use any particular strategy to hook or attract the reader. All it does is make an announcement in a dull sentence. That means that the writer has not spent much time thinking about how to engage the readership. If the introduction creates the first impression that carries through the essay, the first one or two lines is the critical opportunity. Readers of magazine articles, for example, will judge after the first few lines whether the article is worth reading. The writer may have something worthwhile to say but it can go unread unless the essay uses some specific strategies to get the reader to commit to the article.

Insufficient Background Material

The writer has also omitted any specific background to this particular article. Some readers need to know specific terminology or acronyms like BPI, which happens to mean Buying

Power Index. If this is a report, it is not clear in what context it was written or for what purpose. Consequently, it is not clear why this paper is even worth reading.

Lack of Focus

The reader cannot find a focus for this report. Although the subject is Canadian demographics, it is not apparent what the essay is actually doing with the subject. At first, it seems interested in a profile by age, but then it veers into marriage issues. The reader is also not clear on whether the report is a historical treatment, a current profile, or an examination of trends.

Failure to Communicate a Message

The introduction does not provide a clear message about the subject. There is no explicit thesis statement. The reader does not know what the writer is out to demonstrate, prove, or explain. With no message, the report lacks a coherent way to sift the enormous amounts of information on Canadian demographics so that it can say something meaningful rather than just a compilation of assorted information. A thesis statement is essential because it anchors the writing.

With some rewriting, the paragraph might work as a descriptive abstract, but it cannot work as an introduction because it just does not say enough, nor does it establish any kind of tone for the essay to help carry a message. It needs specific opening strategies, a greater focus, more specific information, and a clear thesis. All of that would mean a much longer introduction.

Hint

Give your introductions as much space as necessary to accomplish their purposes. Although the introductions you write for the essay tasks in this book might use single paragraphs, they can be much longer. Some of the examples you will see in this unit use more than one paragraph. The entire first chapter of many textbooks is titled "Introduction." The longer the piece of writing, the longer your introduction will likely be.

The Hook

The first sentence of an essay, sometimes called the *hook*, is the writer's opportunity to grab the reader. The goal is to convince the reader to continue with the introduction, which in turn presents a case that this essay is worth reading.

You can try different strategies for your lead statement. The main thing is to find a way to engage the reader. Vary your approach as you work on different essays in your post-secondary work.

TASK ONE Identifying the Hook

15 minutes

Look at the sample openings below for a chapter on rainforests meant for a textbook on the environment. Identify what the writer does to engage the reader's attention. Explain how that method gets the reader to read further.

Person 2: Please facilitate this task. Be sure everyone has a chance to comment.
Person 3: Please keep track of the time for your group.
Person 4: Please read out the sample paragraphs.
Person 1: Please be ready to give your group answers to the class.

Rainforest Facts reports rainforests once covered 14% of the earth's land surface; now they cover a mere 6% and experts estimate that the last remaining rainforests could be consumed in less than 40 years. Several reasons are behind this disaster including local poverty, multinational corporation greed and short-sighted governments. Whatever the causes, the long term effects of losing our rainforests are devastating and global.

Source: "Rainforest Facts," Wealth of the Rainforest—Pharmacy to the World from Raintree Nutrition, Inc. site, http://www.rain-tree.com/facts.htm. Accessed December 5, 2006.

Method

How it works

What does the destruction of a rainforest in Brazil have to do with you or me? Some just shrug their shoulders. Their attitude is that it is happening a world away, we aren't really responsible, and there is not much we could do about it anyway. The truth is, however, that what happens a world away does affect us where we live. We are responsible, and there are constructive, practical things that we can do.

Method

How it works

In the time that it will take you to read this introduction, 20 acres of rainforest will have been destroyed. In fact, one and a half acres of rainforest disappears every second. Considering that the rainforests are essential for the production of oxygen and support of more than half of the world's species of plants and animals and insects, the world is facing an ecological disaster.

Method

How it works

In the 1992 film *Medicine Man*, Dr. Robert Campbell discovers a cure for cancer from a flower growing in the Brazilian rainforest. The problem is that a logging company is bulldozing the forest with the support of the government. The story ends with a massive forest fire that destroys both the research and the flower, requiring Dr. Campbell to press deeper into the forest to find another cure. This story is not farfetched. Rainforest species are disappearing at an alarming rate, and with them the cures to many diseases. It is vital for medical science to protect these species, which cannot be found anywhere else in the world.

Method

How it works

Identifying Additional Strategies for Starting an Essay — TASK TWO

Task One asked you to identify four different strategies to engage a reader right at the beginning of an essay. This task asks you to consider alternatives. What other ways can you find to start an essay?

Part One

Look at your textbooks and magazine articles for different approaches to beginning an essay. In addition, search the Internet using such search terms as "hook," "introductions," and "writing introductions."

Bring examples and sources for your information to your next group meeting.

Part Two: 20 minutes

Person 3: Please facilitate this task. Ask everyone in turn to give one example of a different strategy for starting an introduction. Continue going around the group until all the different ideas have been presented.

Person 4: Please keep track of the time for your group.

Person 1: Write the first four types of hooks discussed in Task One in the table below. Add the new strategies that your group has discovered.

	Type	Why It Works
1.		
2.		
3.		
4.		

	Type	**Why It Works**
5.		
6.		
7.		
8.		
9.		
10.		

Background Information, Purpose, Scope, and Organization

In most cases, moving directly from a hook to the thesis statement would be too abrupt. The reader, while interested in the subject, may not be well enough prepared to engage the topic just yet. The introduction lays down this preparation in a number of different ways.

Background

Once you have hooked your readers, or at least got them to read a little more, the next thing to do is prepare them for the thesis statement. Ask yourself what the reader needs to know to be able to understand your thesis. Some topics are already widely understood; others are not. Be clear as to who your reader is and just how much that reader needs to be filled in.

Filling in the reader can mean a number of things:

- *Define any special terminology that is key to the thesis.* Avoid gumming up the essay with frequent definitions all the way through, but major terms or acronyms that affect the reading need to be cleared up at the beginning.
- *Briefly give a history of the topic or issue.* The topic might be connected to contemporary events, or have a longer background. Understanding the basic history of the topic helps prepare the reader for whatever take you are going to have on it.
- *Give the context in which your essay is written.* It might be part of a group project, specifically required for a special purpose, or a response to someone else's work. The introduction of a chapter or section in a longer work can make explicit reference to what came before or show how it fits into the larger picture.

Some introductions will need all of this material because the intended reader is unfamiliar with the topic and needs this material to be able to understand what you want to say about it in the body. Other introductions will have only the briefest of introductions because extensive orientation is not needed. What you choose depends a great deal on the intended reader's familiarity and interest with the topic.

Purpose

Some introductions state the purpose of the essay before presenting the thesis statement. That purpose might be to determine which of the root causes of a problem is the most significant. It might be to continue or clarify a discussion in an earlier section of a book. Explicitly setting out what the essay is out to do is part of the limiting process that gives your paper clarity.

Scope

Identifying the scope of the essay tells your reader how broad your treatment is going to be. Are you going to cover all the effects of the disappearing rainforest, or will you focus on three important ones? Is your essay going to look at all the causes of the disappearing rainforest, or will you focus on local ones? That kind of clarity is part of the focusing process that you went through when you developed the thesis statement. For some subjects, particularly large, complex ones, making that process explicit for readers prepares them for the particular slant you will take on the topic.

Organization

Some introductions announce how the paper will be structured. Although this is not necessary for a short paper, such a statement is helpful in a long, complex one like a formal report. It might announce, for example, that it will look at the implications of the disappearing rainforest on people by first looking at the indigenous population, and then at the global one. It might announce that it will look first at the primary cause, a main effect, and the most viable solution. The reader who uses the SQ3R strategy explained in Unit 1 gets a clear idea of what the paper has to say and in what order it will say it before actually engaging the text.

Hint

It is not necessary to include all of these points in an introduction. It is a good idea, however, to consider them and to ask yourself whether your essay would be better if you included that information in your opening.

Placing the Thesis Statement

Put the thesis statement you write for the essays asked for in this book at the end of your introduction. Your essay will be most clear if you make the thesis statement the last line of the opening section. In some cases, you might need a transition line, or a statement or organization just after it. Avoid putting the thesis up too early in the introduction unless the topic is so well understood that little or no background is required.

TASK THREE   Analysis of Introductions: 45 minutes

Look at the following sample introductions taken from various textbooks. As a group, identify and evaluate the strategy the writer uses at the beginning. Determine the kind of background material the writer has provided and evaluate whether it is sufficient. Identify whether the introduction includes information on the scope and organization of the writing. Finally, determine the thesis statement and evaluate whether it is sufficiently focused and if there is a clear message.

Person 3: Please facilitate this task and be sure everyone has a chance to contribute.

Person 4: Please keep track of the time for your group.

Person 1: Please record the group consensus on the discussion in the form below each of the introductions.

Person 2: Please read out the paragraph to the group and be ready to represent your group in a class discussion following this task.

Introduction to "Hereditary Influences on Development"

Hereditary Influences on Development
Can you remember when you were first introduced to the concept of heredity? Although the idea of heredity may seem straightforward, this concept is sometimes a difficult one to understand. The challenges in presenting this information became evident when one of us tried to explain it to her 4-year-old. How would you explain genetics to a 4-year-old? What worked was telling her that all of us have "instructions" that make our bodies

work and that these "instructions" are given to us from our parents. Unfortunately, providing such a simple explanation worked against the mother when the child asked, "What's wrong with your instructions?" when she made a mistake!

This chapter approaches human development from a hereditary perspective, seeking to determine how one's **genotype** (the **genes** that one inherits) is expressed as a **phenotype** (one's observable or measurable characteristics). We first will explore how hereditary information is transmitted from parents to their offspring and why the workings of heredity conspire to make us unique individuals. We then will review the evidence of hereditary contributions to such important psychological attributes as intelligence, personality, and even our inclinations toward displaying mentally healthy (or unhealthy) patterns of behaviour. Indeed, this evidence implies that many (and some would say all) of our most noteworthy phenotypic characteristics are influenced by the genes passed to us by our parents. Yet, the biggest lesson from this chapter is that genes, by themselves, determine less than you might imagine and that the expression "hereditary constraint" is something of a misnomer. As we will see, most complex human attributes are the result of a long and involved interplay between the forces of nature (heredity) and nurture (environment) (Plomin et al., 1997).

Source: From Developmental Psychology: Childhood and Adolescence, Second Edition by SHAFFER. 2005. Reprinted with permission of Nelson, a division of Thomson Learning: wwwthomsonrights.com. Fax 800-730-2215.

Element of the Introduction	Content	Evaluation
Hook		
General background to the topic		
Specific background: purpose, scope, and organization		
Thesis		

Introduction to "The T. Eaton Company: A Community Store"

Timothy Eaton's ability to create Canada's most successful department store by the early twentieth century was due to a variety of factors, but clearly one of the most important was his ability to create a sense of community among his employees. They proudly identified themselves as "Eatonians," an identity that not only linked them to Timothy Eaton and his family but also to a community of fellow workers who had one thing in common: they were employees—or what Eaton preferred to call "associates"—of the T. Eaton Company.

Source: From Journeys: A History of Canada, First Edition 1st Edition by FRANCIS/SMITH/JONES. Reprinted with permission of Nelson, a division of Thomson Learning: www.thomsonrights.com. Fax 800-730-2215.

Element of the Introduction	Content	Evaluation
Hook		
General background to the topic		
Specific background: purpose, scope, and organization		
Thesis		

Introduction to "The Many Faces of Retailing"

How often would a company abandon its well-known corporate name for that of one of its subsidiaries? In May 2001, management decided to drop Suzy Shier as its corporate title and opted instead for La Senza Cor, the name of its popular lingerie chain because it had been so successful. This heralded the beginning of a major overhaul for the company. The company is now focusing on underserved markets and the brands that offer the best chance for expansion beyond Canada.

Source: From Foundations of Marketing, Eight Canadian Edition by BECKMAN. 2003. Reprinted with Permission of Nelson, a division of Thomson Learning: www.thomsonrights.com. Fax 800-730-2215.

Element of the Introduction	Content	Evaluation
Hook		
General background to the topic		
Specific background: purpose, scope, and organization		
Thesis		

Introduction to "Social Welfare and Families with Children"

In proclaiming 1994 the International year of the Family, the United Nations was calling attention to the importance of families and their changing needs and responsibilities. Yet in spite of this recognition, there is no single, universally accepted definition of "family." However, for the purpose of collecting data, Statistics Canada (2003c) defines a census family as a

> Married couple (with or without children of either or both spouses), a couple living common law (with or without children of either or both partners) or a lone parent of any marital status, with at least one child living in the same dwelling. A couple living common law may be of opposite sex.

This chapter focuses on Canadian families with children.

Some organizations prefer to define *family* in terms of the roles that families play in society. The Vanier Institute of the Family (1992, 34–35), for instance, offers the following functional definition of family:
- Any combination of two or more persons who are bound together by ties of mutual consent, birth and/or adoption/placement and which serves the interest of individuals and societies by ensuring the physical maintenance and care of its members; and/or
- Addition of new societal members through procreation or adoption and their relinquishment when mature; and/or
- Socialization of children for adult roles, such as those of spouse, parent, worker, neighbour, voter and community member; and/or
- Social control of members (the maintenance or order within the family and groups external to it); and/or
- Production and consumption of goods and services needed to support and maintain the family unit; and/or
- Maintenance of family morale and motivation to ensure task performance both within the family and the other social groups

This definition of family is highly inclusive and emphasizes the diversity of family activities and tasks; also, this definition does not limit itself to any particular cultural environment. Note, however, that the roles and functions of families change in tandem with changes in society.

Families are recognized for the economic contributions they make: "Families are a basic social unit of production and consumption and, as such, are at the heart of the economic process. Their needs must be intimately connected with the objectives of economic and social development, as a minimum standard of progress" (United Nations, 1999). To strengthen families and foster self-sufficiency, Canadian governments create and support a number of family policies and programs.

Unlike many European countries, Canada has no national family policy that supports a full range of universal family services. Rather, each province and territory is responsible for setting its own priorities for family programs. The result has been considerable disparity in services across the country. Moreover, within each province and territory, family services tend to be poorly coordinated. Quebec is the only province that has developed a comprehensive approach to serving families. In 1997, while other provincial governments were *narrowing* the focus of their family programs to concentrate on low-income families, the Government of Quebec was *broadening* its focus by integrating child allowances, early childhood education, child development services, and parental leave programs and making all of these universally available to all families regardless of income level. Quebec also coordinated its separate public- and private-sector family programs and services so as to establish a cohesive network (Standing Committee, 2000; Canadian Policy Research networks, 2003b).

There are a number of reasons Canada has not yet developed a national family policy. Katherine Scott (1996) suggests that Canadian governments have generally been reluctant to intrude "public policies and programs that infringe on the privacy rights of individuals or families, or to curtail what is viewed as the parents' responsibilities to their children." According to Baker (1997), attempts to develop a coordinated system of family services have been frustrated by the lack of agreement among Canadians regarding what family policy and programs should encompass. In fact, Canadians cannot even agree on a definition of "family." Politicians and social policy-makers tend to avoid making family policy decisions when the issues involved (a) are controversial or (b) are not part of traditional party agendas. Issues such as abortion, same-sex legislation, and wages for homemakers are examples of sensitive policy issues. However, Canadian governments have made some progress with regard to policy developments in these areas.

Source: From Social Welfare in Canadian Society, Third Edition by CHAPPELL. 2005. Reprinted with permission of Nelson, a division of Thomson Learning: www.thomsonrights.com. Fax 800-730-2215.

Element of the Introduction	Content	Evaluation
Hook		
General background to the topic		
Specific background: purpose, scope, and organization		
Thesis		

Putting It All Together

You have worked on different strategies and analyzed introductions from different examples of academic writing. Now apply all this to your own essay writing.

TASK FOUR   Introduction for the Group Essay

You worked as a group to develop an outline for an essay on a topic in your field. Work together to plan and write an introduction for that essay. Use the inverted pyramid as you decide upon your strategies and what kind of background you want to include.

Part One: 30 minutes

Person 4: Please facilitate this activity. Keep everyone on track and give everyone an opportunity to contribute.

Person 1: Please keep track of the time for your group.

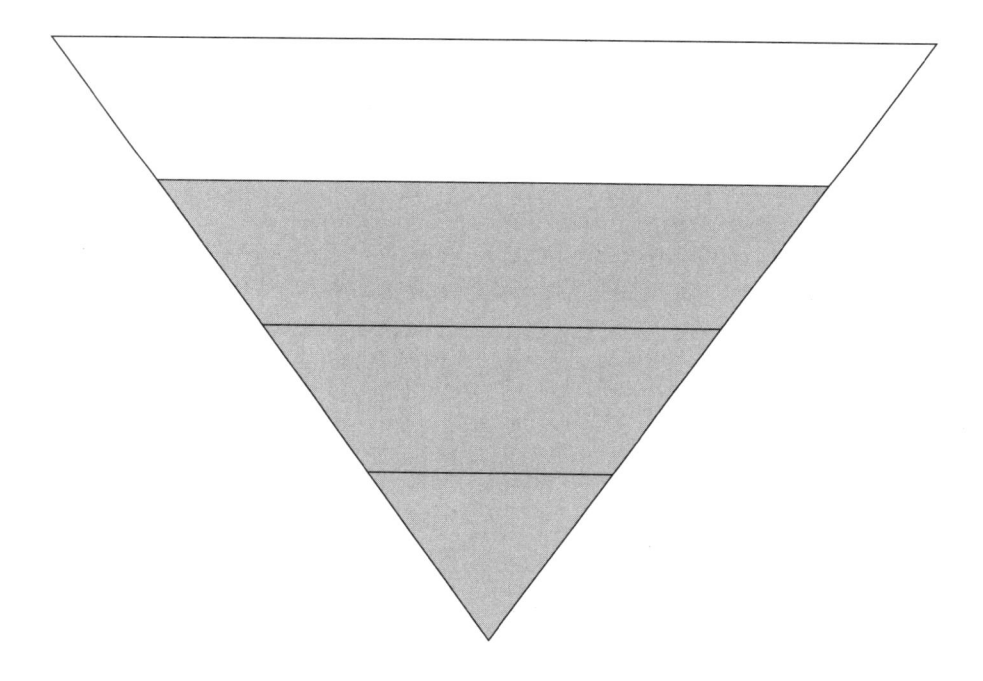

Person 2: Please write out the plan using the inverted pyramid below and the full introduction as the group reaches consensus.

Person 3: Be prepared to take the introduction to other groups for feedback.

Part Two

Person 3: Please take your introduction to another group. Read it to them and take notes of any suggestions they might have as to how to make this introduction even better.

Someone from another group will come to read an introduction to you.

Listen to that introduction and give feedback as to what works well and what might be improved.

Here are some questions you can ask yourself as you listen:

- Does the first line get my attention? Would another strategy be more effective?
- Does the introduction give me sufficient background information? Are there terms or ideas that need clarifying first?
- Does the introduction clearly focus the subject to a topic with an identifiable message?
- Does the introduction need statements of purpose, scope, and organization?

Introduction for the Individual Essay — TASK FIVE

You developed an outline for an individual essay in Unit 4. Write an introduction for that essay that uses the techniques you have worked on in this unit.

Part One: 30 minutes

1. Use the inverted triangle below to determine your opening strategy and what information you are going to put in the introduction.
2. Use the second inverted triangle to plan out a second, alternative introduction for the same essay using a different strategy.

First
Introduction

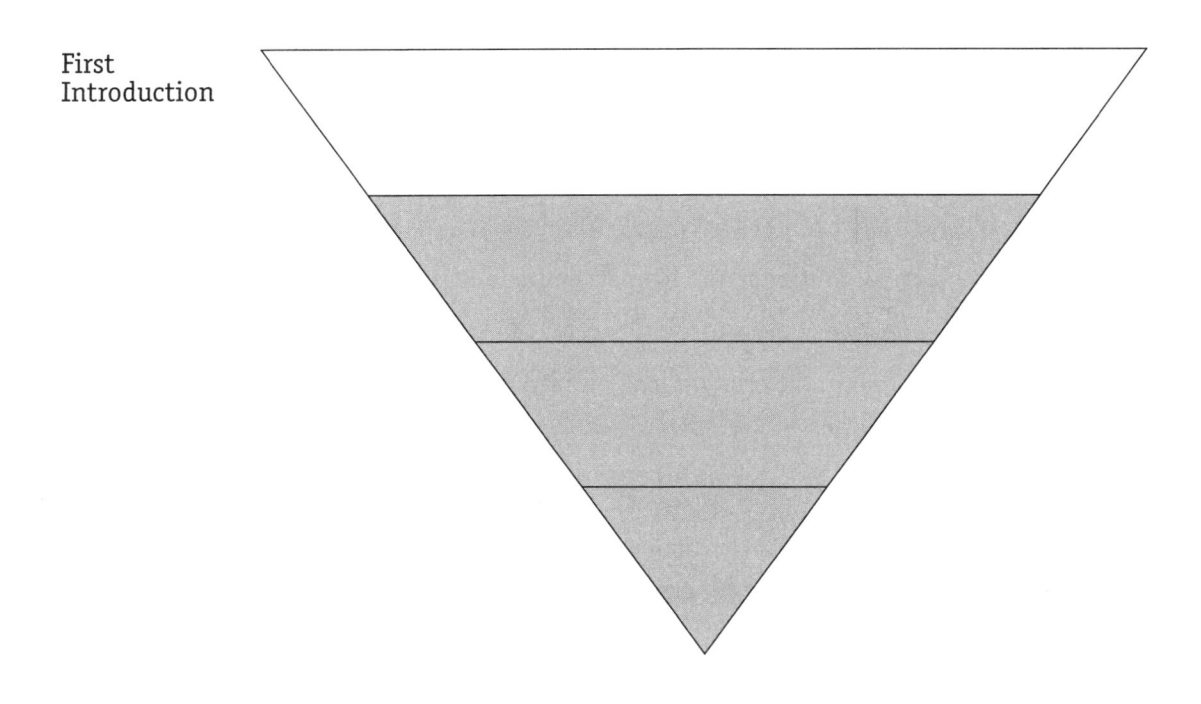

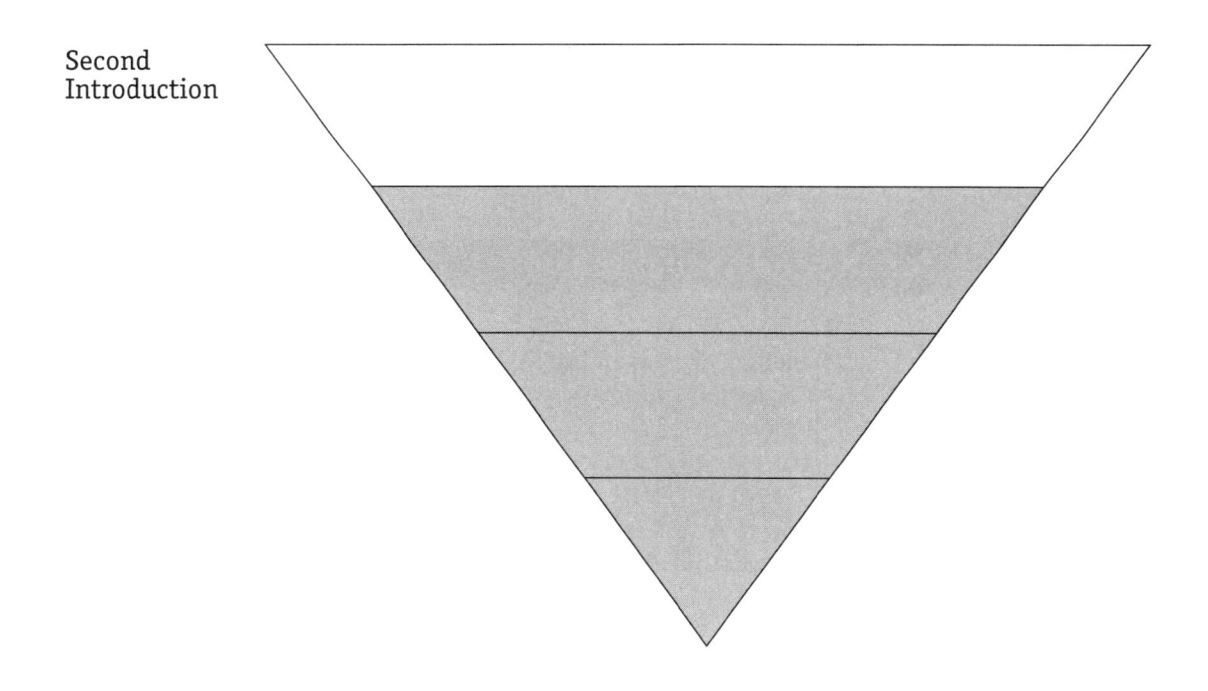

Second
Introduction

Hint

Have a different reader in mind for each essay. The first reader might be a professor or some other expert in the field. The second reader might be a student or a general reader.

Part Two: 15 minutes

Exchange your introductions with a member of your group. Read the introductions given to you. Circle anything that you suspect may be an error. Finally, write a message to the writer at the end of the introductions.

Here are some questions that you can consider:

- Which introduction do you prefer?
- Why does that one work better than the other?
- Is there anything the writer can do to make the introduction even better?

When you have finished, exchange the introductions you have just read for another set. Continue this until everyone in the group has seen everyone's work.

Part Three: 5 minutes

Get your paragraphs back and read the assessments at the bottom. Look at the circles which indicate possible language problems. Repair the ones you can now. Ask about the ones you are unsure of either now or later.

In Summary

Take three minutes to write a summary of what you have learned participating in the tasks of Unit 6.

UNIT 7
Conclusions

Here's what you'll work on in this unit.
- Rephrasing the thesis statement
- Determining a closing strategy
- Crafting clinchers
- Connecting conclusions to introductions
- Writing conclusions for an essay plan

Just as the introduction is your chance to make a strong first impression on the reader, the conclusion is your opportunity to leave a lasting impact. Some writers miss the chance to drive their points home because they see the conclusion as something just tacked on to the end of the essay, almost as an afterthought. However, conclusions require as much strategy and careful planning as introductions.

Unit 4 asked you to think of an introduction as an inverted pyramid that worked from the general to the specific. One way to look at conclusions is to turn that pyramid right side up. Each part of the pyramid structure serves a different purpose in the conclusion.

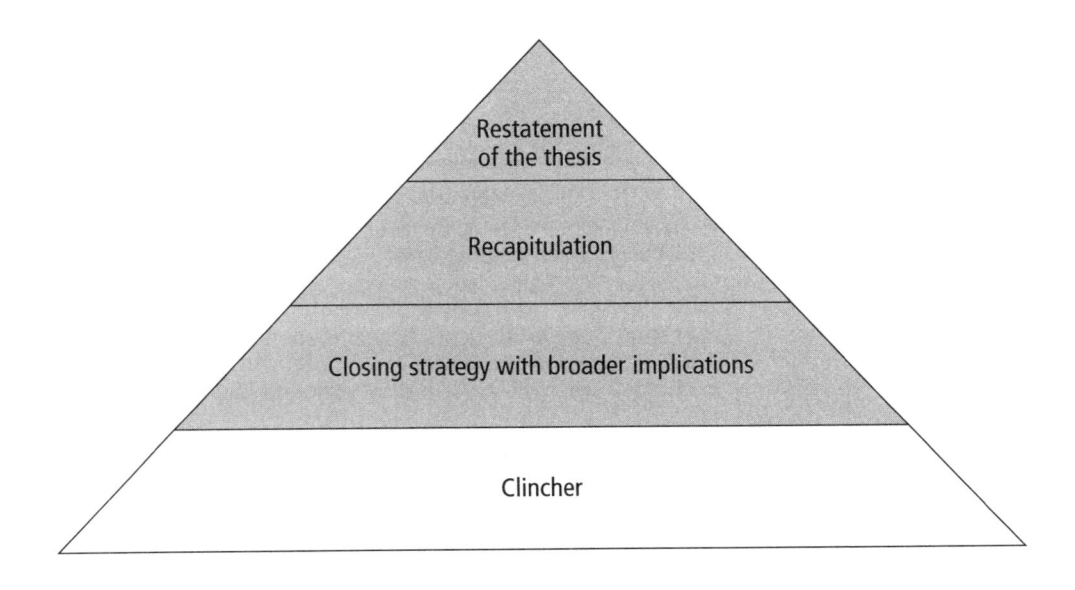

- Restatement of the thesis
- Recapitulation
- Closing strategy with broader implications
- Clincher

This arrangement shows that whereas the introduction progressively tapered the considerations to a specific focus, the conclusion takes the ideas in the essay and opens them up to wider perspectives.

When writing the introduction, you asked yourself what you would find useful if you were reading it. When writing the conclusion, ask yourself whether the essay delivered what it promised. In particular, think about the kind of effect you want to have on the reader. Do you want the reader to leave the essay with a new perspective? Do you want that reader to be left with a sense of urgency? Do you want the reader to stand back convinced about something? As you did when writing the introduction, put yourself in the shoes of the reader. Think about what the particular reader you have in mind would need for a satisfying end to your writing. Students or general readers who want to be sure they have grasped the material might need a concise summary. Professors might prefer statements that tie everything together and give your interpretation. Answering a few basic questions that your specific readership might have will help you meet their needs in your closing section.

Hint

Write your conclusion directly after writing the introduction. This technique will strengthen the links between these two parts of the paper. In this way, the essay will be stronger, better designed, and more effective.

Here's What to Avoid

A wide range of strategies are available for your conclusion, but there are a few things to stay away from. Reread the introduction for the article on rainforests discussed in the last unit, and then take a look at how the writer planned to end the essay.

> **Introduction**
> What does the destruction of a rainforest in Brazil have to do with you or me? Some just shrug their shoulders. Their attitude is that it is happening a world away, we aren't really responsible, and there is not much we could do about it anyway. The truth is, however, that what happens a world away does affect us where we live. We are responsible, and there are constructive, practical things that we can do.
>
> **Conclusion**
> As you have just read in this essay, rainforests are important for all of us. It is unfortunate that an essay of this length can not cover all of the important facts. However, it has shown that we are responsible, and there are constructive, practical things that we can do. We need to do those things because in addition to the benefits of the rainforest discussed in this essay, there may be a cure for cancer hiding in the forests that we are in danger of losing forever.

This closing paragraph is neither satisfying nor particularly helpful for a number of reasons.

Flat Opening Sentence

Just as introductions have lead sentences, so do conclusions. The lead sentence in this conclusion is predictable and unnecessary. It is unnecessary to tell readers that they have just read the essay. All it does is announce the obvious in an unimaginative way. That means that the writer has not spent much time thinking about how to craft the closing in order to leave the reader with a specific impression.

Apology

The flat opening sentence is followed by an apology that highlights the fact that the essay is somehow incomplete or inadequate. This comment is unnecessary, and it weakens the conclusion even more. The body of the essay may have been well written, but this kind of conclusion is undoing the work accomplished earlier. No essay can be comprehensive; that is a given. The writer's position should be, however, that the essay has delivered on what it promised to do. If it didn't, the essay should be rewritten, not apologized for.

Identical Wording

The third sentence in the conclusion picks up the thesis statement from the introduction and reproduces it word for word. The writer has missed the opportunity to drive home the message in a fresh way rather than a repetitive one. Cutting and pasting a sentence from the introduction shows that the conclusion is somehow less of a writing priority for the writer than other sections of the essay. Considering that this is the final contact the reader will have, it misses the chance to emphasize rather than just repeat.

Insertion of New Material

Closing sections are not body paragraphs. Consequently, they should not present brand-new material that is part of the discussion. The conclusion to the rainforest article suddenly introduces a consideration "in addition to" what the body had examined. The information about cancer cures is dropped in suddenly. If the writer wants to bring up the medicinal potential of rainforest plants, he or she needs to add a separate body section that announces the idea and provides sufficient support. As it is, the idea appears right at the end with no explanation, support, or connections to other parts of the article.

Abrupt Ending

Finally, this conclusion just stops at the end of a point. If this sentence happened to be at the bottom of a page, the reader wouldn't know for sure whether the conclusion continued on a missing page. The essay is left hanging.

Although the essay may have started well, it ends weakly. It needs specific closing strategies and more attention to what final impression it is making.

Hint

Write your introductions and conclusions side by side, so that they become like well-matched bookends to the body of your essay. Use the list of items above as a checklist of what to avoid.

Restatement of the Thesis

Recast, rather than repeat, the thesis statement in the introduction. That means sitting back and finding different words to make the message clear. Take, for example, the following thesis statement:

> Construction companies must take immediate steps to address the looming labour shortage.

The first step in recasting the thesis is to think how different parts of that sentence might be restated. The writer might do the following.

construction:	building
companies:	businesses, industry
must:	have to, are obligated to, need to, are required to
take:	enact, perform, introduce, implement
immediate:	urgent, without delay
steps:	measures, programs, policies, plans
address:	solve, deal with, manage
looming:	coming, advancing, menacing
labour:	workers, workforce, builders
shortage:	scarcity, lack

Having thought of different terms for the elements of the thesis statement, the writer could work out a trial restatement:

> The building industry has to enact urgent measures to deal with the lack of workers.

At that point, free from the original wording of the thesis statement, the writer can then explore different ways to rephrase the message. After looking at the idea in several different ways, the writer might settle on the following:

> A scarcity of skilled workers is a serious problem facing the entire building industry that requires urgent action.

That conveys the same message in fresh language. Coming at the beginning of the conclusion, it would signal the reader that the discussion is over and that the writer is wrapping things up.

TASK ONE Rewriting the Thesis Statement

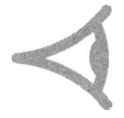

15 minutes

Look again at the sample openings below for a chapter on rainforests meant for a textbook on the environment. Recast the thesis statement in a different way for the conclusion.

Person 2: Please facilitate this task. Be sure everyone has a chance to comment.

Person 3: Please keep track of the time for your group.

Person 4: Please read out the sample paragraphs.

Person 1: Please record the group consensus and be ready to give your group answers to the class.

The website Rainforest Facts reports, "rainforests once covered 14% of the earth's land surface; now they cover a mere 6% and experts estimate that the last remaining rainforests could be consumed in less than 40 years." Several reasons are behind this disaster including local poverty, multinational corporation greed and short-sighted governments. Whatever the causes, the long-term effects of losing our rainforests are devastating and global.

Source: "Rainforest Facts," Wealth of the Rainforest—Pharmacy to the World from Raintree Nutrition, Inc. site, http://www.rain-tree.com/facts.htm. Accessed December 5, 2006.

Restatement

What does the destruction of a rainforest in Brazil have to do with you or me? Some just shrug their shoulders. Their attitude is that it is happening a world away, we aren't really responsible, and there is not much we could do about it anyway. The truth is, however, that what happens a world away does affect us where we live. We are responsible, and there are constructive, practical things that we can do.

Restatement

In the time that it will take you to read this introduction, 20 acres of rainforest will have been destroyed. In fact, one-and-a-half acres of rainforest disappears every second. Considering that the rainforests are essential for the production of oxygen and support of more than half of the world's species of plants and animals and insects, the world is facing an ecological disaster.

Restatement

In the 1992 film *Medicine Man*, Dr. Robert Campbell discovers a cure for cancer from a flower growing in the Brazilian rainforest. The problem is that a logging company is bulldozing the forest with the support of the government. The story ends with a massive forest fire that destroys both the research and the flower, requiring Dr. Campbell to press deeper into the forest to find another cure. This story is not farfetched. Rainforest species are disappearing at an alarming rate and with them the cures to many diseases. It is vital for medical science to protect these species, which cannot be found anywhere else in the world.

Restatement

Recapitulation

Recapitulation means summarizing your own essay. Many beginning writers use their conclusions to simply tell the reader what has just been written. It is not necessary, or even desirable, to do that on a regular basis. Of course, long papers with complex points and ideas might be clearer if the conclusion restates the main points. Many chapters in textbooks list the main points in summary form right at the end. The shorter the paper, however, the less likely that is needed. A one- or two-page essay on a topic of common knowledge probably does not need to rehash the points made. That is a judgment call you will need to make.

If you are writing an academic paper or an essay exam for a professor, you might opt for a concise summary of all the main points, since the most important thing is to demonstrate that you know and understand the material. In other cases, you might want to highlight for the reader the fact that, of several main points in the essay, one or two are really critical. The conclusion might pull this out for special consideration, showing that they stand apart.

If your conclusion does include some kind of recapitulation of main points, keep it concise by eliminating any detail or explanation that properly belongs in the body.

Closing Strategy

Just as good introductions use a definite strategy to engage the reader, good conclusions use a definite strategy to help make a specific impact on the reader.

Identifying Closing Strategies — TASK TWO

15 minutes

Look at the sample conclusions below for the chapter on rainforests meant for a textbook on the environment. Identify what strategy the writer uses and what it accomplishes.

Person 2: Please facilitate this task. Be sure everyone has a chance to comment.
Person 3: Please keep track of the time for your group.
Person 4: Please read out the sample paragraphs.
Person 1: Please record the group consensus and be ready to give your group answers to the class.

> The rate at which the world is losing its rainforest demands attention. The impact on our atmosphere, on irreplaceable species of animals and plants, and on human health is well documented. If industrialized countries fail to take the problem of the disappearing rainforests seriously, they will be responsible for a global disaster. Too much time has already passed without any significant action to solve the problem. Turning a blind eye to the issue only guarantees that we will all suffer the consequences and shortchange our children.

Strategy

What it accomplishes

[ ]

The rate at which the world is losing its rainforest demands attention. The impact on our atmosphere, on irreplaceable species of animals and plants, and on human health is well documented. Getting involved, learning about the problem, making informed choices in how we live, and lobbying the government are ways the average person, even a world away, can do something. We can and must make a difference.

Strategy

[ ]

What it accomplishes

[ ]

Preserving the rare and valuable plants in the rainforest have to be given a high priority. *Medicine Man* might be fiction, but the issue is not. Dr. Campbell might have gone deeper into the rainforest searching for the cure to cancer, but how much time does he or we really have?

Strategy

[   ]

What it accomplishes

[   ]

Identifying Additional Strategies for Concluding an Essay — TASK THREE

Task Two asked you to identify different strategies that you might employ in a conclusion. This task asks you to consider alternatives. What other ways can you find to conclude?

Part One

Look at your textbooks and magazine articles for different approaches to ending an essay. In addition, search the Internet using such search terms as "concluding strategies for essays," "conclusions," or "ending an essay."

Bring examples and sources for your information to your next group meeting.

Part Two: 20 minutes

Person 3: Please facilitate this task. Ask everyone in turn to give one example of a different strategy for ending an essay. Continue going around the group until all the different ideas have been presented.

Person 4: Please keep track of the time for your group.

Person 1: Write the first three types of concluding strategies discussed in Task Two in the table below. Add the new strategies that your group has discovered.

	Strategy	**What it Accomplishes**
1.		
2.		
3.		
4.		
5.		
6.		
7.		
8.		

	Strategy	What it Accomplishes
9.		
10.		

Clincher

The clincher is the last line of your conclusion. Effective writers consider this line as carefully as they consider the hook. The clincher finishes the essay with a strong image, idea, or question that definitively ends the paper. You can do this in several ways.

Asking a Question

The paper can turn over the entire topic of the paper to the reader by asking an open-ended question that requires some thought and ultimately a response. The rainforest paper might end with any number of questions:

- Dr. Campbell might have gone deeper into the rainforest searching for the cure to cancer, but how much time does he or we really have?
- Don't we owe our children a future?
- Can we afford to lose one more irreplaceable species?

Issuing a Challenge

Laying out a challenge either to the reader or to someone else responsible for action can give some muscle to the closing:

- We can and must make a difference.
- All it takes is enough political will to make tough decisions and we will see a difference.
- It is up to consumers to vote with their dollars against any company involved in this tragedy.

Making a Strong Statement

One way of clinching the essay is to leave the reader with a strong statement. That statement can make explicit implications or conclusions that can be drawn out of the body of the essay:

- Turning a blind eye to the issue only guarantees that we will all suffer the consequences and shortchange our children.
- Rainforests are our future. Without them, we won't have one.

Hint

One way to develop an effective clincher is to connect it to the strategy that you used in the hook. References back to images and strategies used in the introduction help frame the essay.

TASK FOUR   Analysis of Conclusions: 45 minutes

Look at the following sample conclusions taken from various textbooks. As a group, identify and evaluate how they have been put together. Here are some questions to consider:

1. What has the writer done, and is it effective?
2. Is there a statement that clearly identifies the message?
3. Does the conclusion include recapitulation?
4. Does the conclusion use a particular closing strategy?
5. Does the conclusion have a satisfying clincher?

Person 3: Please facilitate this task and be sure everyone has a chance to contribute.

Person 4: Please keep track of the time for your group.

Person 1: Please record the group consensus on the discussion in the form below each of the introductions.

Person 2: Please read out the paragraph to the group and be ready to represent your group in a class discussion following this task

Conclusion to "The Case for Complaining in a Restaurant"

Ultimately, it's important to have courage. If something isn't right with your restaurant experience and you say nothing, you're guaranteed to be unhappy as you leave. If you speak up, you may salvage your meal and your evening—and you'll be giving the restaurant a chance to turn a negative experience into a positive one.

Just try it.

Source: Adapted from "The Case for Complaining in a Restaurant", by Talin Vartanian (Broadcasted on Marketplace, February 27, 2002). http://www.cbc.ca/consumers/citizentalin/tips_restaurant.html. © Copyright Canadian Broadcasting Corporation. Reprinted with Permission.

Element of the Conclusion	Content	Comments
Message statement (recasting the thesis statement)		
Recapitulation		
Specific closing strategy		
Clincher		

Conclusion to "Are Extended Warranties Worth It?"

Michael Bailey, Canadian president for Texas-based Warrantech Corp., advises consumers who do choose extended warranties to make sure those warranties are insured, noting that guarantees are no good if they are backed by retail chains that go out of business. He cites stores such as Multitech Warehouse Direct stores as examples: Anyone who bought a warranty from them was out of luck because they are no longer in business. "There is a long list of retailers that have gone down. There are a lot of majors who do not insure their program," says Mr. Bailey.

What will you do the next time an extended warranty is suggested to you?

Source: "Are Extended Warranties Worth it?, by David Stonehouse. *(Financial Post)*. Page IT2. © Copyright March 18, 2002. Reprinted with Permission of the author.

Element of the Conclusion	Content	Comments
Message statement (recasting the thesis statement)		
Recapitulation		
Specific closing strategy		
Clincher		

Conclusion to "Helping Children to Correct Their Mistakes: An Information-Processing Approach"

Perhaps you can see the practical benefits of this approach. By carefully examining the information-processing strategies that children and adolescents use to attack scientific reasoning tasks, math problems, and even reading comprehension exercises, educators can often pinpoint the reasons that their pupils are failing and devise effective interventions to improve their performances (Siegler & Crowley, 1992; Siegler & Munakata, 1993).

Source: From Developmental Psychology: Childhood and Adolescence, Second Edition by SHAFFER. 2005. Reprinted with permission of Nelson, a division of Thomson Learning: wwwthomsonrights.com. Fax 800-730-2215.

Element of the Conclusion	Content	Comments
Message statement (recasting the thesis statement)		
Recapitulation		
Specific closing strategy		
Clincher		

Conclusion to "Smoothing the Rocky Road to Recovery from a Divorce"

Here, then, we have some effective first steps on the path toward a positive divorce experience as well as a better understanding of why divorce is more disruptive for some families than for others. The research also serves as yet another excellent example of the family as a social system embedded in larger social systems. Mother, father, and children will all influence one another's adjustment to divorce, and the family's experience will also depend on the supports available within the neighbourhood, the schools, the community, and family members' own social networks.

From Developmental Psychology: Childhood and Adolescence, Second Edition by SHAFFER. 2005. Reprinted with permission of Nelson, a division of Thomson Learning: wwwthomsonrights.com. Fax 800-730-2215.

Element of the Conclusion	Content	Comments
Message statement (recasting the thesis statement)		
Recapitulation		
Specific closing strategy		
Clincher		

Putting It All Together

You have worked on different strategies and analyzed conclusions from different examples of academic writing. Now, apply all this to your own essay writing.

Introduction for the Group Essay

TASK FIVE

You worked as a group to develop an outline for an essay on a topic in your field. Work together to plan and write a conclusion for that essay. Use the pyramid structure below as you decide upon your strategies.

Part One: 30 minutes

Person 4: Please facilitate this activity. Keep everyone on track and give everyone an opportunity to contribute.

Person 1: Please keep track of the time for your group.

Person 2: Please write out the plan using the pyramid below and the full introduction as the group reaches consensus.

Person 3: Be prepared to take the conclusion to other groups for feedback.

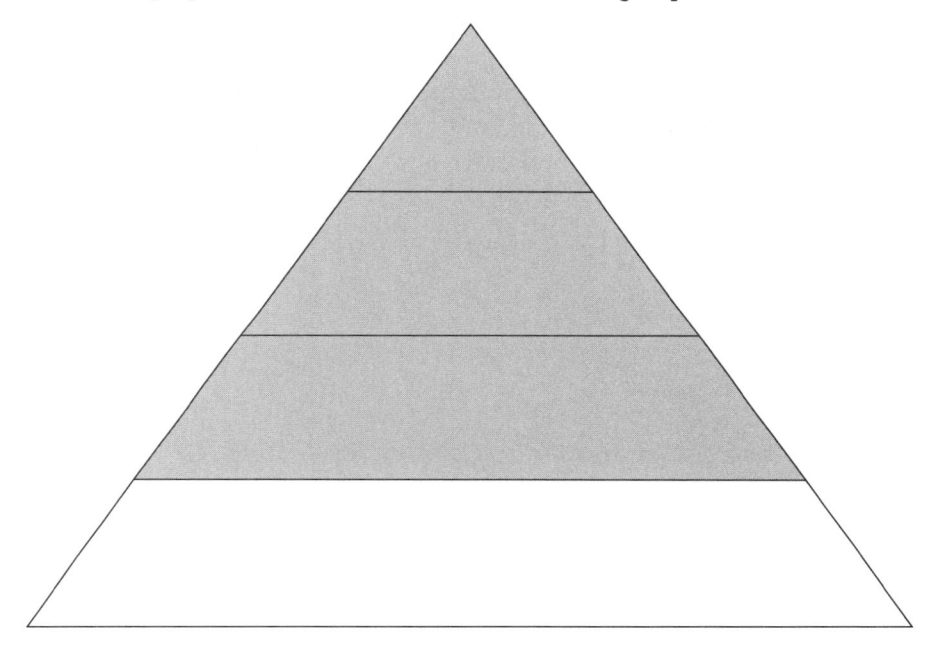

Part Two

Person 3: Please take your conclusion to another group. Read it to them and take notes of any suggestions they might have as to how to make this conclusion even better.

Someone from another group will come to read a conclusion to you. Listen to that conclusion and give feedback as to what works well and what could be improved.

Here are some questions you can ask yourself as you listen:

- Does the conclusion include a sentence that presents the main message?
- Does the conclusion recapitulate main points?
- Does the conclusion avoid introducing new information that should belong in the body?
- Does the conclusion end with a clincher?

TASK SIX   Conclusion for the Individual Essay

You developed an outline for an individual essay in Unit 4. Write a conclusion for that essay that uses the techniques you have worked on in this unit.

Part One: 30 minutes
1. Use the pyramid below to determine your strategy
2. Use the second pyramid to plan out a second, alternative conclusion for the same essay using a different strategy.

Hint

Have a different reader in mind for each essay. The first reader might be a professor or some other expert in the field. The second reader might be a student or a general reader.

First Conclusion

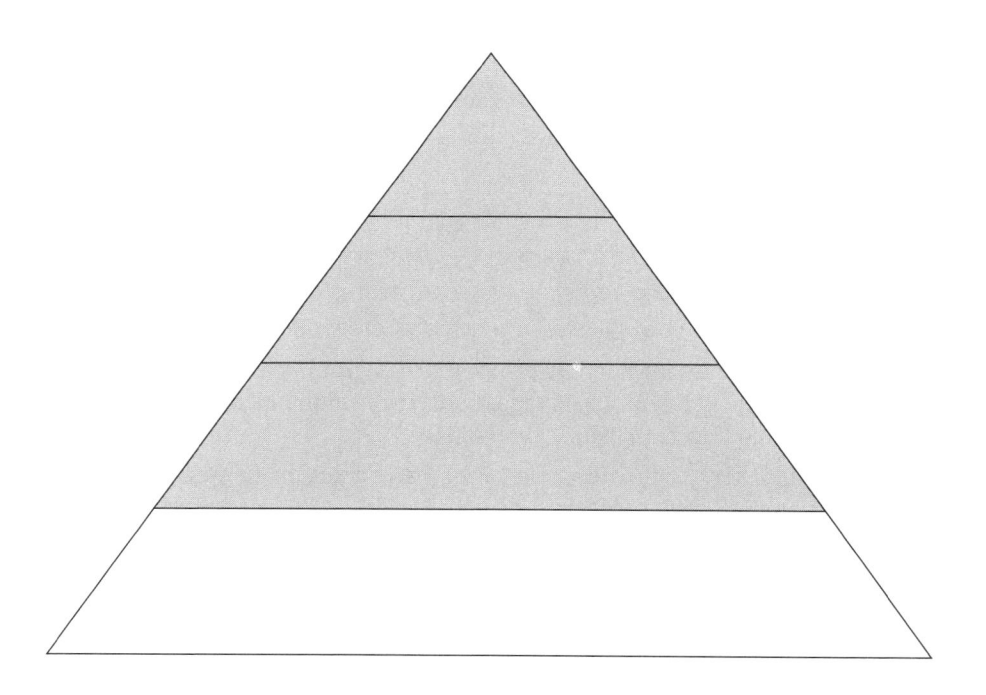

Second Conclusion

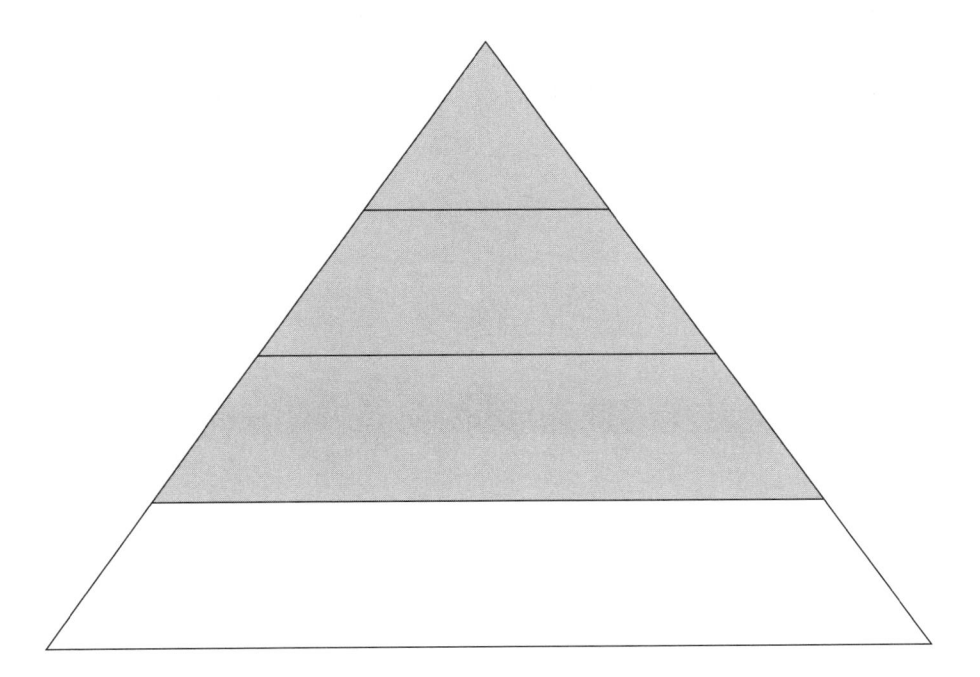

Part Two: 15 minutes

Exchange your conclusions with a member of your group. Read the conclusions given to you. Circle anything that you suspect may be an error. Finally, write a message to the writer at the end of the conclusions.

Here are some questions you can consider:

- Which conclusion do you prefer?
- Why does that one work better than the other?
- Is there anything the writer can do to make the conclusion even better?

When you have finished, exchange the conclusions you have just read for another set. Continue this until everyone in the group has seen everyone else's work.

Part Three: 5 minutes

Get your paragraphs back and read the assessments at the bottom. Look at the circles that indicate possible language problems. Repair the ones you can now. Ask about the ones you are unsure of either now or later.

In Summary

Take three minutes to write a summary of what you have learned participating in the tasks of Unit 7.

UNIT 8

Drafting, Revising, and Editing

Here's what you'll work on in this unit.

- Drafting the college essay
- Evaluating support
- Checking for unity
- Ensuring coherence
- Improving sentences
- Improving word choice

Now that you have a full plan for the essay as well as a working introduction and conclusion, it's time to put together the first draft of the paper. It is tempting for busy students to write down their thoughts in one shot and submit, so they can get on with other tasks. The problem with that approach, however, is that writers often miss their own mistakes after a quick read-through. In addition, it shortchanges them, because they lose the chance to polish their work. That extra step can make a huge difference in the presentation, the effectiveness, and ultimately the grade of the paper.

Even experienced writers polish their work through several stages. Allowing yourself time to reread your work, see it with fresh eyes, and make improvements pays off. That is true of essay exams as well. Just as you set aside some time to sketch out an outline that you can submit along with the essay exam, give yourself a little time at the end of the allotted time to go through your essay and make whatever corrections necessary to take your work up a notch.

Try this three-step process: drafting, revising, and editing.

Drafting

You have already done considerable thinking about your topic and produced a point-form outline. Drafting is your chance to get it all down on paper. Here are a few things to keep in mind while you do that.

Follow Your Outline

Aim at continuous writing so that you get as much as possible down in a free-flowing manner. The drafting period is not the time to second-guess yourself or revisit the plan of the essay. For the moment, free yourself from thinking about content and pour your energy into expressing the content that you have already worked out. The best way to do that is to treat your outline as a map. Follow the map; explain the twists and turns of that road to the reader who may not have been there. Nothing is permanent at this stage, and if you want to revisit the ideas, you will have the chance to do that later.

Hint

Although the drafting stage depends on following your outline, it is not necessary to always follow that outline in order. If you are writing a long paper out of class as a major submission for a course, you might find it more appealing or stimulating to write the paper out of order. For example, you might feel particularly motivated to write point 4.0 first. Later, you might be more inclined to write 2.0. And so on. You can use your word processing program to rearrange the ideas later.

Avoid Correcting Yourself

Just as the drafting stage is not the time to rewrite the outline, neither is it the time to worry about correcting sentence structure or errors in language mechanics. Just keep writing in a way that does not stifle this important step in producing your essay.

Hint

If you are not sure of the spelling of a word, simply spell it the first way that makes sense to you. If you are using a word processor and see underlining indicating spelling or grammar errors, ignore it. The goal is to write, not to correct. Avoid stopping to check out a word or rewrite a phrase. If you have trouble finding the right word, just leave a blank, draw a line, or write a series of X's. You will have time to settle those issues later.

Aim at Completing the Draft in a Specific Time Frame

The purpose of the first draft is to get down a form so that you have something to work with. You create the essential structure which you then mould later on. You need to be able to stand back and see the whole structure, at least in its first incarnation, as soon as possible. If the writing project is a short one, block out a suitable period of time during which you will complete the whole draft. If the writing project is a longer one, schedule two or three sessions. The idea is to get the whole draft completed as soon as possible.

Hint

You need to adjust your time for completing the rough draft according to your own writing level. It is likely that you will find that you will need less time for the first draft as you write more academic work.

Indicate on Your Draft Where You Need More Material

You may discover as you write the draft that you are missing some detail of support or information that the essay needs to make a convincing argument. Just as you left blank spaces for words that you couldn't find at the moment, leave a space or indicate with a quick note what you want to put in at this spot of the essay but do not have at your fingertips right now. In this way, the intention becomes part of the essay and you don't interrupt your writing flow.

Hint

Avoid stopping the flow of the writing to make these points. Instead, switch to capital letters to insert whatever note you need to make to yourself. Switch back to regular case when the note is done.

Drafting — TASK ONE

You developed an outline for an individual essay in Unit 4. You completed an introduction and a conclusion for that outline in Units 5 and 6. Now, write a first draft for the body of that essay using the technique discussed above. Please write the draft double-spaced.

Keep your draft for group work later on in this unit.

Revising

Lay your rough draft aside for a day or so and work on other projects. Putting some space and time between readings helps you see your work with fresh eyes. What seemed so clear before may not seem so obvious now. What seemed to flow smoothly from your fingertips may not read so smoothly now. In addition, your mind is working on the ideas and the essay on a subconscious level. You are in a better position now to bring more insight to the topic. This is the stage where you might want to change around some of the ideas, remove some information or sections, and possibly add new ones.

The critical thing to keep in mind during the revision stage is that this is still not the time to be overly concerned with mechanics like punctuation. Right now, think about content and how the ideas hang together. Here are some ways to do that.

Evaluate the Support

Evaluating the support for your paper starts with considering the audience. Read the paper through as if you are the intended reader. The essays you write in the tasks of this book are academic and therefore aimed at a professor. Other pieces of writing, however, may be aimed at clients, colleagues, students, and other groups. Start off with a clear idea of how the intended reader is likely to assess the paper. If the professor or the client or the colleague were to put a grade on it, what would the main criteria, at least in terms of content, be? What is it that would make a satisfying read for them? What are their needs? For a professor, it may be that the criteria have all been laid out in an assignment sheet. If not, ask ahead of time what he or she might be looking for in an essay. Does the professor want you to demonstrate breadth of research, a facility with analyzing a primary text, or simply that you have read, fully understand, and are able to explain a topic? With that clear picture of your reader in mind, you will be in a good position to evaluate your own work.

Hint

As you read through your essay in the role of the intended reader, ask yourself whatever question the reader would likely have at any particular point in your paper. It might be a question about what something means, or about any examples, or about how you know something to be true. Make a note of the questions you have in the margin.

Check for Unity

Unity in essay writing simply means that everything is on topic. Look through the topic sentences again to ensure that they actually fit the purpose of the essay and match the message of the thesis statement. A topic sentence that does not fit those parameters, even if the information is correct, needs to be removed along with its accompanying paragraph.

The next test for unity is each individual paragraph. Remember to treat the essay as a train. Each section is a separate unit that can stand on its own, like boxcars, but that also connect to a greater whole. You have ensured that the topic sentences make a greater whole by double-checking whether they match the thesis statement. Now, check for unity by verifying that all the information, ideas, and arguments in each particular paragraph fit the topic sentence to which they are attached. Remove anything that does not belong.

Check for Gaps

Read through the paper to identify your assumptions. Do any ideas need explaining? You may have included support for a topic sentence, but is it adequate? Do you need to elaborate on the explanation by providing more details? Write a note in the column to check for information on any point.

Hint

If you have difficulty actually finding what you need to demonstrate a point, that is a signal to omit it completely. You might want to replace the point with one that has a more solid foundation. Alternatively, you might find that the paper is better with one fewer idea.

Check for Coherence

Coherence refers to how well a paper hangs together. A paper or a section of paper that seems scattered, going abruptly from point to point, is jarring. In addition, if you have several points in a paper or several items of support in a section, the arrangement should make sense. Think of taking your reader by the hand step by step through your work. What should come first? What should follow naturally from that step? How do you get from one point to another?

In some cases you might decide to move in order of importance—that is, from the least important to the most important idea. In other cases you might want to move from the most familiar to the more unfamiliar ideas. Some detail might be arranged chronologically—that is, according to time. You make the choice on the basis of the material you have and what makes sense for the reader. The important thing, however, is to have a clear order in mind rather than just dropping in the material as it occurs to you. The more structure you can build into your essay, the more you maximize understanding, particularly for a reader who might be unfamiliar with your essay's topic.

Hint

Different sections of your essay will likely use different principles of organization depending on the kind of support they have. Identify the organizing principle for each section and then verify that the placement of your material is consistent with that principle.

TASK TWO   Evaluating for Support, Unity, and Coherence

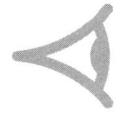

20 minutes

Look at the sample body paragraphs below for the chapter on rainforests meant for a textbook on the environment. Evaluate the paragraphs for adequacy of support, unity, and coherence.

Person 2: Please facilitate this task. Be sure everyone has a chance to comment.

Person 3: Please keep track of the time for your group.

Person 4: Please read out the sample paragraphs.

Person 1: Please record the group consensus and be ready to give your group answers to the class.

The rainforests are precious because they are the most biologically diverse environments on earth. One small pond in Brazil contains more different kinds of fish than all of the varieties of fish found in Europe. A single plot of rainforest land could contain more than the total number of tree varieties in all of North America. A tree in Peru contained forty-three species of ants, about the same number of ant species in the British Isles. Certainly, some of the plants in the rainforest have yet yield to medical cures for serious disease. Finally, the number of species of fish in the Atlantic ocean is smaller than the number that can be found in the Amazon.

Source: "Rainforest Facts," Wealth of the Rainforest—Pharmacy to the World from Raintree Nutrition, Inc. site, http://www.rain-tree.com/facts.htm. Accessed December 5, 2006.

Is the support adequate?

Is the paragraph unified?

Is the paragraph coherent?

The rate at which the world is losing its rainforest is staggering. According to *Rainforest Facts*, "Scientists estimate that we are losing more than 137 species of plants and animals every single day. ..." The loss has accelerated in modern times. Whereas 15% of the world's surface was covered by rainforest in 1950, only about 6% remains. To put that in perspective, we lose 200,000 acres a day. More than 99% of the species in the forest have yet to be properly evaluated for their uses. The twenty-first century is seeing an unprecedented demand on rainforest resources. The effects are serious on plant life, wildlife and human beings. Since the early 1900s more than 90 tribes have been lost because of the exploitation.

Source: "Rainforest Facts," Wealth of the Rainforest—Pharmacy to the World from Raintree Nutrition, Inc. site, http://www.rain-tree.com/facts.htm. Accessed December 5, 2006.

Is the support adequate?

Is the paragraph unified?

Is the paragraph coherent?

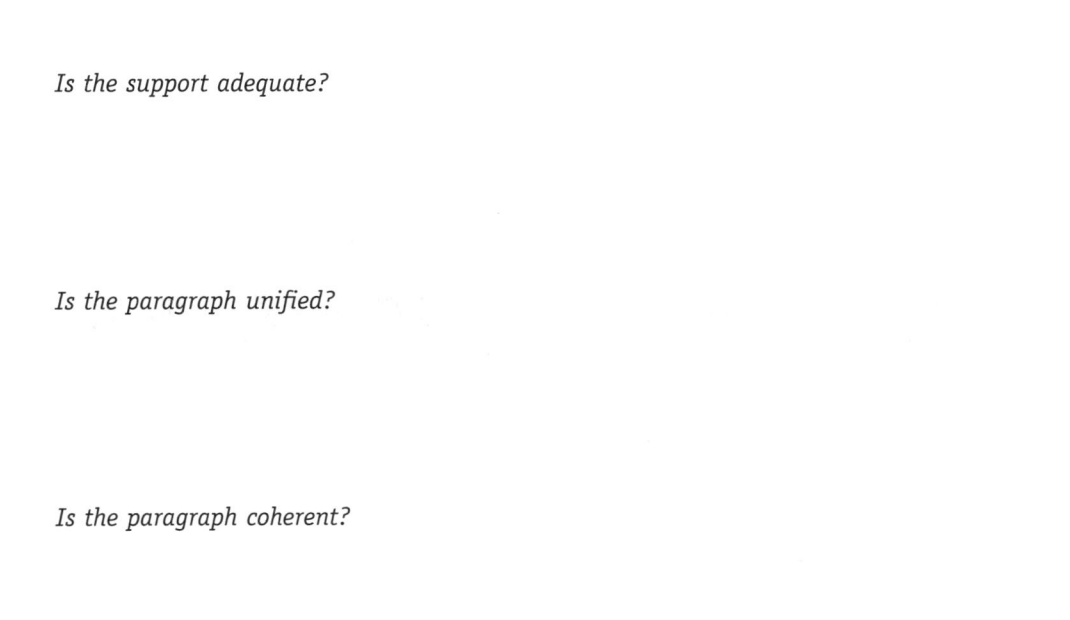

Fixing the problem of the disappearing rainforests depends on clearly identifying the part that wealthy western countries have played. The truth is that the pressure from industrialized countries for wood products is one of the most significant causes of deforestation in countries like Brazil. Poachers would not be driving species to extinction if there were not buyers in Europe and North America willing to pay well for animal hides. North American forests have already been over-exploited to produce paper, shingles and other wood products. That is why companies turn to less developed countries that still have extensive forests. In addition, local people who are at or below subsistence standards of living cannot afford to be concerned with global issues. They cut the forests for fuel, materials and farming purposes just to survive.

Source: "Rainforest Facts," Wealth of the Rainforest—Pharmacy to the World from Raintree Nutrition, Inc. site, http://www.rain-tree.com/facts.htm. Accessed December 5, 2006.

Is the support adequate?

Is the paragraph unified?

Is the paragraph coherent?

TASK THREE   Revising Your Essay

Task Two asked you to evaluate different body paragraphs in terms of adequate support, unity, and coherence. This task asks you to evaluate the full text of an essay written by individual members of your group.

Part One

Exchange the rough draft of your individual essay with a group member. When you receive a paper, read through the body paragraphs and evaluate it for adequate support, unity, and coherence.

Write your comments in the right-hand margin of the paper. Use the following considerations as a guideline:

- Indicate any questions that you have about the material.
- Is there anything that you do not completely understand? Is any more explanation needed? Are there clear examples and supporting detail so that the reader can see what the writer means?
- Indicate any material that breaks the unity either of the whole essay or of a particular section.
- Is there any information that is off topic? Are there any ideas that do not really belong in this essay? Is there anything that you recommend the writer strike out?
- Indicate if there is anything that needs rearranging.
- Is there any material that seems to be in the wrong place? Does the writer have a clear organizing principle for each section that is followed consistently?

Part Two

Exchange your paper with one other person in your group. When you get the next paper, evaluate it in the same way you evaluated the last one. This time, write your comments in the left-hand column.

Part Three

Give the paper back to the writer. When you get your paper, look at the comments in the columns. Read your paper over again and make your own decisions on how you will revise the draft.

Part Four

Write a new draft of the paper taking into account the comments made to you, your observations of other people's work, and your own rereading of your paper.

Editing

Revision has to do with the content of your essay and its overall structure. Editing has to do with the language in which you express all that. Use editing to find more effective ways to put your sentences and correct any errors in language mechanics. Holding this stage right to the end means that you have had the opportunity to focus on getting your essay down on paper. Now you have the opportunity to put on the finishing touches.

Finding More Effective Ways to Put Your Sentences

Improving your sentences means attending to style. Sentences in a particular section of your essay may be correct but not necessarily effective or memorable. One way to help you identify any places needing improvement is reading out loud. If you find you stumble over any part of the reading, or if any section seems flat, you have found a place that needs rewriting. Here are some of the things you can do:

Vary the Sentence Length and Type. Modern writing style prefers short, crisp sentences. At the same time, that observation should be taken as a guideline rather than as a fixed rule. An essay which was a series of short sentences all written in the same subject-verb-object order would be repetitive, dull, and unimpressive. If you find a string of such sentences, choose an appropriate place to break up the repetition with some variety. You can vary the sentence length by combining two or more sentences. You can vary the sentence structure by switching the order and introducing supporting components.

> **Vary the Sentence Length**
> One-and-a-half acres of rainforest disappear every second. The effects are disastrous.
>
> **Rewrite**: One-and-a-half acres of rainforest disappear every second with disastrous effects.
>
> About 25% of Western pharmaceuticals are based on species found in the rainforests. Less than 1% of the rainforest species have been tested.

Rewrite: While 25% of Western pharmaceuticals are based on rainforest plants, less than 1% of species have been tested for their potential.

Vary the Sentence Structure

The Amazon produces more than 20% of the world's oxygen. The loss of the rainforests there has a huge impact on health.

Rewrite: Sometimes called the "lungs of our planet," Amazon rainforests are crucial to everyone because they produce 20% of the world's oxygen.

One-fifth of the world's fresh water is in the Amazon. The Amazon produces more than 20% of the world's oxygen.

Rewrite: Just as the Amazon holds a significant 20% of the world's fresh water, it also produces an astounding 20% of the world's oxygen, which makes the Amazon key to supporting life on earth.

Concentrated action must be taken soon by companies and governments to save this endangered resource.

Rewrite: Companies and governments must take immediate steps to preserve the rainforests.

Hint

Prefer simple, direct writing to complex sentences. Use longer, complex sentence only occasionally for variety.

Replace Worn-Out Phrases. Many writers use canned terms or phrases. Such phrases can seem mechanical and uninspiring, or, even worse, pompous. An essay that uses these misses the chance to express the voice of the writer in a personal style. Rather than picking up jargon, coined phrases, or clichés, try to express your ideas directly in your own words.

Replacing Canned Phrases

at this moment in time	**replace with**	now, immediately
state-of-the-art	**replace with**	modern
at the end of the day	**replace with**	finally
the bottom line	**replace with**	the essential fact, the most important fact
in the event that	**replace with**	if
in this day and age	**replace with**	today

Eliminate Wordiness. Wordiness means that the sentence uses empty words. Empty words serve no function, but are often repetitive or simply state the obvious. These words will often appear in a rough draft, but the work of polishing strengthens the sentences by making each word choice valuable. Ask yourself if your writing uses words that do not really contribute to meaning. In most cases, you can just remove the word, but sometimes you will need to do some rewriting.

Eliminate Wordiness

The Amazon rainforest is enormous in size, covering over a billion acres.

Rewrite: The Amazon is enormous, covering over a billion acres.

Scientists have identified rainforest plants that number 3,000 that fight cancer.

Rewrite: Scientists have identified 3,000 rainforest plants that fight cancer.

Ecological and environmental groups have called for and asked that governments take serious actions and steps to rescue and save the rainforests of Brazil.

Rewrite: Environmental groups have called on governments to take serious steps to save the Brazilian rainforest.

There are many species of rainforest plants that fight cancer.

Rewrite: Many species of rainforest plants fight cancer.

One species in particular, periwinkle, is very unique because it produces an extremely powerful anticancer drug.

Rewrite: One species, periwinkle, is unique because it produces a powerful anti-cancer drug.

Hint

Prefer simple, direct words to inflated, overly complex ones unless you are writing in a particularly formal setting.

Improving the Sentences in a Body Paragraph — TASK FOUR

20 minutes

Examine the following paragraphs and make suggestions on how the writer could improve the sentences.

Person 1: Please facilitate this task and be sure everyone has a chance to contribute.

Person 2: Please keep track of the time for your group.

Person 3: Please make the changes, upon which the group decides, above the sentences in the boxes below.

Person 4: Please read out the paragraph to the group and be ready to represent your group in a class discussion following this task.

Paragraph 1

> The loss of the rainforest is an ecological disaster. It produces 20% of the world's oxygen. It contains 1/5 of the world's fresh water. It has produced 80% of the world's diet. It has medicinal plants. Many of these plants can fight cancer. The bottom line is that the rainforest is irreplaceable.

Paragraph 2

> The rainforest is disappearing at an alarming and scary rate. In the year 1950, 15% of the world's surface was covered by rainforest which is large in size. In this day and age, the rainforest is vanishing at the incredibly fast rate of 78 million acres every year. At this point in time, very little is being done to solve or rectify this catastrophe which is a disaster for all of us.

Paragraph 3

> There is certainly no doubt that the entire planet earth is facing a very serious crisis. At this point in time, the disappearing and vanishing rainforests pose threats to human survival because of their importance to our air and water supply. In addition to all of that, there are also further considerations. Those considerations have to do with the species, thousands in number, of both plant and animal that are completely irreplaceable. That is why something must be urgently and immediately done to turn the tide. As the old saying, goes, where there is a will there is a way, and where there isn't a will, there isn't a way.

Correcting Errors

The final step is to go through your work to correct any sentence mechanics errors. These range from spelling to punctuation to grammar mistakes. If you wrote your paper on a computer, you would likely have noticed that the word processing program prompted you to fix certain errors that it had picked up. You will find those errors underlined and colour-coded. Use the language tools functions on your computer to do a thorough spelling and grammar check. Be careful, however, not to simply accept every change the computer recommends. Be sure to read the prompts and make your own decisions. Sometimes it does not pick up acceptable differences in spelling. In addition, it may simply not analyze your sentence correctly. You may find the program identifying an error where there isn't one. Conversely, some of your errors will not be picked up at all. Consequently, a computer check is good place to start but not to finish.

One of the most effective ways to correct your errors is to have a designated reader or readers. Most people cannot see their own typos. They tend to just automatically fill in a missing word or mentally correct a mistake. Other people will be able to pick up things that you miss. In addition, readers can give you helpful feedback on how clearly the ideas are really coming through.

Ask your readers to circle anything they suspect might be an error. Ask them to put a question mark beside anything that is not clear to them. In that way, you will have a valuable proofread draft that highlights where you can make significant improvements to your work.

Unit 4 discusses several common errors in writing. Use that section to repair any language mechanics problems that your readers uncover for you.

Revising and Editing Your Essay — TASK FIVE

Task Three asked you to read papers written by your group members and make suggestions for revision. This task asks you to make suggestions on how to improve the writing.

Part One

Exchange the rough draft of your individual essay with a group member. When you receive a paper, read through the body paragraphs. Make suggestions for improving the writing.

Circle any errors that you suspect. Write your suggestion for changes above the phrase or sentences and any comments in the right-hand column. Use the guidelines in this unit regarding sentence variety, canned phrases, and wordiness as you evaluate the writing.

Part Two

Exchange your paper with one other person in your group. When you get the next paper, evaluate it in the same way you evaluated the last one. Write your suggestion for changes below the phrase or sentences and any comments in the left-hand column.

Part Three

Give the paper back to the writer. When you get your paper, look at suggestions your readers have offered. Read your paper over again and make your own decisions on how you will correct the draft.

Part Four

Write a final draft of the paper, taking into account the comments made to you, your observations of other people's work, and your own rereading of your paper.

In Summary

Take three minutes to write a summary of what you have learned participating in the tasks of Unit 8.

Part 3

Applications

Unit 9: Comparison and Contrast
Unit 10: Argument
Unit 11: Classification
Unit 12: Cause and Effect
Unit 13: Research

Part 2 of this book asked you to work on the parts of an academic paper. Part 3 gives you an opportunity to apply your skills to specific purposes. Keeping readership in your thinking will help you plan writing that succeeds. Your academic writing in postsecondary programs is primarily, although not exclusively, aimed at professors. That means you use a formal tone and Standard English. It also means that you need to demonstrate that you understand the subject to someone who likely knows it much better than you do. You will have to define, explain, and support as you go on, not so much so that the professor can understand as to show the reader that you have mastered the material.

Keeping your purpose clear during the planning stages is also critical. Ask yourself what the paper sets out to do. The units in this section take you through academic essay writing focused on specific tasks. An essay that compares two different approaches or theories in your field is different from one that intends to trace the causes of a problem or from one that intends to argue a position. Each requires a specific strategy tailored to the writing situation.

UNIT 9

Comparison and Contrast

Here's what you'll work on in this unit.

- Differentiating between comparison and contrast writing
- Determining the purpose of comparison and contrast writing
- Selecting comparison and contrast criteria
- Employing different organization strategies
- Outlining a comparison and contrast essay
- Writing a comparison and contrast essay

Comparison and contrast writing is common in academic work. A professor may ask you to look at two or more competing theories or approaches to a subject. In one case, the assignment may be simply to clarify what sets them apart. In another, the purpose of the writing may be to get the writer to step out and state a preference. Both these situations require that the writer know what comparison and contrast requires, choose appropriate criteria, and employ an effective organizational strategy.

Differentiating Between Comparison and Contrast Writing

Consider what the following three tasks ask for:

- Compare the British medical system with the Canadian medical system.
- Contrast the British medical system with the Canadian medical system.
- Compare and contrast the British and the Canadian medical systems.

Your first task as a writer is to determine how to handle a task. Each of these writing assignments asks for a different focus. Determining the focus and writing to provide what was asked for depends on differentiating between the terms "compare" and "contrast."

Compare

Any assignment or exam question that stresses the term "compare" wants you to highlight similarities. In other words, how are these subjects of comparison similar to each other? What do they have in common? The writer who compares the British and Canadian medical systems will likely focus on the philosophical assumptions of socialized medicine, similar approaches, benefits, and challenges. That does not mean that differences are ruled out of the essay, but they take second place to the main task of demonstrating how the two systems have common elements.

Contrast

An assignment or exam question that stresses the term "contrast" wants you to emphasize differences. This kind of writing focuses on what sets the subjects apart from each other. How do they diverge? The writer who contrasts the British and Canadian medical systems will likely focus on such items as doctor-led walk-in clinics and provincial responsibilities over the system. Similarities are raised in this paper as background for the main work of ferreting out how things are done differently.

Compare and Contrast

If the professor asks you to write a comparison and contrast paper, provide a balanced treatment of both the similarities and the differences. Explore both fully rather than allowing one to take over as the primary purpose. The writer who both compares and contrasts the British and Canadian medical systems will discuss philosophical assumptions and government funding through taxation and the differences in how the systems are managed.

Hint

If you are in doubt about what focus the assignment asks for, clarify expectations with the professor.

Determining the Purpose of Comparison and Contrast Writing

After having determined what emphasis you need to take, consider what purpose the writing serves. Clarifying the purpose is essential to making decisions about what to include in your paper. Comparison and contrast writing has two basic purposes.

Informative

An informative paper focuses on presenting a comprehensive picture that demonstrates that you have done the research, understand the subjects of your paper, and are able to relate what you have learned. No action is recommended or expected in this kind of work. Both the writer and the reader stand back as observers.

Evaluative

An evaluative paper focuses on making a decision about the subjects being compared and contrasted. The writer uses the information presented to make a clear recommendation. In fact, the essay was written so that the reader could make an informed choice. In this case, the writer and the reader are not simply observers but involved with the subject in a closer manner.

Hint

If the assignment is not clear about whether it is informative or evaluative, clarify with the professor just what is being asked for in the task. This kind of clarification will help you plan out a paper that is on target.

Selecting Comparison and Contrast Criteria

Now that you are clear as to the emphasis and purpose of your paper, you can determine just what kind of comparison and contrast criteria you will use. These criteria are the points of comparison. What is it that you are interested in finding out about your subjects? In what ways do you want to show your subjects as similar or dissimilar? It is normally not possible or even desirable to compare and contrast your subjects in every single way possible. On the one hand, that would make your paper far too long. On the other, comparing and contrasting everything would only obscure what is really important for whatever you have set out.

Your choice of criteria depends on answering three questions:

- How long is the paper?
- What is the purpose of the paper?
- Who is the reader of the paper?

If you were writing a short two-page paper comparing two houses, you would have to narrow your number of criteria. You could not compare and contrast all the details of two houses in such a short piece. It would be more reasonable to aim at three points. Here is how a writer might determine those points to suit particular writing situations:

Reader	Purpose	Criteria
First-time home buyer	A recently married couple wants to choose a house in which to raise a family.	**Condition** • Extensive renovations are not possible if money is an issue. **Price** • The asking price will determine whether they can even consider the property. **Location** • Transportation to work, schools, and shopping will be important considerations.
Home owner	A long-established owner of a house wants to appeal the municipal assessment by comparing the house to the neighbour's house.	**Renovations** • How much work has been done to the houses is key. **Features** • In-ground swimming pools, basement apartments, and lot size change the assessment. **Value** • How real estate agents price the houses is an important factor.
Architectural department professor	A second-year student is required to write an academic paper for a professor comparing two different kinds of houses in Toronto.	**Special Architectural Details** • Design elements set one house apart from the other. **History of the Structures** • When the houses were built, the designer, and the builder are factors in the style. **Materials** • The materials used in the house are part of what makes it distinctive.

TASK ONE   Selecting Comparison and Contrast Criteria

15 minutes

This task asks you to compare and contrast two hotels in Toronto for different purposes in a short two-to-three-page paper. Determine the criteria of comparison and contrast that you would use in the paper. Be ready to defend your choices.

Person 2: Please facilitate this task. Be sure everyone has a chance to comment.

Person 3: Please keep track of the time for your group.

Person 4: Please record the group consensus in the table below.

Person 1: Please be ready to give your group answers to the class.

Reader	Purpose	Criteria
Postsecondary students	A committee of students is selecting a hotel to run a party for graduation.	
Investor	A foreign investor wants to buy a hotel to run as an ongoing business.	
Hospitality and tourism professor	A first-year student is required to write a report and prepare a PowerPoint presentation for a mid-term grade on two luxury hotels in Toronto.	

Employing Different Organization Strategies

You saw in Task One that a different readership and different purposes changed the criteria the essay would use to compare and contrast the subjects. Having decided on the points of comparison, the next step is to decide how they should be ordered and then organized.

Ordering Your Points

Look through your points and decide what principle you might use for arranging their order. You might, for example, want to work in order of priority from most to least important. Think about what makes most sense for the particular case on which you are working. The essay for the first-time home buyers, for example, will consider three points:

1. Condition

    Extensive renovations are not possible if money is an issue.

2. Price

    The asking price will determine whether they can even consider the property.

3. Location

    Transportation to work, schools, and shopping will be important considerations.

You might decide to rearrange the points as follows:

1. Price

    The asking price is the starting point. There is no use considering other details if the price is beyond what they can afford.

2. Location

    A great house at a great price is not ideal if transportation is a serious issue. The family is going to be very busy and needs a certain convenience in getting around.

3. Condition

    Although this factor is important, it likely could be placed at the bottom of the list. A good price for a house in the perfect location might make some renovation work acceptable.

Once you have selected and ordered your points, you can then decide on the best way to organize the essay. You have several options.

Whole-by-Whole

This method of organization treats each of the subjects separately. The reader learns everything the paper is going to provide about the first subject before learning about the next.

In the case of the first-time home buyers, a whole-by-whole organization of the paper might look like this:

1.0 Introduction
2.0 House 1
    2.1 Price
    2.2 Location
    2.3 Condition
3.0 House 2
    3.1 Price
    3.2 Location
    3.3 Condition
4.0 Recommendation

The advantage of the whole-by-whole system is that it gives the reader a total picture of each subject. The disadvantage is that if you try to apply it to a longer paper with several criteria, the reader might forget what you wrote about the first subject in an earlier section and thus lose the sense of comparison and contrast.

Part-by-Part

This option asks the reader to consider both subjects at the same time through the lens of one particular comparison and contrast criterion. The essay constantly compares and contrasts the subjects for the reader.

In the case of the first-time home buyers, a part-by-part organization of the paper might look like this:

1.0 Introduction
2.0 Price
    2.1 House 1
    2.2 House 2
3.0 Location
    3.1 House 1
    3.2 House 2
4.0 Condition
    4.1 House 1
    4.2 House 2
5.0 Recommendation

The advantage of the point-by-point system is that it makes the comparison and contrast immediate and explicit. The reader can see the subjects side by side. The disadvantage is that the reader loses the sense of the larger picture in which one item may compensate for another.

Similar-Dissimilar

As the name implies, this kind of organization uses two main sections. The first section provides a comparison, while the second section provides the contrast.

In the case of the first-time home buyers, a part-by-part organization of the paper might look like this:

1.0 Introduction
2.0 Similar
    2.1 Price
    2.2 Location
3.0 Dissimilar
    3.1 Condition
4.0 Recommendation

The advantage of using a similar-dissimilar organization is that the essay emphasizes whether or not the subjects are more alike. In particular, it draws the reader's attention to the third section, in which the differences are highlighted. It is likely that the rationale for a recommendation will come out of this part of the essay. Like the part-by-part organization, however, it fragments both subjects so that the reader does not get a total picture.

Reorganizing a Comparison and Contrast Essay TASK TWO

20 minutes

The following three body paragraphs are from a comparison and contrast section in a marketing textbook. This section compares and contrasts different media that a company can use in marketing its product. Identify the comparison and contrast organization strategy that the authors have selected. Produce an outline for two alternative articles with the same information using the strategies discussed above. Finally, decide as a group which of the three approaches you would use if you were writing the text, and why you would choose it.

Person 4: Please facilitate this task. Be sure everyone has a chance to comment.
Person 3: Please keep track of the time for your group.
Person 1: Please record the group consensus in the form below.
Person 2: Please be ready to give your group answers to the class.

Television

Television is the largest advertising medium. It now accounts for about 26 percent of total advertising volume. Since 1991, it has grown by 22 percent. Television advertising can be divided into three categories: network, national spot, and local spot. The Canadian Broadcasting Corporation, the Canadian Television Network, and Global Television are the three national networks. Network advertising usually accounts for over two-thirds of the total television advertising expenditures. A national "spot" refers to non-network broadcasting used by a general advertiser. For example, Black & Decker might choose to place an advertisement in several cities across the country without buying time from a television network. Local spots, primarily used by retailers, consist of locally developed and sponsored commercials. Television advertising offers the following advantage: impact, mass coverage, repetition, flexibility, and prestige. Its disadvantages include the temporary nature of the message, high costs, high mortality rates for commercials, some evidence of public distrust, and lack of selectivity.

Newspapers

Newspapers are approximately the same as television in size as an advertising medium. About 28 percent of Canada's total advertising revenues are spent on newspaper advertising. Dailies account for 19 percent and community newspapers represent 9 percent. The primary advantages of newspapers are flexibility (advertising can vary from one locality to the next), community prestige (newspapers have a deep impact on the community), intense coverage (in most places, about nine out of ten homes can be reached by a single newspaper), and reader control of exposure to the advertising message (unlike audiences of electronic media, readers can refer back to newspapers). The disadvantages are a short lifespan, hasty reading (the typical reader spends only 20 to 30 minutes on the newspaper), and poor reproduction.

Radio

Radio continues to hold its share of advertising revenue. Advertisers using the medium of radio can also be classified as network or local advertisers. Radio accounts for about 11 percent of total advertising volume. The advantages of radio advertising are immediacy (studies show that most people regard radio as the best source for up-to-date news); low cost; flexibility; practical, low-cost audience selection; and mobility (radio is an extremely mobile broadcast medium). Radio's disadvantages include fragmentation (for instance, Montreal has fifteen AM and FM stations), the unavailability of the advertising message for future reference, and less available research information than for television.

Source: From Foundations of Marketing, Eight Canadian Edition by BECKMAN. 2003. Reprinted with Permission of Nelson, a division of Thomson Learning: www.thomsonrights.com. Fax 800-730-2215.

Original text	Organization method used

Alternative 1

Alternative 2

Group's preferred model

```
┌─────────────────────────────────────────────────────────┐
│                                                         │
│                                                         │
│                                                         │
│                                                         │
└─────────────────────────────────────────────────────────┘
```

Reasons

```
┌─────────────────────────────────────────────────────────┐
│                                                         │
│                                                         │
│                                                         │
│                                                         │
│                                                         │
└─────────────────────────────────────────────────────────┘
```

━━━━━━━━━━━━━━━━▷━━━━━━━━━━━━━━━━

Outlining a Comparison and Contrast Essay

Having selected your points and settled on an organization strategy, you can now outline your paper. Use the box outline described in Part 2 of this book. Fill in the thesis statement at the bottom of the introduction and the topic sentences at the beginning of each body paragraph. List in bullet form the main information you will use. Here is a box outline for the essay for the first-time home buyers:

Lead or Hook: Buying your first house is one of the most important decisions you will make.

Background
- Criteria: Price, location, condition
- Reasons for selecting these criteria

Thesis: House 1 is the better choice.

Topic 1: Both houses fit well within the budget.

House 1
- Slightly lower price
- Lower taxes
- Similar utilities fee

House 2
- Slightly higher price
- Slightly higher taxes
- Similar utilities fee

Topic 2: The location of each house has its own advantages.

House 1
- Near shopping
- Near schools
- 20-minute drive to rapid transit

House 2
- Near highway
- Near rapid transit
- 40-minute drive to shopping and schools

Topic 3: One house is in better condition than the other.

House 1
- Clean
- Bedrooms need painting
- Floors need sanding

House 2
- Immaculate
- Basement renovated

Recommendation

Cost of painting and sanding offset by lower price, taxes, and utilities.

Planning a Comparison and Contrast Paper

TASK THREE

Your department is assessing the textbooks used in your program. Each person in your group will write a two to three page submission for the committee that compares and contrasts any two textbooks that you are currently using. The department wants to know what works well with its students and what needs to be improved. It is particularly interested in feedback on special features and how helpful the texts are in the courses. The committee will use this information to make recommendations about what textbooks to assign next term.

Part One
1. Select two textbooks that you are using.
2. Identify the number of criteria of comparison and contrast that would be appropriate for this paper.
3. Consider what points of comparison you want to use and which suit the task.
4. Order the points.
5. Select an organization method.
6. Sketch out a preliminary numbered outline like one of those above.

Part Two
Work out a box outline for your paper.

Part Three
Exchange the outline of your individual essay with a group member. When you receive a paper, read through the outline and evaluate it for clarity and organization.

Write your comments on the right-hand side of the paper. Use the following considerations as a guideline:

- Does the outline have a clear set of comparison and contrast criteria?
- Are the criteria arranged in an order that makes sense to you?
- Does the outline use a whole-by-whole, part-by-part, or similar-dissimilar pattern?
- Does the supporting evidence fit the topic sentences?
- Does the introduction indicate the hook, the criteria, and the thesis statement?

Now that you have seen the outlines of other people working on the same project and have had a chance to get feedback on yours, work through the rough and final-draft process.

Part One

Use your outline, the suggestions given to you by group members, and your own insights when reading other outlines to write a first draft of your paper.

Hint

Keep in mind that you are writing for a committee of faculty who teach in your department. Think about what that means in terms of tone and wording.

Part Two

Exchange your draft with someone in your group. When you get a paper, evaluate it for support, unity, coherence, and language mechanics. Circle any errors that you suspect and write your comments in the right-hand margin.

Part Three

Exchange the draft you have with one other person. When you receive a paper, evaluate it in the same way you evaluated the first draft given to you. Write your comments in the left-hand margin. Give the paper back to the writer.

Part Four

When you get your paper, look at the suggestions that your readers have offered.

Put your rough draft aside for a day or so, and work on other projects. Then use your draft, the suggestions your group members made, and your own insights from reading other papers to produce a final draft. Submit that draft for grading.

In Summary

Take three minutes to write a summary of what you have learned participating in the tasks of Unit 9.

UNIT 10

Argument

Here's what you'll work on in this unit.

- Defining the characteristics of an argument
- Determining claims
- Identifying assumptions
- Using thesis and antithesis
- Recognizing logical fallacies
- Outlining an argument
- Writing an argument

Some of the academic writing you will do will be purely informative. Its goal is to convey information. Other academic writing will be argumentative. That does not mean the writing equivalent of shouting and getting angry. It means, instead, putting together a convincing essay that persuades the reader to accept your point of view. A good argument depends on a number of criteria.

Defining the Characteristics of an Argument

Making a Claim
Arguments are based on claims rather than on self-evident facts. Essentially, your thesis statement is a claim about your subject. Some people will sign on to your claim while others will not. The essay's job is to clarify the claim and convince the reader to accept it.

Building a Case
Think of an argumentative essay as presenting a case in a law court. The writer is the lawyer, the essay content is the evidence, and the reader is the judge. The writer connects facts and demonstrates that they support the claim made in the essay. The case interprets the evidence

and draws out the conclusions. How convincing the essay is depends on how compelling the argument is.

Using Evidence

Argumentative writing is built upon facts. These facts are the basic material with which the writer builds the larger structure of the essay. The information must be precise and verifiable if it is to carry any weight.

Employing a Structure

A lawyer not only has to provide convincing evidence, but has to employ a convincing strategy. The way in which the material is handled is crucial to how the reader receives it.

The Claim

A *claim* is an assertion that cannot just be looked up in a book or checked out on a Web page. That British Columbia is Canada's most western province is a fact, not a claim. It is not something around which you could form an argument. A claim is also something that goes beyond personal taste. To say that olives taste terrible is simply expressing a personal preference, but is not a claim that can be supported by evidence. You do not have to prove to the reader whether you like something or not. On the other hand, you do have to prove any claim to truth. An argument can support a number of different kinds of claim.

Claim of Policy

A claim of policy advocates for a way of managing an issue or organization. It claims that one way of doing things is better than another.

>Medication should be included in provincial health plans.

>The college should provide day care facilities for the children of staff members.

>Voting, drinking, and driving ages should be consistent.

Claim of Value

A claim of value asserts that the subject has a definite value beyond a matter of taste. The claim is more universal than personal.

>Pornography is unhealthy.

>Homeschooling is a positive alternative to institutionalized education.

>Video games are good for developing critical-thinking skills.

Claim of Fact

Although an argument cannot be based on a fact that is immediately verifiable, it can be based on something that is not yet clear. The claim is either right or wrong, but there is no authoritative source available to clarify the matter. A case still needs to be built.

>Aliens from outer space have been visiting the earth for centuries.

>The universe began with the Big Bang.

>Sexual orientation is primarily genetic.

Determining Claims

TASK ONE

15 minutes

This task asks you to examine several statements proposed as claims for an argument. Look at each one and determine whether it is a claim upon which a writer might build a persuasive paper. Explain why you have ruled out any statements. Identify what type of claim the writer is making. Be ready to defend your decisions.

Person 4: Please facilitate this task. Be sure everyone has a chance to comment.

Person 3: Please keep track of the time for your group.

Person 2: Please record the group consensus in the table below.

Person 1: Please be ready to give your group answers to the class.

Statement	Is it a claim?	If it is an acceptable claim, what kind of claim is it? If it is not an acceptable claim, why not?
More people died in World War I than in World War II.		
Drivers should have to take a driving test every five years.		
Most of the Canadian television I have watched is boring.		
Students should have a voice on the curriculum development committee of their departments.		
Pornography should be permitted in public libraries.		
The college should have a sports centre.		

Statement	Is it a claim?	If it is an acceptable claim, what kind of claim is it? If it is not an acceptable claim, why not?
The pyramids were built by aliens.		
New York is the theatre capital of the world.		
We should allow doctors who have immigrated to Canada to practise medicine as soon as they arrive.		
Slasher movies are harmful to society.		

Identifying Assumptions

You will be required at different points in your studies to stake out a point of view and defend it. That means working with a claim about your field of study. You will also read different pieces that argue for a particular claim. The writer may argue for a particular theory or advocate a particular way of doing things. Whether you are writing or reading an argument, it is important to look behind the claim for any unstated assumptions. Your readers might share those assumptions with you, in which case you can start building your case. If they do not share those assumptions, however, the argument is not likely to be convincing. Recognizing assumptions is also essential for careful academic reading. It can help you determine any weaknesses in a case.

One way to identify assumptions is to cast an argument in three parts: major premise, minor premise, and conclusion. The *major premise* is the large principle, conviction, or assumption that lies behind the argument. Many arguments do not explicitly state the major premise. Sometimes it is a given that the reader and the writer agree with a basic principle. At other times the absence of a major premise is evidence of bad reasoning. The *minor premise* is a particular focus. The *conclusion* is the claim that grows out of your reasoning.

Hint

Both the major premise and the minor premise must be true if the claim is to be true.

Take a look at the following claim.

> We must dramatically increase the military budget so that Canadian troops can play a more effective role in international peacekeeping.

This claim provides both the conclusion and the minor premise.

Minor Premise: An increased military budget would permit Canadian troops to play a more effective role in international peacekeeping.

Conclusion: We must dramatically increase the military budget.

If the argument continued on this basis, it would sidestep the assumption upon which the whole claim depends. That assumption is the major premise. Stepping back from the minor premise helps a reader discover that assumption. In this case, the argument can be mapped out this way.

Major Premise: Canadian troops should play a more effective role in international peacekeeping.

Minor Premise: An increased military budget would permit Canadian troops to play a more effective role in international peacekeeping.

Conclusion: We must dramatically increase the military budget.

If the writer were writing this paper for an identified readership that was already committed to the assumption of the major premise, the article could continue as planned. On the other hand, if the readership is not committed to this idea, moving ahead with the claim for increasing the military budget is not likely to go very far.

Identifying Assumptions — TASK TWO

15 minutes

This task asks you to determine assumptions behind an argument. Look at each of the following claims and break them down into major premise, minor premise, and conclusion.

Person 2: Please facilitate this task. Be sure everyone has a chance to comment.

Person 1: Please keep track of the time for your group.

Person 3: Please record the group consensus in the table below.

Person 4: Please be ready to give your group answers to the class.

1. We should raise taxes so we can enact more anti-terrorist security measures.

    Major premise: _____
    Minor premise: _____
    Conclusion: _____

2. If we cut taxes, social services will suffer.

    Major premise: _____
    Minor premise: _____
    Conclusion: _____

3. If we have a fully stocked bar at the college, students will be happy.

    Major premise: _____
    Minor premise: _____
    Conclusion: _____

4. The Canadian building industry needs to switch to green materials in order to construct more environmentally friendly structures.

    Major premise: _____
    Minor premise: _____
    Conclusion: _____

5. Canada and the United States should adopt a single currency as Europe has done, in order to rationalize our economies.

    Major premise: _____
    Minor premise: _____
    Conclusion: _____

Using Thesis and Antithesis

Many beginning writers mistake expressing an opinion for arguing. These are, in fact, two very different things. Expressing an opinion does not aim at persuading, but simply at letting the reader know why the writer thinks a certain way. Arguing focuses on convincing the reader. The writer needs to start where the reader is in order to be able to maximize any opportunity to win agreement. Writing an argument means, then, assessing where the intended reader stands on the issue and incorporating that into the essay.

Take, for example, the abortion debate. Both sides of that debate have a clear main point that defines the position. Those against abortion on demand call their movement *pro-life* because the main point is that abortion is the killing of a human life. On the other hand, those who support access to abortion call their movement *pro-choice* because the main point is that women have a right to make their own choices. If a writer or speaker is not aware of what the other side's concerns are, little will be accomplished except explaining why he or she holds that opinion. If the pro-choice writer puts together an argument that simply presents that view, the pro-life reader may agree with many points including the importance of choice in a free society, but all the time will also think, "Yes, but what about the life of the child?" Similarly, if the pro-life writer puts together an argument that simply presents the life argument, the pro-choice reader may agree with some or even much of what is said, but all the time will also think, "Yes, but what about a woman's right to choose?" In both cases, the articles have explained a position but have not worked to change minds by focusing on the needs of the reader. The opinions for both these essays might be diagrammed as follows.

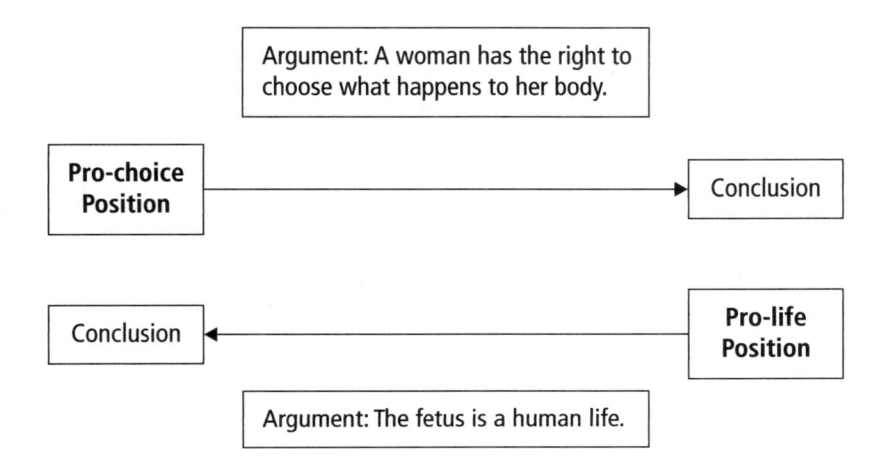

```
                  ┌─────────────────────────────────┐
                  │ Argument: A woman has the right to│
                  │ choose what happens to her body.  │
                  └─────────────────────────────────┘
  ┌──────────────┐                                    ┌──────────────┐
  │ Pro-choice   │ ─────────────────────────────────▶ │  Conclusion  │
  │ Position     │                                    │              │
  └──────────────┘                                    └──────────────┘

  ┌──────────────┐                                    ┌──────────────┐
  │  Conclusion  │ ◀───────────────────────────────── │  Pro-life    │
  │              │                                    │  Position    │
  └──────────────┘                                    └──────────────┘
                  ┌─────────────────────────────────┐
                  │ Argument: The fetus is a human life.│
                  └─────────────────────────────────┘
```

The thesis–antithesis method is a strategy for persuasive writing that helps the reader present an argument and address the specific concerns of an identified reader. Essentially, the essay makes its case, then frankly addresses the main concern or argument on the other side. It does this by stating the main objection as fairly and objectively as possible, then refuting that objection. In other words, the writer shows why the main argument on the other side is not convincing enough. The other side hears its concerns voiced and treated seriously. The two abortion arguments might be diagrammed as follows.

Pro-choice Argument

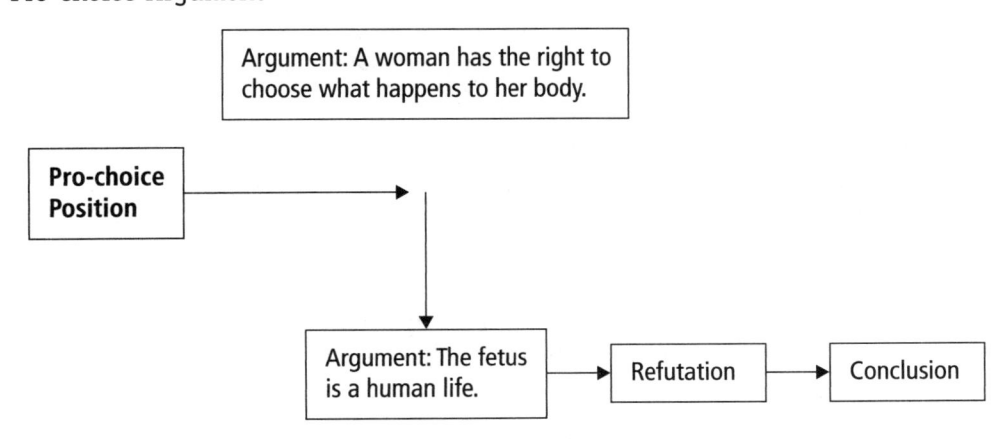

```
                    ┌─────────────────────────────────┐
                    │ Argument: A woman has the right to│
                    │ choose what happens to her body.  │
                    └─────────────────────────────────┘
  ┌──────────────┐             │
  │ Pro-choice   │─────────────▶
  │ Position     │             │
  └──────────────┘             ▼
                    ┌──────────────┐   ┌────────────┐   ┌────────────┐
                    │ Argument: The fetus│──▶│ Refutation │──▶│ Conclusion │
                    │ is a human life.   │   │            │   │            │
                    └──────────────┘   └────────────┘   └────────────┘
```

Pro-life Argument

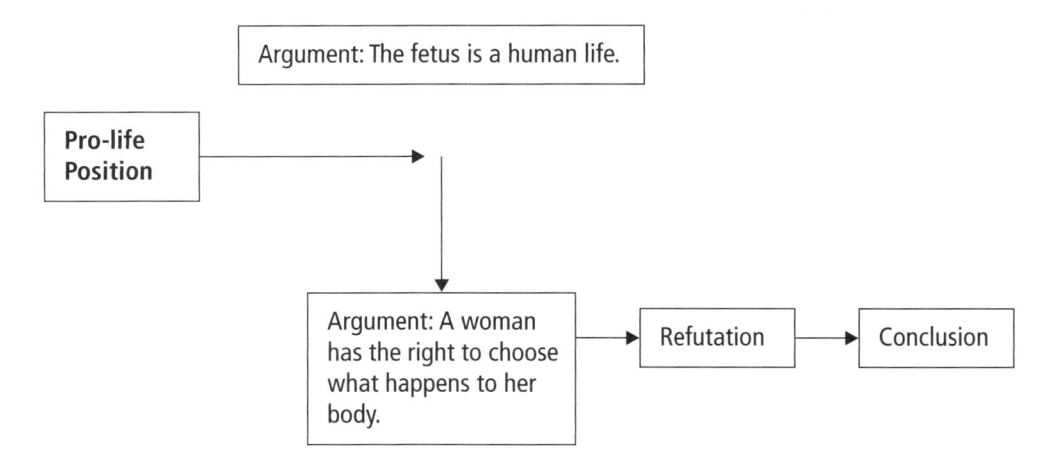

```
                    ┌─────────────────────────────────┐
                    │ Argument: The fetus is a human life. │
                    └─────────────────────────────────┘
┌──────────┐                    │
│ Pro-life │ ──────────────→    │
│ Position │                    ▼
└──────────┘        ┌─────────────────┐   ┌────────────┐   ┌────────────┐
                    │ Argument: A woman│ → │ Refutation │ → │ Conclusion │
                    │ has the right to │   └────────────┘   └────────────┘
                    │ choose what      │
                    │ happens to her   │
                    │ body.            │
                    └─────────────────┘
```

Your position is the thesis. The other side's position is the antithesis. It is important in this model to choose the strongest argument from the other side rather than choosing weak arguments that are easy to knock down. A longer paper might deal with more than one argument against your position.

Hint

The strongest argument from the other side is the one that you have the most difficult time dealing with. If, in fact, you cannot adequately refute that argument, you may need to do some more research or rethink your own position. If you cannot clearly refute the antithesis, you are not ready to argue your position.

TASK THREE Identifying the Antithesis and Stating a Refutation

15 minutes

Each of the following situations identifies a particular readership and a thesis. Determine what the main objection from that readership would be, and the best way to refute it.

Person 3: Please facilitate this task. Be sure everyone has a chance to comment.

Person 4: Please keep track of the time for your group.

Person 2: Please record the group consensus in the form below.

Person 1: Please be ready to give your group answers to the class.

1. Audience: Board of Governors of the college

    Thesis: The college should build a multi-storage parking garage.

Objection

Refutation

2. Audience: Cafeteria manager

    Thesis: The college cafeteria should stop selling coffee in paper or plastic cups, and use ceramic mugs instead.

Objection

Refutation

3. Audience: MPPs

   Thesis: Corner grocery stores should be allowed to sell beer and wine.

   Objection

   Refutation

4. Audience: Student group

   Thesis: We should advocate for a repeal of the law that permits Sunday shopping.

   Objection

   Refutation

Recognizing Logical Fallacies

Although the argument is based on facts and an objective presentation of the antithesis, it is the quality of reasoning that holds everything together. After reading or writing an argument, look at the reasoning to see if it is sound or if there are any flaws. Flaws in reasoning are called *logical fallacies*. Here are some of the main logical fallacies that creep into persuasive essays.

False Cause

The *false cause* fallacy connects two events without demonstrating that one event indeed caused another:

> This is an excellent government because ever since it came into power the economy has done very well.

Problem: The economy might have improved because of the government's policies, but it might have improved for other reasons related to global conditions. The mere fact that the economy is good does not validate the claim that the government is excellent.

Circular Argument

The *circular argument* is sometimes called *begging the question*. It sets the reader up by anticipating the conclusion.

> Ineffective security measures like alarm systems are not necessary in this building.

Problem: Naturally, ineffective measures of any kind are unnecessary. This claim does not deal with the question of whether the building needs an alarm system.

False Dichotomy

False dichotomy forces the reader to choose between two options without recognizing that other options are available.

> We must either adopt these emission standards or accept the inevitable consequences of global warming.

Problem: This claim eliminates the possibility of another approach or of different standards. It tries to close down any argument against it by forcing a quick decision.

Straw Man

A *straw man* argument sets up a false target—a "scarecrow" that is easy to knock down. It essentially works by exaggerating the other side's arguments. The exaggerated argument is refuted instead of the actual case that the other side makes.

> The government has gone too far in making smoking illegal in restaurants and bars. Smoking has been made illegal just about everywhere. The next step would be to make it illegal even in the privacy of your own home. That would be an intrusion of privacy by the government and a loss of your freedom to choose.

Problem: The claim is that the government is wrong in prohibiting smoking in restaurants and bars, but the reasons for the claim, intrusion and loss of choice, are made discussing a totally different and exaggerated case.

Attacking the Person

This fallacy, which some call *ad hominem* (Latin for "to the man"), takes the reader's attention away from the argument and moves it to the person. It calls the person's credibility into question so that whatever he or she says loses value. It fails to look at the integrity of the claim on its own.

> As celibate clergy, he cannot offer any positive ideas in marriage counselling.

Problem: The focus is taken off whatever the ideas might actually be. Instead of evaluating those ideas, the writer makes an unsupported claim that only married people could have something to say about marriage counselling.

False Comparison

Many arguments draw analogies or comparisons to make things clear. Although this can be helpful, it can also be dangerous to make a *false comparison*—to over-identify one thing with another—because that minimizes the differences. Such oversimplification misses what is special to each situation.

> The criminal element in this neighbourhood is like an infestation of pests that must be eliminated before the soundness of the structure of society gives way.

Problem: Criminals are human beings, not insects. Society is a community of people, not a wooden building. It is reasonable to exterminate an infestation of bugs, but not reasonable to eliminate people. Communities can work on issues, but buildings cannot.

Hasty Generalization

Hasty generalization is making sweeping statements based on few examples. Such conclusions then become the major premise or assumption of a larger argument. The flaw is that the assumption was really never borne out by the facts to begin with.

> The recent case of street gunfire along with the one earlier this year shows just how dangerous our streets have become and how much violent crime has escalated.

Problem: Two cases do not establish a crime wave or an enormous escalation in violence. More evidence is needed before any general conclusion can be drawn.

TASK FOUR   Identifying the Logical Fallacies

15 minutes

Read through the following text. Separate your views on the subject from the ways this writer has tried to build the case. Identify any errors or fallacies in reasoning. Explain why they are errors. Be prepared to explain your answers in the larger class setting.

Person 2: Please facilitate this task. Be sure everyone has a chance to comment. Read out the text to the group.

Person 1: Please keep track of the time for your group.

Person 4: Please record the group consensus in the form below.

Person 3: Please be ready to give your group answers to the class.

When an animal is suffering it is a common practice to "put it down." We shoot an injured horse, or put a sick dog to sleep and see it as an act of mercy. Yet we do not have the same consideration for people. We treat our animals better than people. People have the same right to euthanasia as our pets.

Some people argue that euthanasia is against the will of God. But how can this be? There are many examples in the Old Testament of God sending plagues that kill people, and of ordering the Israelites to slaughter other people. And if there is a God, isn't it better to send people to be with Him than to keep them here? Everyone wants to go to heaven, but nobody wants to die or let other people die. Shirley MacLaine, the American actress and singer, in her book *Out on a Limb*, shows clearly that people survive after death and many come back again in new bodies. General George Patton and automobile manufacturer Henry Ford also firmly believed in it. In that case, what is the problem with letting people go?

I suppose those against euthanasia are in favour of keeping people alive for hundreds of years as living skeletons or vegetables hooked up to machines that cost society millions of dollars. That is so immoral when there are people starving in other corners of the world. It is so immoral to spend money on keeping them alive when we could all have a higher standard of living.

Some societies already permit euthanasia. Holland is an example. What is interesting is that the recent studies show that the Dutch are among the happiest people in Europe. One of the biggest opponents of euthanasia is the Church, but as everyone knows, it is preoccupied with suffering and actually encourages suffering so that it can keep control over its adherents. Consequently, we must either recognize euthanasia as a way of bringing loving mercy to the sick, which frees them from pain, or give in to being manipulated by organized religion.

I urge you to stand up and be counted. Insist that the government fulfill its responsibilities by legalizing euthanasia so that no one ever need suffer again.

Fallacy	Problem

Fallacy	Problem

TASK FIVE Identifying Additional Logical Fallacies

Give your group members at least more three logical fallacies apart from the ones we have considered. Your group will put a list of logical fallacies together for everyone else in the class.

Part 1: Research

Explore the Net and the library to see what additional logical fallacies you can discover. One place for you to start to look is the Fallacy Files site, at http://www.fallacyfiles.org/wanalogy.html. You can also conduct research using the terms "logical fallacies" or "errors in reasoning." Identify the name and give an example for each type of fallacy you find.

Part 2: Group Meeting

Person 2: Facilitate the task. Be sure everyone has an opportunity to present the different fallacies in turn.

Person 1: Record the different fallacies discovered.

Person 3: Prepare a word-processed version of the different fallacies for your group portfolio.

Person 4: Be prepared to present the results to the class.

Outlining an Argument

Having determined a claim, a case, the antithesis, and a refutation, it is time to outline the argument. The first part of the organization can use the questioning system discussed in Unit 4.

1. Determine your claim.
2. Turn the claim into a question.
3. Answer the question in as many ways as possible.
4. Select the appropriate number and type of answers appropriate to your readership and length of paper.
5. Turn each of the answers into a full topic sentence.

At that point, put this information into a box outline. The claim is the thesis statement and goes at the bottom of the introduction. Each of the topic sentences goes at the beginning of a body box. When this is done, itemize support for each of the topic sentences using bulleted points.

So far, the outline should look like this:

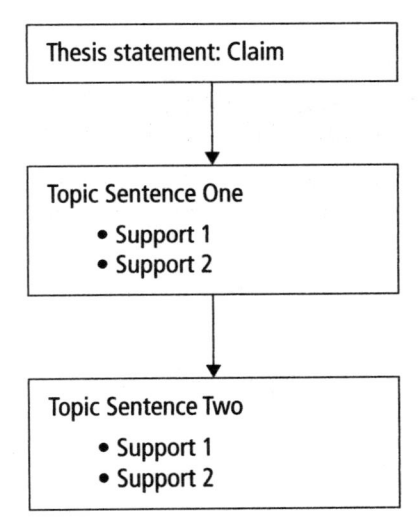

```
┌─────────────────────────┐
│ Thesis statement: Claim │
└───────────┬─────────────┘
            ▼
┌─────────────────────────┐
│ Topic Sentence One      │
│    • Support 1          │
│    • Support 2          │
└───────────┬─────────────┘
            ▼
┌─────────────────────────┐
│ Topic Sentence Two      │
│    • Support 1          │
│    • Support 2          │
└─────────────────────────┘
```

The number of body paragraphs for your case depends on the length and purpose of your paper. This example uses two, because the assignment asks the paper to be no more than six paragraphs long.

The next step is to outline the antithesis and the refutation:

1. Determine the antithesis. What claim would the other side make?
2. Identify the strongest reason that the other side would put in its case.
3. Refute that argument. Is it a fallacy? Does it lack evidence? Is it weaker than the arguments you make?

Add this information to the box outline, which should now look this:

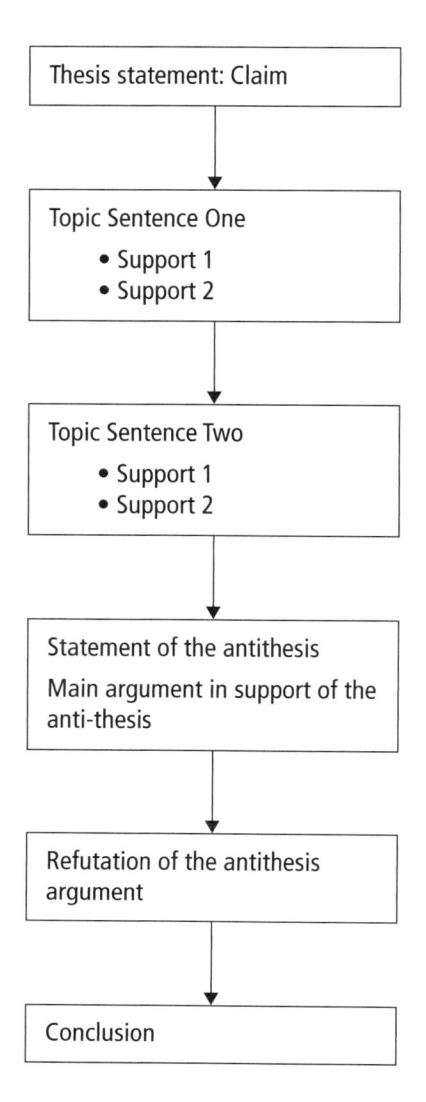

```
┌─────────────────────────────┐
│   Thesis statement: Claim   │
└─────────────────────────────┘
              │
              ▼
┌─────────────────────────────┐
│   Topic Sentence One        │
│     • Support 1             │
│     • Support 2             │
└─────────────────────────────┘
              │
              ▼
┌─────────────────────────────┐
│   Topic Sentence Two        │
│     • Support 1             │
│     • Support 2             │
└─────────────────────────────┘
              │
              ▼
┌─────────────────────────────┐
│  Statement of the antithesis│
│  Main argument in support of│
│  the anti-thesis            │
└─────────────────────────────┘
              │
              ▼
┌─────────────────────────────┐
│  Refutation of the antithesis│
│  argument                   │
└─────────────────────────────┘
              │
              ▼
┌─────────────────────────────┐
│   Conclusion                │
└─────────────────────────────┘
```

Fill in the introduction box, indicating your hook and background. Finally, indicate what kind of closing strategy you will use in the conclusion.

Outlining an Argument

TASK SIX

This task gives you the opportunity to develop an outline for an argument.
A professor in one of your courses has asked for a six-paragraph argument on a topic in your field.

Part One

Spend some time brainstorming topics for this paper with your group. Here are some guidelines:

1. Select a topic in your field that interests you and that has more than one point of view, approach, or theory.
2. Consider a topic discussed in your texts, or on the curriculum, which can be approached in various ways.
3. Everyone in the group can work on something different. It is all right, too, if more than one person is working on the same subject.

Here are some examples from different fields:

Solar power should be/should not be incorporated more fully into Canadian home building.

People should/should not avoid high-protein diets.

Canadian provinces should/should not have greater autonomy and a looser connection to Ottawa.

Police departments should/should not engage in collecting statistics connected to race, ethnicity, or religious affiliation.

People do/do not have the right to demolish or renovate historical buildings.

Free trade should/should not be extended to more countries.

Use the method discussed in this unit to complete a box outline. Use the blank form below.

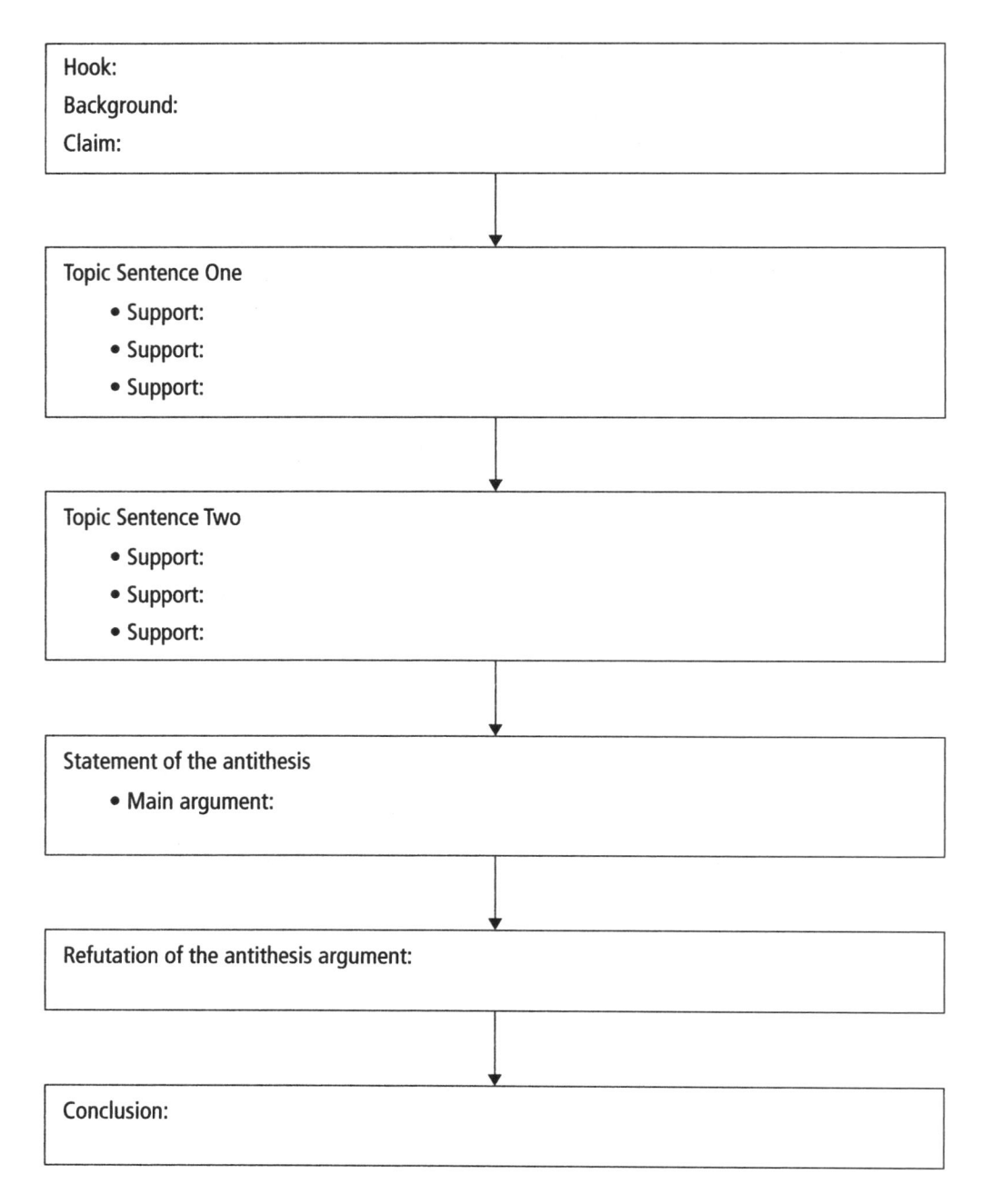

```
┌─────────────────────────────────┐
│ Hook:                           │
│ Background:                     │
│ Claim:                          │
└─────────────────────────────────┘
                │
                ▼
┌─────────────────────────────────┐
│ Topic Sentence One              │
│    • Support:                   │
│    • Support:                   │
│    • Support:                   │
└─────────────────────────────────┘
                │
                ▼
┌─────────────────────────────────┐
│ Topic Sentence Two              │
│    • Support:                   │
│    • Support:                   │
│    • Support:                   │
└─────────────────────────────────┘
                │
                ▼
┌─────────────────────────────────┐
│ Statement of the antithesis     │
│    • Main argument:             │
└─────────────────────────────────┘
                │
                ▼
┌─────────────────────────────────┐
│ Refutation of the antithesis argument: │
└─────────────────────────────────┘
                │
                ▼
┌─────────────────────────────────┐
│ Conclusion:                     │
└─────────────────────────────────┘
```

Part Two

Exchange your box outline with each person in your group. Read through each of the box outlines that they give you. Write a brief assessment for each one using the following guidelines:

- Does the outline present a clear claim?
- Does each of the topic sentences serve the claim in the thesis sentence?
- Does each of the support points in the different boxes support the topic sentence to which it is connected? Is the support free from logical fallacies? Is it convincing?
- Has the writer clearly stated the antithesis?

- Has the writer presented the strongest reason possible for the antithesis?
- Has the writer effectively refuted the antithesis argument?
- How can the writer improve the outline?

Writing the Argument — TASK SEVEN

Part One
Use your outline to write a first draft of the argument.

Part Two
Exchange the rough draft of your individual essay with a group member. When you receive a paper, read through the body paragraphs and evaluate it for adequate support, unity, and coherence. In addition, determine whether the paper is convincing.

Circle any language mechanics errors that you see or suspect. Write your comments in the right-hand margin of the paper beside each of the sections. Use the following considerations as a guideline:

- Indicate any questions that you have about the case. Is there anything that you do not completely understand? Is any more explanation needed? Are there clear examples and supporting detail so that the reader can see what the writer means?
- Indicate if the antithesis is clearly and objectively presented. Has the writer presented a fair version of the other side of the issue? Has the writer selected a strong argument for the other side's point of view? Has the writer presented clear support for that argument?
- Indicate if the refutation is adequate. Does the writer convincingly show the problem with the antithesis argument?

Part Three
Exchange your paper with one other person in your group. When you get the next paper, evaluate it in the same way you evaluated the last one. This time, write your comments in the left-hand margin.

Part Four
Give the paper back to the writer. When you get your paper, look at the comments in the margin. Read your paper over again and make your own decisions as to how you will revise the draft.

Part Five
Write a final draft of the paper for submission taking into account the comments made to you, your observations of other people's work, and your own rereading of your paper.

In Summary

Take three minutes to write a summary of what you have learned participating in the tasks of Unit 10.

UNIT 11

Classification

Here's what you'll work on in this unit.

- Identifying the principles of a classification system
- Assessing classification articles
- Outlining a classification paper
- Writing a classification paper

Classification writing puts your subject into categories. If your field is building management, you might write about the different types of construction management systems. If your field is fitness training, you might write about the different types of exercise. If your field is nursing, your might write about different types of treatment or care for a particular kind of patient.

Putting together a classification system is like putting together a filing system. Different people can look at the same subject and come up with different systems. Each of those classification systems needs to follow a few basic principles.

Identifying the Principles of a Classification System

Take a look at the following classification system.

A Classification of Music

Classical
Jazz
Vocal
Baroque
Instrumental

This kind of classification system is not helpful, for a number of reasons:

1. *A classification system must use a single basis.* If the content is not equal, the classification system will not work. The classification of the music above starts off with musical styles, classical and jazz, but then suddenly switches the basis of classification to how the

music is produced—voice, and then later, instrumental. Either basis is fine, but the writer needs to be consistent by using only one. If the writer wants to use musical style, for example, the system has to continue by identifying other styles, for example rock.

2. *A classification system must use consistent levels.* Not only must the content be equal, but the levels need to be equal as well. Whereas classical is a separate style that is equal in level to jazz, baroque is a subgroup of classical and not equal to a main category at all. If the writer were classifying types of classical music, the writing could have groups like baroque and romantic. In the system above, however, the subgroup is mixed with a larger group, which makes for an inconsistent system.

3. *A classification must be complete.* If classification is a filing system, then the writer needs to provide a place for every example that could fit under the general title. The classification system above does not have folders in which to place specific show tunes or dance music titles, for example.

Hint

The basis you choose for classification will determine how many categories you need for a complete system. A classification system of cars based on where they are produced would require many more categories than one based on wheel-drive systems.

4. *A classification system must not overlap.* A classification is complete when every example that fits the general subject title can be filed. At the same time, however, the system needs to be organized so that the example is filed in only one place—that is, the system provides *mutually exclusive categories*. If the system permits you to put the same example in a number of different places, the system loses its value. Readers will have difficulty finding an example or understanding why, if there were many ways to file the example in the system, the writer chose one rather than another. Opera, for example, will fit in both the vocal and the instrumental category.

TASK ONE   Principles of Classification

20 minutes

This task asks you to assess a number of classification systems. Identify at least one problem in each of the following systems. Be ready to explain why the system does not work.

Person 2: Please facilitate this task. Be sure everyone has a chance to comment.

Person 3: Please keep track of the time for your group.

Person 1: Please record the group consensus in the table below.

Person 4: Please be ready to share your answers in the larger group.

A classification of camera lenses:
    Telephoto
    Closeup
    Expensive
    Fisheye
	Classification problem

A classification of major world religions:
    Islam
    Hinduism
    Catholicism
    Christianity
    Buddhism
	Classification problem

A classification of stage productions:
    Dramatic performances
    Performances with music
    Comedic performances
    Concerts
	Classification problem

A classification of wines:
    Canadian
    South African
    Italian
	Classification problem

Assessing Classification Articles

Textbooks use classification to help readers more readily grasp material. Apply the principles of classification to the material you read as well as to the material you write.

TASK TWO Assessment of Classification Articles

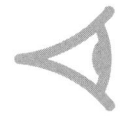

Part One: 20 minutes

Part One of this task asks you to assess two classification articles from a textbook for students in community service. Identify the basis of classification. Assess the articles in terms of the principles identified in Task One.

Person 3: Please facilitate this task. Be sure everyone has a chance to comment.
Person 2: Please keep track of the time for your group.
Person 1: Please record the group consensus in the table below.
Person 4: Please read the following articles to your group.

The types of help provided in the social welfare field can be classified as either formal or informal. **Informal help** is provided by volunteer or "natural" helpers. This type of help includes unpaid care and support given through structured social agencies, as well as unstructured help given by family, friends, neighbours, or co-workers. **Formal help** can be divided into professional and self-help:

- **Professional help** is given by paid individuals, who bring a recognized knowledge base, formal training, and relevant experience to their practice. Often, this type of help is guided by a Code of Ethics that is specific to the worker's profession. Professional helpers include social workers, social service workers, psychiatrists, and psychologists.
- **Self-help** refers to mutual aid provided through formally organized yet non-professional groups. Self-help groups are run by the members rather than professionals. Even so, they are regarded as formal collectives because they usually have a set procedure for conducting meetings, and because meetings are often coordinated by an organization. Meetings for Overeaters' Anonymous, for example, are coordinated by intergroups, regional offices, and a World Service Office (Pape, 1990).

Source: From Social Welfare in Canadian Society, Third Edition by CHAPPELL. 2005. Reprinted with permission of Nelson, a division of Thomson Learning: www.thomsonrights.com. Fax 800-730-2215.

Items of Assessment	Comments
Equal in content	
Equal in level	
Complete	
Does not overlap	
Additional comments	

> In a democratic country like Canada, the policy-making process invites the participation of a wide range of groups from both government and non-governmental sectors. The various groups can be viewed as a policy community. This community comprises several concentric rings and overlapping systems. At the centre of the action are the government bodies that are ultimately responsible for enacting policy. The next ring includes major interest or pressure groups; government departments and opposition parties whose actions may greatly influence social policy decisions; and foreign bodies that influence Canada's economic policies and therefore affect social policy. In the outermost ring are the individuals and groups (such as the media) that carefully follow the policy process. Each system involved in the policy community constantly interacts with and influences the others. In Canada, no single entity dominates at all times the social policy-making process (Pross, 1995).
>
> From Social Welfare in Canadian Society, Third Edition by CHAPPELL. 2005. Reprinted with permission of Nelson, a division of Thomson Learning: www.thomsonrights.com. Fax 800-730-2215.

Items of Assessment	Comments
Equal in content	
Equal in level	
Complete	
Does not overlap	
Additional comments	

Part Two

Select an article or chapter from one of your textbooks. Outline the classification system it uses in the box on the following page. Identify the basis of classification. Assess the articles in terms of the principles identified in Task One, and submit the results.

Title of section:
Page numbers:
Textbook title:
Author:
Classification system:

Items of Assessment	Comments
Equal in content	
Equal in level	
Complete	
Does not overlap	
Additional comments	

Outlining a Classification Paper

A helpful way to outline a classification system is to indent each level. The table of contents in a textbook uses indention to make categories and subcategories clear. This kind of formatting makes it easier to verify that the system consistently follows the principles of classification.

Here is how such an outline might look on the subject of "research sources":

Research Sources

Introduction
    Secondary
    Print
    Electronic

Primary
> Surveys
> Site Observations
> Interviews
> Experiments

Conclusion

It is clear from this outline that there are two main categories of research material. Each of those has a number of subgroups. Depending on the purpose and length of the paper, each of the subgroups could be further divided as far as necessary. The introduction makes clear what the basis of classification is, and how detailed this classification system is going to be.

Outlining a Classification Article: Individual Essay — TASK THREE

Your professor has asked you to investigate the different types of professions in your field.

Part One
Use the boxes below to prepare an outline of the article.

Introduction
Hook
Background
Basis of classification
Thesis

Classification System

Conclusion

Restatement of thesis

Closing strategy

Part Two

Exchange your outline with each person in your group. Read through each of the outlines that your group members give you. Write a brief assessment for each one using the following guidelines.

- Does the outline present a clear introduction with background, hook, and thesis?
- Does the classification system use a consistent basis?
- Does the system avoid mixing main categories with subcategories?
- Does the system provide a place for every example?
- Does the system provide mutually exclusive categories, so that an example would fit only in one place?
- Does the outline indicate a concluding strategy?

Writing the Classification Paper

TASK FOUR

Part One
Use your outline to write a first draft of the classification paper.

Part Two
Exchange the rough draft of your individual essay with a group member. When you receive a paper, read through the body paragraphs and evaluate it for adequate support, unity and coherence. In addition, determine whether the paper is convincing.

Circle any language mechanics errors that you see or suspect. Write your comments in the right-hand margin of the paper beside each of the sections. Use the following considerations as a guideline:

- Is there anything that you do not completely understand?
- Is any more explanation needed?
- Are there clear examples and supporting detail so that the reader can see what the writer means?
- Does the classification system work?

Part Three
Exchange your paper with one other person in your group. When you get the next paper, evaluate it in the same way you evaluated the last one. This time, write your comments in the left-hand margin.

Part Four
Give the paper back to the writer. When you get your paper, look at the comments in the margins. Read your paper over again and make your own decisions as to how you will revise the draft.

Part Five
Write a final draft of the paper for submission taking into account the comments made to you, your observations of other people's work, and your own rereading of your paper.

In Summary

Take three minutes to write a summary of what you have learned participating in the tasks of Unit II.

UNIT 12

Cause/Effect

Here's what you'll work on in this unit.

- Differentiating between immediate and related causes and effects
- Determining probable causes and effects
- Outlining a cause/effect paper
- Writing an cause/effect paper

Some academic writing asks you to analyze an event in order to determine how it came about or what kind of impact it has. A cause/effect paper can work in one of three ways:

1. It can start with something that happens and treat it as an event or an effect. The essay then works backward to determine the reasons that produced that event or effect.
2. It can start with something that happens and treat it as a cause. In that case, the essay works forward to determine what future effects or events will occur.
3. It can do both. The paper looks at an event as both the result of causes and also as part of a chain of cause—producing future effects.

For example, a general education essay in modern history that focuses on the sinking of *Titanic* in 1912 might:

1. Examine the causes of the sinking
2. Look at the impact of the sinking
3. Present both the causes and the effects of the sinking

Differentiating Between Immediate and Related Causes and Effects

No matter which one of the cause/effect papers approaches the writer chooses, one task is to differentiate between immediate and related causes and effects.

Causes

The immediate cause of the sinking of *Titanic* was that it was hit by an iceberg. Related causes, however, include:

- A course in North Atlantic waters
- The speed of the ship in order to reach New York early
- The quality of the steel and rivets
- The design of the bulkheads
- Pride evident in the claim that *Titanic* was unsinkable

In some cases, related causes can be organized in a series from proximate to remote; that is, the proximate cause is the closest cause to the event which has behind it a string of causes. In other cases, several related causes work at the same time to contribute to the event.

Effects

The immediate effect of the sinking was a terrible loss of life. This resulted in an inquiry. Other events influenced by all this were changes to White Star ship designs, and the establishment of new safety regulations. As with causes, some of effects become causes of more distant effects. In other cases, several different effects occur as the result of the same cause.

Determining Probable Causes and Effects

In some academic writing, there is no doubt about the main cause or main effect of an event. In other writing situations, the situation is not so clear, and the writer argues for one interpretation over another. Was the design of *Titanic* more of a cause than faulty materials? Was human error the primary cause? Was the loss of life primarily the result of pride evidenced in the lack of lifeboats, or class discrimination as evidenced by blocking exit routes to third-class passengers until late in the sinking? Whether dealing with definite or probable causes or effects, using a diagram can help you organize the material in preparation for outlining your essay.

The following excerpt from a college Canadian history text is an article on the causes and projected effects of the free-trade agreement between Canada and the United States.

The Great Free-Trade Debate

The conclusion of a comprehensive trade agreement with the United States became the Mulroney government's most passionately debated initiative during its first mandate.

Canada has always sought wide access to foreign markets for its exports, while simultaneously using tariffs to reduce imports to protect Canadian jobs in industries unable to withstand competition from abroad. When multilateral trade negotiations discredited protective tariffs, Canada, like many other countries, erected a host of non-tariff barriers such as quotas in an effort to impede the entry of cheap imports of goods such as clothing and footwear. The downward slide of the Canadian dollar after 1976 helped less productive Canadians compete in foreign markets. It also meant that imports cost more.

> As trade increased with the United States, Canada insistently proclaimed its belief in diversification. Nevertheless, the numerous "Team Canada" trade missions to Asia, Europe, and Latin America, organized by Ottawa, failed to have any fundamental impact. Indeed by 1985, fully 80 percent of Canada's exports went to the United States, and 70 percent of its imports originated there.
>
> Prime Minister Brian Mulroney now argued in favour of even closer trade relations with the Americans. He asserted that a free-trade agreement with the United States would create jobs. Increased sales of goods in that market would also diminish Canada's burgeoning balance of payments deficit in relation to the flow of investment income, tourism, services, and interest payment to foreign lenders to finance the growing mountain of federal debt. Many sectors of the business community favoured free trade. Polls showed that, in the early stages of the debate, a solid majority of Canadians backed it, too. Consumers were generally convinced that free trade would bring lower prices.
>
> As the debate heated up, public support for free trade cooled. American protectionist measures weakened Canadian enthusiasm, though at the same time they seemed to make some form of agreement even more urgent. Labour unions, farmers, the churches, the federal New Democratic and Liberal parties, and several businesses warned that free trade would cost thousands of jobs. They argued that American companies might close their higher cost branch plants in Canada and serve the Canadian market from their more cost-efficient American Bases. Anti–free traders further warned that a deal could endanger Canada's more generous social programs. It even risked jeopardizing Canada's political sovereignty.
>
> **Source:** From Journeys: A History of Canada, First Edition by FRANCIS/SMITH/JONES. Reprinted with permission of Nelson, a division of Thomson Learning: www.thomsonrights.com. Fax 800-730-2215.

This article starts from an event, the trade agreement between Canada and the United States, and works both backward and forward. It works backward to look at how the agreement arose. It looks forward from both Brian Mulroney's and the anti–free traders' viewpoints to the possible effects.

Outlining a Cause/Effect Paper

Outlining a cause/effect paper begins with making a diagram. Place the event in the centre of the page. From there, draw arrows to the immediate causes and effects. You can continue to work as far back in the chain as necessary for your project. At the same time, indicate contributory causes and effects with additional arrows connected to the main event. This kind of diagram is useful for articles that you are writing as well as for ones that you are reading.

Here is one way to diagram the article on free trade:

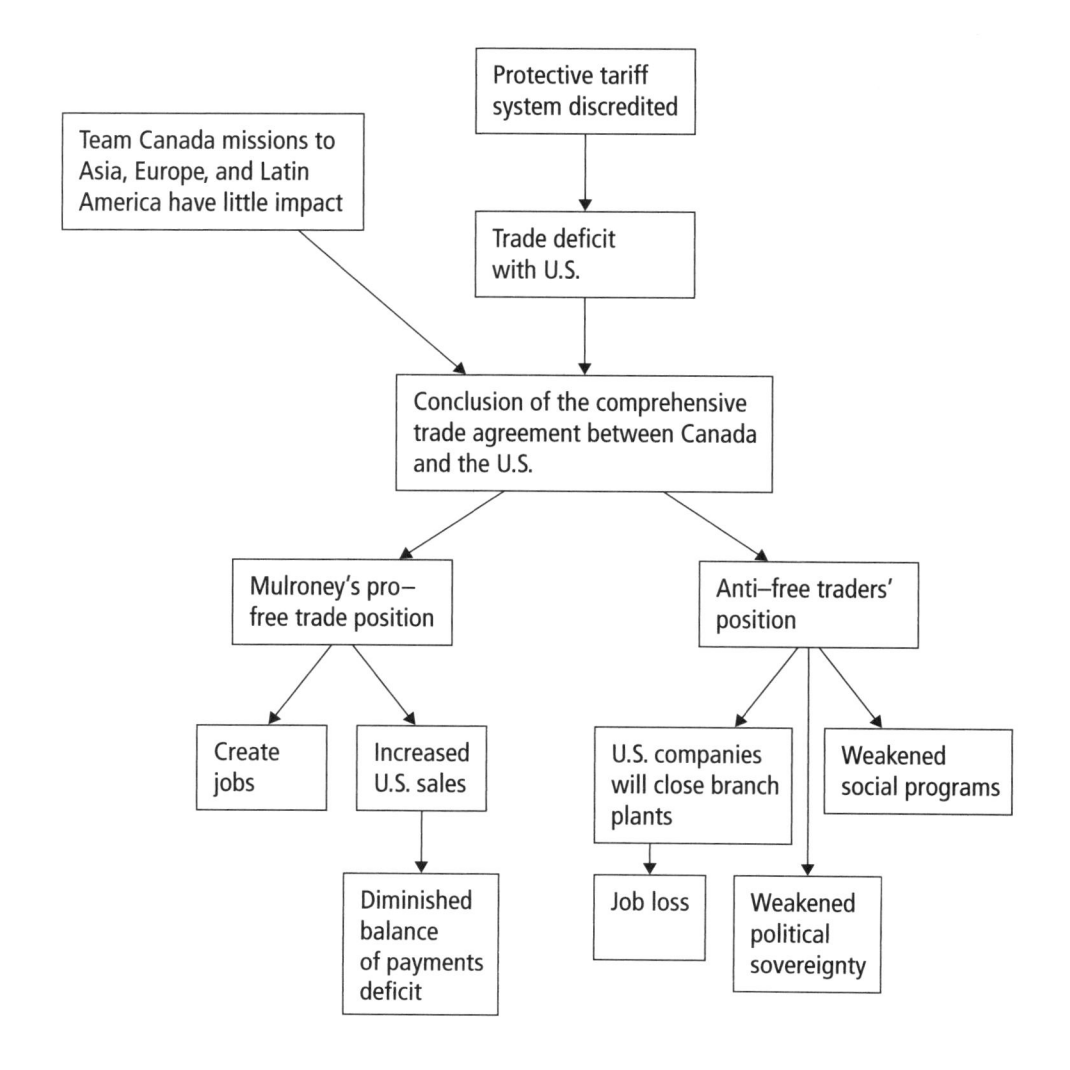

```
                          ┌─────────────────┐
                          │ Protective tariff│
                          │ system discredited│
                          └────────┬────────┘
┌──────────────────────┐           │
│ Team Canada missions to│          ▼
│ Asia, Europe, and Latin│    ┌──────────┐
│ America have little impact│  │ Trade deficit│
└──────────┬───────────┘      │ with U.S.  │
           │                  └─────┬─────┘
           │                        │
           ▼                        ▼
    ┌─────────────────────────────────────────┐
    │ Conclusion of the comprehensive         │
    │ trade agreement between Canada          │
    │ and the U.S.                            │
    └──────────┬──────────────────┬───────────┘
               │                  │
               ▼                  ▼
      ┌───────────────┐     ┌───────────────┐
      │ Mulroney's pro-│    │ Anti–free traders'│
      │ free trade position│ │ position        │
      └───┬───────┬───┘     └────┬───────┬──┘
          │       │              │       │
          ▼       ▼              ▼       ▼
     ┌──────┐ ┌────────┐   ┌──────────┐ ┌──────────┐
     │Create│ │Increased│  │U.S. companies│ │Weakened │
     │ jobs │ │U.S. sales│ │will close branch│ │social programs│
     └──────┘ └────┬───┘   │ plants    │ └──────────┘
                   │       └────┬─────┘
                   ▼            │
            ┌──────────┐        ▼         ┌──────────┐
            │Diminished│    ┌────────┐    │Weakened  │
            │balance   │    │Job loss│    │political │
            │of payments│   └────────┘    │sovereignty│
            │deficit   │                  └──────────┘
            └──────────┘
```

TASK ONE Diagramming a Cause and Effect Article

Select a section from one of your textbooks that traces causes, indicates effects, or shows both. Create a diagram of that article in the space below.

Person 4: Please facilitate this task. Be sure everyone has a chance to comment.

Person 3: Please record the group consensus in the table below.

Writing your own paper begins with a diagram. Once you have put the diagram together, make decisions on what strategies you will use in the introduction and conclusion.

Outlining a Cause and Effect Essay

TASK TWO

Your professor has asked you to write a cause/effect essay in your field. Select an event or development in your area of study mentioned in your texts or in class. Decide if you will trace the causes, determine the effects, or work with both.

Part One

Use the boxes below to prepare an outline of the article.

Introduction

Hook

Background

Thesis

Diagram

Conclusion

Restatement of thesis

Closing strategy

Part Two

Exchange your outline with each person in your group. Read through each of the outlines that your group members give you. Write a brief assessment for each one using the following guidelines:

- Does the outline present a clear introduction with background, hook, and thesis?
- Does the diagram show clear relationships between causes and effects?
- Does the diagram indicate immediate, proximate, and related causes and/or effects?
- Does the outline indicate a concluding strategy?

Writing the Cause and Effect Paper

TASK THREE

Part One
Use your outline to write a first draft of the cause and effect paper.

Part Two
Exchange the rough draft of your individual essay with a group member. When you receive a paper, read through the body paragraphs and evaluate it for adequate support, unity, and coherence. In addition, determine whether the paper is convincing.

Circle any language mechanics errors that you see or suspect. Write your comments in the right-hand margin of the paper beside each of the sections. Use the following considerations as a guideline:

- Is there anything that you do not completely understand?
- Is any more explanation needed?
- Are there clear examples and supporting detail so that the reader can see what the writer means?
- Are the causes and effects connected in such a way that you can see how they relate?
- Does the paper end with a clear concluding strategy?

Part Three
Exchange your paper with that of one other person in your group. When you get the next paper, evaluate it in the same way you evaluated the last one. This time, write your comments in the left-hand margin.

Part Four
Give the paper back to the writer. When you get your paper, look at the comments in the margins. Read your paper over again and make your own decisions about how you will revise the draft.

Part Five
Write a final draft of the paper for submission taking into account the comments made to you, your observations of other people's work, and your own rereading of your paper.

In Summary

Take three minutes to write a summary of what you have learned participating in the tasks of Unit 12.

UNIT 13

Research

Here's what you'll work on in this unit.

- Identifying the research question
- Conducting secondary research
- Evaluating secondary sources
- Evaluating Web pages
- Conducting primary research
- Providing in-text references
- Determining when to document
- Using quotations and paraphrases
- Assembling a bibliography
- Taking notes
- Outlining a research paper
- Writing a research paper

The personal essay presents a writer's experience and thoughts. A research essay focuses on uncovering facts and other writer's perspectives. That does not mean that the writer of the research paper disappears. In some cases, the purpose of the paper is to find an answer that requires putting different material from different sources side by side and then showing what together it all means. The writer's perspective comes through in the analysis and the conclusions. In other cases, the purpose of the paper is to speculate or propose based on solid, verifiable data in which the reader can have confidence.

Research writing is formal and employs conventions that make it easy for a reader to track down sources. Rather than a separate mode of essay writing like the informative essay in Part 2, the comparison and contrast essay in Unit 9, or the persuasive essay in Unit 10, research writing is employed in whatever mode requires research to meet the specific needs of that particular task.

Identifying the Research Question

Academic writing generally requires research. The professor may set out a specific research question for you. In that case, you conduct your investigation to fit the focused problem. That focus saves you a great deal of time as you are able to filter irrelevant material right at the start.

Other research tasks may be open-ended. You have a topic to research but no specific research problem connected with it. In that case, you will need to do general research first and then look for a particular focus that begins to emerge from the material you find.

You can also propose your own research topics from the questions you have during your course of study. Textbooks and class lectures cannot possibly deal with every aspect of every topic related to your field. Identify what questions might be asked about the topics that are not answered in your texts. Those questions may be about specific aspects or applications. Here are some examples.

If you were in a business program using Beckman's *Foundations of Marketing*, you would find discussion of the benefits of free trade in Chapter 20 in the section "The Case for Open Trade." One possible research question you might have after reading it is: What is the case made by those strongly opposed to free trade?

If you were in a law and security program using Sacco's *The Criminal Event*, you would find discussion of domestic violence in the section "Measuring Women's Victimization" in Chapter 3. One possible research question you might have after reading that section is: To what extent are men victims of domestic violence?

Some writing tasks will require more research than others depending on the situation and the readership. The more unfamiliar or contentious a topic, the more solid research required. If you are writing on a topic that presents information or ideas completely out of either your or the reader's experience, you need to carefully demonstrate that your material is accurate. If you are presenting a point of view on a subject with which the reader is likely to strongly disagree, you need to show that every step of the essay is firmly rooted in verifiable evidence and that the paper is using the data accurately.

In both cases, a professor is looking for solid sources that show an appropriate breadth of research for the scope of the paper. Some academic projects you work on will have guidelines on the number and type of sources expected. If not, ask what those expectations are.

TASK ONE Determining the Project

20 minutes

This task asks you to craft a number of research projects in your field. As a group, determine eight different research tasks connected with your studies. Identify topics that are touched upon in your texts or in your curriculum but that are not treated extensively.

Part One

Person 4: Please facilitate this task. Be sure everyone has a chance to comment.

Person 3: Please keep track of the time for your group.

Person 2: Please record the group consensus in the table below. Leave the fourth column blank for now.

Topic	Something Known	Possible Research Questions	

Part Two (10 minutes)

Sign up for one of the research topics to use throughout the rest of the tasks in this unit. Write your name in the blank cell beside the research questions.

Person 1: Please facilitate this part. Work out a group consensus that assigns one research question to each person in the group.

Conducting Secondary Research

Secondary research focuses on finding the research that has already been conducted and made available on a topic. The key to uncovering excellent material is to move from general to specialized sources.

Hint

Resisting the temptation to use the first material that comes to hand will help you avoid writing superficial research papers.

General Sources

Get a general overview of your subject by looking at reference works in your college library. These works cannot be checked out. They include sources like encyclopedias, handbooks, dictionaries of the field, and similar material. For example, here are some general sources that a student in architecture might consult.

Abramovitz, A.	Architect's essentials of contract negotiation
Butler, R.	Standard handbook of architectural engineering: a practical manual for architects, engineers, contractors, and related professions and occupations
Cole, E. (ed.)	The grammar of architecture
Harris, C. (ed.)	Dictionary of architecture and construction
Ricketts, S., Maitland, L. and Hucker, J.	A guide to Canadian architectural styles

Specialized Sources

Material in general reference material can help you get a handle on the subject and also provide useful search terms that you can use as you refine your research with specialized sources.

Print

The next step is to drill down into the topic using the online catalogue of your college library. Think of the *keywords* of your research project—words that name aspects of your topic. Enter those words as your search terms. This research will give you two results. First, you will discover what material your library has on its shelves that uses your keywords. Second, you will find suggestions for alternative search terms that you can use throughout the whole research process. An architectural student with questions about the application of solar power to residential designs would find whatever material the library has by entering the keywords "solar power." What may be even more valuable, however, is that the online catalogue might give the following alternative search terms:

- renewable energy resources
- photovoltaic power generation
- solar panels
- solar cells
- solar collectors
- solar air conditioning

That student would now have keywords to access even more specific information.

In many fields like technology, information on certain topics changes so quickly that even books with a recent publication date are already behind the latest developments. If your topic is concerned with these latest developments, the next step is to find out what periodicals have to offer. Special-interest magazines will have articles current to the month. Journals from professional organizations will present papers written by experts on highly specialized topics. The key to finding the article you need is using a *periodical index*—a record of what articles have been published in a number of magazines or journals. Locate what indexes are available to you in your library. Here are some examples:

- *The Wilson Applied Science and Technology Index* lists the articles in hundreds of scientific and technology publications.
- *PsycINFO*, from the American Psychological Association, covers thousands of publications regarding psychological and similar subjects.
- *Medline* provides millions of citations of articles in the health care field from the 1950s to the present.

Use the keyword search that you entered in your library's online catalogue. Try the alternative search terms that you discovered as well.

Electronic Sources

Electronic sources have the ability to provide the most current material. One of the difficulties, however, is ferreting through everything that is available and tracking down something right on target.

The Internet

The first place many people go when researching a topic is the Internet. It may be a place to start, but it is important to explore sources beyond the Web as well. The Internet is convenient and fast, but it also has its limitations:

- Most of the articles available in periodicals cannot be accessed through an Internet search engine.

- Material in private databases cannot be accessed through an Internet search engine.
- Much material on the Internet cannot be validated.
- Much material on the Internet comes from commercial sites.

These are serious limitations. Although a search often yields thousands of results, an enormous number of valuable articles written by specialists simply will not appear. The difference in the sources is the difference between a superficial and a superior research paper. And it is important for the credibility of your research writing that you check out your sources.

- If you cannot locate who generated the material on the Web, don't use it. If the information is just what you want, find it in another more reputable source.
- If you come across a page that doesn't provide the information you need, go up in the website's file structure in your browser's address box by deleting the various folder names after the slashes one by one, until you arrive at the *home page*. If you still cannot find clear information about who wrote the material and when it was generated, move on.
- Prefer sites that end in *.edu*, *.ca*, or *.org*. These are educational sites and organizations that carry more weight than a *.com* site.

Try This Out. Virginia Tech offers an excellent website devoted to evaluating Web page material. It gives specific techniques for assessing authority, coverage, objectivity, accuracy, and currency. It also provides sample Web pages from different fields for you to assess using those techniques. You will find it at:

http://www.lib.vt.edu/help/instruct/evaluate/evaluating.html

The University of California at Berkeley also provides a useful site with a set of questions to ask when you are thinking of using a website. It clearly lays out the implications of the answers to those questions as you put together your research paper. Go to:

http://www.lib.berkeley.edu/TeachingLib/Guides/Internet/Evaluate.html

Databases

Databases are like a private club or electronic research circle. You have to be a member to gain access. Different postsecondary institutions offer you access to different databases. Searching these databases is similar to searching the library catalogue. You can enter keyword searches and refine those searches according to specific parameters such as date. These databases make material available that cannot be readily obtained elsewhere.

Here are a few examples:

- *EBSCO* is a company based in Birmingham, Alabama. It offers access to over one hundred databases, including thousands of e-journals on a huge variety of subjects.
- *ProQuest* is run by Bell and Howell. It has negotiated agreements with more than 9,000 publishers to offer more than five billion pages of information.
- *LexisNexis* provides search options for thousands of news, business, legal, industrial, and other research publications. In addition, it enables researchers to search millions of companies worldwide.

These databases permit you to locate, download, and email full-text articles along with their bibliographic information.

Identifying Secondary Sources

TASK TWO

Locate at least 10 different sources for your research paper. Your professor has specified that only one source can come from the Web. Indicate your sources in the form below and submit. Download and save electronic sources. Photocopy the pages of print sources that you will use.

Title	Author	Date	Source

Reading with a Critical Eye

Developing critical reading skills is crucial for evaluating what you read. You can employ them to make judgments on the reliability and usefulness of your sources.

Purpose

Identify what the purpose of the text is right at the start. Most will fit into one of the following categories.

Type	What It Does
Informative	The author intends to convey facts and figures.
Persuasive	The author promotes a position and attempts to convince the reader.
Inspirational	The author aims at an emotional response that encourages the reader.
Entertaining	The author wants to amuse the reader.

Research writing for an academic paper will most often depend on writing in the first two categories. Being clear as to what the author wants to accomplish will help you step back from the reading to evaluate whether the writing succeeds.

Credibility

Determine the source and credentials of the article. Is the writer a recognized expert in the field? People without demonstrable credentials can, of course, write valuable insights, but a lack of credentials should alert the reader to be extremely careful. Statements will need to be checked out in other sources before you can use them in your own research writing. Does the material come from a reputable organization? Does the organization have a stake in the subject of the article? If you are writing about a new drug treatment, for example, you might find a scientific article written by someone with many credentials. If you also discover that the writer works for the company that makes the drug, you need to be on alert. The material may be accurate and just what you need, but you will need to verify if there is another side to the story, because the writer might be too invested to give you a balanced, objective view. Look for what the publication itself tells you about the writer. An Internet search on the writer, organization, or company connected with the article will also help you determine just how credible, and therefore reliable, it is.

Message

When you have identified an author's purpose, the next step in evaluating the text is to be clear on the main message of the whole text. The article may have many points, but determine what they are serving. Sometimes, that main point is not as obvious as a thesis statement at the end of an introduction. The message might come out from the whole tone of the article, which has a particular agenda.

Tone

How has that message been expressed? Is the message and tone in which it is conveyed reasonable, or does it sound extravagant? An excited, emotional extreme message may be valid but will require solid and ample evidence to justify that. An extreme tone which is sarcastic or angry is an alert to reader to verify that the writer has based those responses on critical reasoning with good support.

Support

Read the paper in two contrary ways.

First, read the paper as an advocate for the writer trying to understand with an open mind. See if you can supply your own examples for support from your own reading that validates the points in the article.

Second, read the article from a contrary point of view, even—indeed, especially—if you actually agree with the writer. Determine whether the writer has left out any explanation or support that someone who would disagree might need. Think about the evidence and other support provided. Would it convince those in disagreement with the message? Would they find it weak, lacking in detail, or too sparse?

Source of Support

Verify that the author has clearly identified the source of all the material used for support. A line that begins "Studies show ..." or "Experts agree ... ," but then does not provide either in-text documentation or references at the end to point the reader to those studies or experts, is problematic. The writer might be correct in the information, but if it cannot be traced down, it has no value for your research.

Evaluating Your Research Material — TASK THREE

Choose three of the sources you listed in Task Two. Examine each one critically by filling out the following form.

SOURCE 1

Title and author:	
Credentials	
Purpose	
Message	
Tone	
Quality of support	
Identifiable sources	

SOURCE 2

Title and author:	
Credentials	
Purpose	
Message	
Tone	
Quality of support	
Identifiable sources	

SOURCE 3

Title and author:	
Credentials	
Purpose	
Message	
Tone	
Quality of support	
Identifiable sources	

Conducting Primary Research

Primary research means getting material first-hand, as opposed to second-hand as you did with secondary research. That means finding material that is not available on a library shelf or in a database. You can conduct this kind of research in several ways. Interviewing, surveying, and experimenting are three main methods.

Interviewing. An effective primary research method is to interview experts. Conduct your secondary research first so that you understand the topic as much as possible. That will help you put together targeted questions not answered in your reading, and make the material you gain from the interview a valuable addition rather than just restatement of what is available in print. Ideally, interviews should be conducted face to face, to maximize personal contact. Short interviews, however, can also be conducted over the telephone or even through email.

Surveying. Some academic work requires collecting first-hand statistics. Surveying involves putting together a questionnaire and administering it to a target group. You may want to target consumers, professionals, students, or academics. The survey's credibility increases the larger the sample size. Here are some guidelines for conducting a survey:

- *Keep the survey form simple.* Your respondents may be unwilling to go through a survey that goes beyond a page.
- *Identify the purpose of the survey and how it will be used.* Cooperation depends on clarity that puts your respondents at ease.
- *Provide a series of answers that can be checked off.* This technique makes it easy to add up the results and produce numbers that can be changed into bar or pie charts.
- *Administer the survey in person and collect it immediately.* This strategy helps you get a higher response rate.

Experimenting. Another form of primary research is to run an experiment. You can personally try out a method, material, or tool over time and report on the results.

Providing In-text References

Research writing requires you to *document* your work as you go. Assume that your reader is skeptical of what you have to say, and is constantly challenging you about where you got that information. In-text references keep the record straight all the way through. The traditional system for *documentation* is putting numbered footnotes at the bottom of the page or endnotes at the end of the essay. It is now common in academic writing to use either the Modern Language Association (MLA) or the American Psychological Association (APA) format. Both of them use bracketed information instead of footnotes.

Hint

Check with your professor to determine what system is expected for any research writing that you do.

MLA In-text Citation. Place a round opening bracket before the period at the end of the sentence that has information you need to document. Put the author's last name, a space, and a page number, then close the brackets—also known as *parentheses*.

> Opening the roof of the Roger's Centre in Toronto takes only 20 minutes, while moving the lower stands so that the centre can be converted from baseball to football takes 10 to 12 hours (Grunner 25).

APA In-text Citation. Again, open the parentheses before the period at the end of the sentence that has the information you need to document. Put the author's last name, a comma, and the date inside the parentheses.

> Opening the roof of the Roger's Centre in Toronto takes only 20 minutes, while moving the lower stands so that the centre can be converted from baseball to football takes 10 to 12 hours (Grunner, 2006).

If your sentence actually quotes the original, add the page number after the date.

> Opening the roof of the Roger's Centre in Toronto takes only 20 minutes, while "it takes 10 to 12 hours to change from baseball to football by rolling the lower stands" (Grunner, 2006, p. 307).

Research writers often identify the source in the sentence. In this case only the date is needed in the parentheses.

> Grunner (2006) notes that "it takes 10 to 12 hours to change from baseball to football by rolling the lower stands."

Determining When to Document

Just as it is wrong to steal material property, it is also wrong to take intellectual property and pass it off as one's own. *Plagiarism*—lifting whole sections of someone else's writing and dropping it into an essay without giving credit by means of references—is a serious offence. Academic institutions have penalties for this ranging from failing grades to expulsion.

Some plagiarism is unintentional. Some writers are surprised to find themselves accused of it because they were not completely clear at the beginning on just when they are supposed to document. Here is how you know:

SITUATIONS REQUIRING IN-TEXT DOCUMENTATION

Reference to facts	If you come across a fact that is not generally known, you need to document it even if you are not using the original text word for word. If you write, for example, that there is enough stone in the Great Pyramid in Egypt to build a three-metre-high wall around France, you need to provide the information a reader might want in order to check out that assertion.
Reference to opinions found in another source	If you express an opinion that you did not arrive at independently, tell the reader where you first came across it.

Direct quotation	If you lift a phrase or more from a text, put quotation marks around the words and provide an in-text citation at the end.
Paraphrase	If you put a sentence or section of another work entirely into your own words, you still need to tell the reader where the information came from.

Using Quotations and Paraphrases

Use quotations sparingly. Resist the temptation to string a series of quotations together. Generally, unless a sentence is said so well that it just has to be kept, it is better to recast it entirely in your words as a *paraphrase*. Here are some guidelines for doing that using APA style.

Using Quotations

> China experienced a construction boom in the 1990s. "There were more major construction projects in Shanghai than in all of North America" (Bromley, 2006, p. 34).

> China experienced a construction boom in the 1990s. Bromley (2006) notes that "there were more major construction projects in Shanghai than in all of North America" (p. 34).

An Extended Quotation. Any quote of 40 words or more must be set off from your own text. Frame the quotation with space by indenting it five spaces, type single-spaced, and omit quotation marks. In this situation place the reference in parentheses after the period (to exclude it from the quotation).

> The fully retractable roof is made up of two sliding rectangular parabolic arches, a fixed quarter-dome at the north end of the stadium, and a rotating quarter-dome that will roll around the top of the stadium and nest with the other panels. The measurements, movement, and scope of this quarter-dome are staggering.
>
> > The roof area measures 339,343 sq. ft. and rises 279 ft. above field level. It can be fully opened in 20 minutes. In the full open position 91% of the seats will be exposed to the sky. The dome stadium is the world's first major sports stadium with a retractable roof. (Creighton, 1998, 67)

Paraphrasing

> **Not acceptable:** China experienced a construction boom in the 1990s. Shanghai had more major construction projects than in all of North America combined (Bromley, 1999, p. 34).

The above example uses a large chunk of the original word for word. "... more major construction projects than in all of North America ..." is taken directly from Bromley but without quotation marks to indicate that the phrasing has been lifted. Even though the writer makes a reference to Bromley's information, this constitutes an unacceptable paraphrase.

> **Acceptable:** China experienced a construction boom in the 1990s. Shanghai, in particular, boasted large construction contracts that exceeded the number of contracts in Canada and the United States combined (Bromley, 2006, p. 34).

Documentation of Works Without Authors

If you are citing a text produced by an organization, use the organization's name as the author. If you are citing an anonymous text like an article from a magazine or newspaper, use the title instead of an author's name.

> **Example:** It is clear that "the next generation of television watchers will use an entirely different technology which provides a qualitatively different experience" (Tricom, 2006).

> **Example:** "It once was necessary to learn DOS, then it was necessary to learn html, but as the technology becomes more user friendly, it is unnecessary for the average person to invest time in arcane computerese" ("Computer Dumb," 1999, p. 2).

Assembling a Bibliography

The last page of your research project provides a list of the sources you used in the paper. A reader who wants to track down an in-text citation can find the full listing there. Keep the following guidelines in mind:

- This list needs to be in alphabetical order according to the first letter of the listing.
- The first line of a citation begins at the left hand side of the page. Additional lines are indented. This is called a *hanging indent*.

TASK FOUR — Formatting a Bibliography

This task asks you to determine the proper format technique for a variety of sources and apply them to the material you are using for your research paper.

Here are some Web sources for this task:

APA source at McMaster University	http://library.lib.mcmaster.ca/guides/apa.htm
APA source at Long Island University	http://www.liu.edu/CWIS/CWP/library/workshop/citapa.htm
MLA source at McMaster University	http://library.mcmaster.ca/guides/mla.htm
MLA source at Long Island University	http://www.liu.edu/CWIS/CWP/library/workshop/citmla.htm

Part One

Use either the APA system or the MLA as determined by your professor.

Person 4: Investigate how to properly format a bibliographic entry for a book (1) by one author and (2) by several authors. Prepare a short, five-minute lesson with examples for your group.

Person 3: Investigate how to properly format a bibliographic entry for a website. Prepare a short, five-minute lesson with examples for your group

Person 2: Investigate how to properly format a bibliographic entry for (1) a print journal article and (2) a database journal article. Prepare a short, five-minute lesson with examples for your group

Person 1: Investigate how to properly format a bibliographic entry for (1) a brochure and (2) class handouts. Prepare a short, five-minute lesson with examples for your group

Part Two: 20 minutes

Each person beginning with person number one teaches the mini-lesson to the group. Sign and submit your notes and examples in the group portfolio.

Part Three

Use the techniques you have learned in Parts One and Two of this task to format a bibliography for your research project. Use the materials you collected in Task Two.

Sign and submit in your group portfolio.

Taking Notes

Take notes highlighting information, opinions, or possible quotations that you will use in your paper. You have a number of ways to do this.

Computer Log

1. Open a separate file for each source.
2. Enter the bibliographic information at the top.
3. If you are working from electronic documents, cut and paste the pieces you want.
4. Identify the content or purpose of each piece with a title.
5. Remember to put information such as section or page numbers at the end.
6. Collect similar content together.
7. Later, you can assemble information from various sources with the same content title.

Double-Entry Journal

1. Create a two-column table in your word processing program.
2. Put the bibliographic entry information at the top.
3. Enter the information from the original in the left-hand column.
4. Put any comments, observations, or connections that you want to make in the right-hand column.

Note Cards

1. Use separate slips of paper for each piece of information that you want to use.
2. Either write out the complete citation at the top of each sheet or mark it in such a way that you will always be clear on which source produced it.
3. Sort the note cards into piles according to content.

Outlining a Research Paper

After having collected and sorted your information, organize the groups in order. That order might suggest what sections you want to have in your paper. In that case, give a subtitle to each pile of information, and then write a topic sentence that expresses what that information shows. Remove all information from any section that does not directly relate to the controlling idea.

Alternatively, use one of the outlining systems described earlier including questioning, comparison and contrast, and argument. Take the information that you have collected and sorted, and determine where it best fits into your research essay. Finally, remove any information that is unnecessary for any particular section.

TASK FIVE   Outlining the Research Essay

Part One

Put together an outline for your research essay using the techniques discussed in this unit.

Part Two

Exchange your outline with each person in your group. Read through each of the outlines that they give you. Write a brief assessment for each one using the following guidelines:

- Does the outline present a clear introduction with background, hook, and thesis?
- Does each of the topic sentences serve the thesis sentence?
- Does each of the support points in the different boxes support the topic sentence to which it is connected? Is the support clear and convincing?

Writing the Research Paper

TASK SIX

Part One
Use your outline to write a first draft of the research paper.

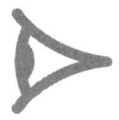

Part Two
Exchange the rough draft of your individual essay with a group member. When you receive a paper, read through the body paragraphs and evaluate it for adequate support, unity, and coherence. In addition, determine whether the paper is convincing.

Circle any language mechanics errors that you see or suspect. Write your comments in the right-hand column of the paper beside each of the sections. Use the following considerations as a guideline:

- *Indicate any questions that you have about the topic.* Is there anything that you do not completely understand? Is any more explanation needed? Are there clear examples and supporting detail so that the reader can see what the writer means?
- *Indicate if any of the support is not adequately documented.* Has the writer indicated where special information or quotations come from? Have all the paraphrases been properly documented?
- *Indicate any changes the writer needs to make to the bibliography.* Does the writer use the correct APA or MLA system throughout?

Part Three
Exchange your paper with one other person in your group. When you get the next paper, evaluate it in the same way you evaluated the last one. This time, write your comments in the left-hand column.

Part Four
Give the paper back to the writer. When you get your paper, look at the comments in the columns. Read your paper over again and make your own decisions about how you will revise the draft.

Part Five
Write a final draft of the paper for submission taking into account the comments made to you, your observations of other people's work, and your own rereading of your paper.

In Summary

Take three minutes to write a summary of what you have learned participating in the tasks of Unit 13.

Part 4

Editing your drafts involves identifying and fixing problems with language mechanics. Those problems can concern spelling, grammar, and punctuation. One of the reasons the writing process in this book involves your group is that it can be difficult for you to spot your own errors. You automatically tend to fill in the blanks as you read through your drafts by supplying a missing word, or seeing a misspelled word spelled correctly.

Part 4 of this book presents the most common issues in language mechanics that come up in college writing. As you become familiar with the material in this section, you can identify the problem on any rough draft that you read by referring to the subsection number. Circle the problem on the draft and write the reference in the column so that the writer can check it out later.

You may find that you have one or two issues that you need to get a handle on. Keep a record of your errors. Use this section to find out what your particular problems are and how to solve them. This section does not present a comprehensive grammar review, but rather treats problems that are likely to come up in a college classroom. Read the explanation of each problem, look at the solutions, and try your hand at the exercise that follows. You will find the answers to all the exercises at the back. If your answers match the solutions, then you know you've got it. If they do not, ask for some one-on-one help from your group members who do not have that same problem, at a language tutoring centre, or from your professor. Keep track of the kinds of mechanics errors that your reviewers identify for you. If they begin to drop out in later essays, you know that you have got those issues under control.

If you have a language mechanics issue not covered in this section, you can try one of these excellent resources. The website Guide to Grammar and Writing is sponsored by the Capital Community College Foundation. It is a user-friendly site with drop-down menus concerning the sentence, paragraph, and essay. It provides slide shows and exercises with instant feedback. It is available at http://grammar.ccc.commnet.edu/grammar/index.htm. Another helpful site is Grammar Bytes, at http://www.chompchomp.com/exercises.htm.

4.1 Sentence Fragment

Explanation

A fragment is simply an incomplete sentence. It doesn't work because it leaves necessary information out. Think of it this way. Imagine coming into a room and finding a piece of paper on a desk. You pick it up and read:

> After having finished lunch

What do you do with a message like that? What is supposed to happen after finishing lunch? Who is to have finished lunch anyway? Student writers often miss their own sentence fragments because they are filling in information from the sentences around the fragment, but in academic writing every sentence must be able to stand on its own.

Causes

Your sentence fragment can have one of three causes:

Cause 1. It is missing a subject.

> Walked into the room. (Who walked into the room?)

Cause 2. It is missing a verb.

> Janice in the classroom. (What was Janice doing in the classroom?)

Cause 3. It is missing a complete message.

> Before we begin today's assignment. (What do we have to do before beginning today's assignment?)

Solution

The solution is to provide what is missing. You have two ways to do that:

First Method. Insert the missing words.

Walked into the room.	The professor walked into the room.
Janice in the classroom.	Janice studied in the classroom.
Before we begin today's assignment.	Let's review before we begin today's assignment.

Hint

A verb with *to* in front of it is an infinitive. The subject still requires a verb.

Janice to study in the classroom.   Janice tried to study in the classroom.

Hint

Imperative verbs imply the subject *you* and so don't need an explicit subject.

Sit down. Turn on the computer. Open the file.

Second Method. Combine the fragment with another sentence.

Having finished the essay. She asked for some peer review.	Having finished the essay, she asked for some peer review.
She wanted to submit the essay right away. But her reviewer said she needed to make some changes.	She wanted to submit the essay right away, but her reviewer said she needed to make some changes.

Try it on your own and see how you do.

Fragment Exercise

1. Underline the sentence fragment in each of the examples below.
2. Circle the cause.
3. Correct the fragment in the space provided.

Underline the Fragment	Circle the Cause	Correct the Fragment
1. Ran the marathon race. Training took the better part of a year.	Missing subject Missing verb Incomplete message	
2. She to relax in the garden. It seemed, though, that she just couldn't find the time.	Missing subject Missing verb Incomplete message	

Underline the Fragment	Circle the Cause	Correct the Fragment
3. I have many reasons for wanting to leave. The hot weather during last summer.	Missing subject Missing verb Incomplete message	
4. She drank a cup of coffee. While she worked out the problem.	Missing subject Missing verb Incomplete message	
5. I like this novel the best. The only one that had a strong plot line.	Missing subject Missing verb Incomplete message	
6. Doesn't make any sense. I have to take a closer look.	Missing subject Missing verb Incomplete message	
7. The course involves a lot of work. And the exams are difficult, too.	Missing subject Missing verb Incomplete message	

Underline the Fragment	Circle the Cause	Correct the Fragment
8. The college facilities have been updated. A new language lab, an expanded computer centre, and a redecorated student centre.	Missing subject Missing verb Incomplete message	
9. The textbook's difficult reading level. The visuals, however, are useful.	Missing subject Missing verb Incomplete message	
10. His peer reviewer went through the essay carefully. Identifying every sentence error and making several suggestions.	Missing subject Missing verb Incomplete message	

4.2 Run-on Sentence

Explanation

A run-on sentence goes on longer than it should. It doesn't stop at the end of a complete thought, but runs into another.

> She worked on her essay for her English class it seemed an easy task until she actually worked out the outline and saw how much research it really would take.

You would likely run into trouble trying to read that sentence out loud without taking a breath. It is not the length, however, that makes it a run-on sentence. Short sentences can be run-ons, too.

> I want to go she doesn't.

In both cases, two complete thoughts push into each other.

> She worked on her essay for her English class.

> It seemed an easy task until she actually worked on the outline and saw how much research it really would take.

I want to go.

She doesn't.

Causes

Your run-on sentence can have one of two causes:

1. Two complete sentences have been fused without punctuation.

    The writer spent two weeks researching electronic sources she did not check out the library holdings.

2. Two complete sentences have been joined by a comma.

    She worked through a rough and final draft, she submitted her work in the classroom folder before the deadline.

Solution

You can solve your run-on sentence in one of four ways.

First Method. Put a period after the first complete thought and begin the next sentence with a capital letter.

  The writer spent two weeks researching electronic sources. She did not check out the library holdings.

Second Method. Put a comma and a word like *but, and, so, yet, or, for,* or *nor* after the first sentence. These words are called *coordinating conjunctions* and indicate the kind of relationship the two sentences have with one another.

  The writer spent two weeks researching electronic sources, but she did not check out the library holdings.

Third Method. Rewrite the sentence completely to indicate how one sentence depends upon the other.

  Even though she did not check out the library holdings, the writer spent two weeks researching electronic sources.

Fourth Method. Use a semicolon to connect two closely related sentences.

  I want to go; she doesn't.

Try it on your own and see how you do.

Run-on Exercise

Correct each of the run-on sentences in two ways.

Run-on	Two Corrections
I had difficulty putting the essay together the group feedback was helpful.	
The meeting went on for hours, the afternoon appointments had to be rescheduled.	
The service was poor the food was overpriced.	
The report was beautifully written the PowerPoint presentation was well designed.	

Run-on	Two Corrections
Using an outline is a good way to prepare an essay it helps ensure a tight structure.	
She worked on the project day and night, however she missed the deadline.	
The environment is changing there is no doubt about that.	
A cause and effect essay can trace the reasons behind an event it also can predict the effects of an event.	

Run-on	Two Corrections
The textbook has several positive features the index is not one of them.	
A healthy diet is essential to managing medical problems heart disease and diabetes can be significantly improved if you choose the right foods.	

4.3 Pronoun Shifts

Explanation

A pronoun replaces a noun mentioned earlier on.

> John loves his guitar. He takes it everywhere.

The second sentence uses the pronoun *he* to replace *John* and *it* to replace *guitar*. A pronoun shift happens when the wrong pronoun is used.

> John loves his guitar. He takes them everywhere.

We often don't notice a pronoun shift because we automatically understand what was meant. In some cases, though, a pronoun shift can cause a great deal of confusion. The reader is no longer sure what the writer is referring to.

Causes

1. Modern sensitivity to gender issues means that writers often want to avoid gender-specific references. In the past, it was common to read sentences like:

   > Each student must submit his textbooks to the main office before he can receive his final grade.

The pronoun *he* was used to stand in for everyone. Some writers have tried to solve this problem in various ways:

> Each student must submit her or his textbooks to the main office before she or he can receive her or his final grade.

Such sentences are unwieldy. Many people have got into the habit of solving it this way:

> Each student must submit their textbooks to the main office before they receive their final grade.

It seems simpler, but the problem is that it doesn't make sense. *Each* is singular, but *their* is plural. You would not write, "Each student are here."

2. Some writers treat a group as several individuals instead of recognizing its function as one unit. They think of a rock band or an audience as many people, and so write:

   > The rock band played their concert last night.
   >
   > The audience roared their approval.

The band members did not play individual concerts, but rather one concert as a single group. The audience roared together with one voice. So in both cases, the writer has a pronoun shift from a single unit, band, or audience, to a plural pronoun, *their*.

3. Some writers get confused about what the subject of the sentence actually is. For example, in this sentence:

   > Neither of the women will give their secrets away.

The writer thinks that the subject is *women*, but it isn't. The real subject of this sentence to which the pronoun must refer is *neither* as in *neither one*. That means the subject is singular and does not match the plural pronoun "their."

Hint

Nothing in a phrase that begins with a preposition like *in*, *of*, or *among* can be a subject of a sentence. Strike out the phrase and see what is left. If you did that with the sentence "One of the children is here," you would strike out *of the children*, which would leave you with *one* as the subject.

4. Some writers forget to keep a consistent focus. They will start out writing about *you*, but then switch to *they* or some other focus.

   > New drivers must be careful not to get overconfident and forget what they have learned. All you have to do is let your guard down for a moment and you could have an accident. Such drivers then suffer from a bad insurance record that will plague them for a long time.

This paragraph starts off talking about a group, a *they*, but then suddenly switches to addressing the reader, a *you*, but then flips back again to *they* in the last sentence. It is not that one focus is necessarily better than the other; but the writing needs to be consistent.

Solutions
Here are two solutions for your pronoun shift:

First Method. Use the plural form of a noun when you want to avoid awkward gender expressions.

> Students must submit their textbooks to the main office before they receive their final grades.

Second Method. Trace the pronoun back to its noun and verify that the number and gender agree.

> The rock band played its concert last night.
>
> The audience roared its approval.

Third Method. Choose a clear focus at the beginning. Check each pronoun you use against that focus.

> New drivers must be careful not to get overconfident and forget what they have learned. All they have to do is let their guard down for a moment and they could have an accident. Such drivers then suffer from a bad insurance record that will plague them for a long time.
>
> As a new driver, you must be careful not to get overconfident and forget what you have learned. All you have to do is let your guard down for a moment and you could have an accident. You will then suffer from a bad insurance record that will plague you for a long time.

Try it on your own and see how you do.

Pronoun Shift Exercise
1. Underline the pronouns.
2. Correct each of the pronoun shifts.

The student committee made their decision on who should get the contract.	
Either Judith or Marilyn will present their credentials at the head office tomorrow.	
Every participant in the marathon must register his vital statistics before obtaining his number.	

An operator must not engage the machine before the safety guard is down so that you don't risk injury.	
A movie extra has a harder job than it looks. They have to stand around for hours and stick out many tedious retakes.	
Neither the professor nor his students were able to solve the puzzle.	
When someone wants to lose weight, they often make the mistake of choosing a crash diet.	
Anybody who thinks dieting is easy should have their head examined.	
When he fit the two computer pieces on the desk, it broke.	
The crew had to get their work done by closing time.	

4.4 Modifier Problems

Explanation
Modifiers are words or phrases that describe. Some describe nouns, as in "*red* house," and others describe verbs as in "run *quickly*." It is critical to clear writing to ensure that the reader understand just what the modifiers are meant to describe.

Causes
Your modifier problem can have one of four causes, as discussed below.

1. The writer does not place the modifier as close as possible to what it is describing risks transferring the description to another noun:

   There are many photographs of my beautiful children standing on my desk.

   There are "many" photographs and the children are "beautiful." These modifiers stand right beside what they describe. On the other hand, the modifying phrase at the end, *standing on my desk*, points to *children*, suggesting that the photographs are pictures of children standing on top of the desk. Common sense corrects this mistake for us so naturally that most people don't even notice it. If this same kind of mistake occurred in a highly technical sentence about some subject which the reader knew little, it would not be so clear.

2. English word order has a lot of flexibility. That flexibility opens the language to ambiguity, especially when a writer neglects to put limiting words directly in front of what they modify. Limiting words include *often*, *not*, *almost*, and *nearly*, among others.

   He almost ate all of the candy.

   This sentence would be correct if the writer meant that he came very close to deciding to eat the whole batch but in the end did not eat at all. The word *almost* modifies *ate*, meaning that it was the eating that was almost. On the other hand, if the writer really meant that he ate a great deal of the candy, leaving only a little, the sentence should be:

   He ate almost all of the candy.

   In this case, the *almost* is now referring to the batch of candy. The same is true with all limiting words. For example:

   In my family, all the children were not musical.

   This sentence suggests that there is no musicality at all in the family. It means something quite different if the word order is changed:

   In my family, not all the children were musical.

   Now it becomes clear that most of the children were musical, but a few were not. This radical difference comes about purely because of word order.

3. Putting a modifier right in the middle of two nouns or verbs points in two directions.

   The doctor said if my friend didn't take a vacation tomorrow he would die.

   The modifier is *tomorrow*, but does the placement mean that the vacation is tomorrow or that the death is tomorrow?

4. Dangling a modifier at the front of a sentence and failing to put the noun right after the comma misleads the reader.

> Typing furiously at the keyboard, the essay got done in record time.

The modifying phrase is *typing furiously at the keyboard*. It hangs at the beginning of the sentence and is followed not by whoever did the typing but by the word *essay*. But an essay did not do any typing at all.

Solutions

You can solve your modifier problems using these solutions:

First Method. Move the modifiers so that they are beside what they modify.

> There are many photographs standing on my desk of my beautiful children.

Second Method. Place limiting words directly in front of what they describe.

> He wants only one piece of cake.
>
> She is even willing to work on the weekends.

Third Method. Rewrite any sentence so that modifiers point only to one place.

> The doctor said that my friend would die if he didn't take a vacation beginning tomorrow.

Fourth Method. Identify any modifying phrases followed by a comma. Be sure that the next word is the subject of that modifying phrase.

> Typing furiously at the keyboard, I got the essay done in record time.

Try it on your own and see how you do.

Modifier Problem Exercise

1. Underline the modifiers.
2. Correct each of the sentences.

Sentence	Correction
Reaching for the salad, the wine glass tipped over.	
Judy looked for her boyfriend dressed in a blue evening gown.	

Sentence	Correction
Only I want to eat a hamburger.	
My girlfriend told me today she loves me.	
I gave a birthday cake to my wife laced with chocolate icing and sprinkles.	
Failing the exam again, the professor called him into her office.	
After working out a settlement, the contract was signed by both labour and management.	
The old man drove the car wearing a toupee.	
The woman I meet for lunch occasionally picks up the cheque.	
Only solar power is one alternative to traditional sources.	

4.5 Improper Comma Use

Explanation

The comma is often overused because many writers are not clear as to just when it is really needed. A good rule of thumb is to avoid using a comma unless you can state the reason it should be there. Chances are you will have fewer errors with commas by leaving them out than putting them in without a clear reason to do so.

Causes

1. Many people put in commas when the sentence starts to get long just to break it up. This kind of approach can easily lead not only to unnecessary punctuation but also to comma splices (see section 4.2 above).

   > The longest river in the world is the Nile, but there are other impressive rivers, including the Mississippi in the United States, and the Yangtze in China, in each case, these rivers have become an important part of the culture, and the mythology of those countries, that show the importance of waterways to the life of a nation.

2. Some writers use commas in the same way they would take a breath. They use them to indicate natural breaks in the writing.

   > It is hard to say, with any certainty, just why, or how, the Mayan civilization disappeared, seemingly overnight. Several theories have been advanced, but none of them, is really completely satisfactory, because there are too many unexplained aspects, to this intriguing part of history.

Solutions

The best way to solve unnecessary comma issues is to compare the writing situation to the ones outlined below. If they do not match, avoid using the comma.

Use a comma to link items one after another.

> I need to double-check comma splices, fragments, pronoun shifts, and misplaced modifier problems in my essay.

You will find differing advice about the comma before the *and* in this sentence. Some writing handbooks require it while others do not. Check the requirements of your professor for this one.

Hint

Do not put commas before or after the items. In this example, there is no comma before "comma splice" or after "misplaced modifier problems."

Use a comma between adjectives that individually describe a noun.

> He is an efficient, effective, and dedicated worker.

You can break up that sentence into three separate messages:

1. He is an efficient worker.
2. He is an effective worker.
3. He is a dedicated worker.

In a situation like that, put commas between the adjectives. On the other hand, do not put commas between adjectives if they work together as one unit.

Two tiny black ants crept over the breadcrumbs.

Two, *tiny*, and *black* work together as a single modifying comment.

Use a comma after an introductory phrase.

If they do not match, avoid using the comma.

After carefully sifting the evidence, the archaeologist can make some pretty shrewd guesses about what happened.

The main message in the first sentence is "Avoid using the comma." Everything before it sets the scene. The main message in the second sentence is "The archaeologist can make some pretty shrewd guesses about what happened." That message is rooted in the observation made in the introductory phrase that the archaeologist sifts evidence carefully.

Hint

Do not use a comma in an inverted sentence. The opening phrase in an inverted sentence is not an introductory element but actually the end of the sentence brought to the front.

On the top of my book shelf is an expensive first edition copy of *Treasure Island*.

Use a pair of commas to mark additional, unessential information.

My son, who is a pilot, is coming this Christmas.

My son who is a pilot is coming this Christmas.

In the first sentence, *who is a pilot* is additional information that is interesting but *not essential* to the message. The second sentence, however, does not have commas around that phrase, which means that it is *essential* information. In that case, the writer likely has more than one son and wants to indicate that it is the son who is a pilot, rather than the son who is a teacher, who is coming for Christmas.

Use a comma to emphasize a contrast with words like *not* or *unlike*.

Chinese medicine is gentle, unlike Western drugs, which can be very powerful.

Her musical preference is jazz, not rock.

Use commas in dates and addresses.

We will celebrate on December 20, 2008, in Europe.

He will change his address to 587 Constance Road, Mississauga, Ontario.

Use a comma when you include quotations in your writing.

Professor Traverian explained, "We have no conclusive evidence yet that permits us to even start making recommendations."

Use a comma when you join two complete thoughts with *and, but, so, for, yet, nor, or*.

I thought I had the essay word perfect, but discovered a number of errors when I edited it.

She hopes to win a scholarship to study music, and I plan to apply to the same school.

Hint

Do not put a comma after conjunctions. Notice that there is no comma after the *but* or the *and* in these examples.

Try it on your own and see how you do.

Comma Problem Exercise

1. Remove any unnecessary commas.
2. Add commas where necessary.

Sentence	Correction
I need, vegetables fruit and dairy products, for this menu.	
"The cost of the project is prohibitive" said a company representative.	

Sentence	Correction
At the end of the day, he wrote his final report.	
The world will never forget, June 6, 1944 and all the soldiers who gave their lives.	
The house, which was renovated, is the one for sale rather than the other one.	
Before writing a final draft of an essay it is a good idea to work through the rough draft, with some peer editors.	
The old, wooden, Chinese box contained, a hidden compartment.	
He wrote a thorough thoughtful and fascinating research paper.	
The textbook presents a practical not a theoretical approach to the subject.	
I would rather spend my summers travelling, than taking care, of a pool and garden.	

4.6 Article Problems

Explanation

English generally uses the articles *a*, *and*, and *the* before nouns. The problem for many writers is knowing the exceptions.

Causes

Your article problem can be prevented by using the following guidelines:

1. The articles *a* and *an* are not used with nouns that cannot be counted.

   A sugar is on the table. **should be** Sugar is on the table.

   An orange juice is in the refrigerator. **should be** Orange juice is in the refrigerator.

   It is possible to count cups of sugar or bottles of orange juice. Use the articles only in those cases.

2. The article *the* is not used for plural or uncountable nouns that stand for a general group.

   The swimming pools are a lot of trouble to keep. **should be** Swimming pools are a lot of trouble to keep.

   The bread is a staple food in Western culture. **should be** Bread is a staple food in Western culture.

   The article *the* means that a certain number of swimming pools are a lot of trouble, whereas the writer wants to convey that swimming pools in general are difficult.

3. The article *the* is not used with names of people or most places.

   The Toronto is in the Ontario in the Canada. **should be** Toronto is in Ontario in Canada.

   Proper names generally do not require the article, but there are exceptions.

   Countries that are a collection or unity:

   the United States, the Philippines

   Oceans and seas:

   the Atlantic, the Pacific

   Mountain groups:

   the Himalayas

Solutions

Method 1. Determine whether the sentence is dealing with something that can be counted or whether it needs something else to count it. Countable nouns go with the word *many*, whereas uncountable nouns go with the word *much*. Use *a* or *an* for countable nouns.

I enjoy drinking tea. (much tea)

I enjoy drinking a cup of tea. (many cups of tea)

Method 2. Determine whether the sentence is dealing with a specific known item or referring to a noun that was mentioned earlier. If so, use the article *the*.

I ordered a cup of tea. (The specific cup of tea is not known yet.)

The cup of tea is too hot. (The tea is now in front of you and is known.)

A little girl ran out into the street after her ball. A car almost hit the little girl. The car managed to pull over in time.

At first, the little girl is countable, but she is unknown, so the writer uses the article *a*. The car is also countable but unknown and likewise uses the article *a*. The second sentence is now referring to a girl identified earlier, so the article now becomes *the*. The third sentence refers to a particular car mentioned in the sentence before it, so the article also switches to *the*.

Try it on your own and see how you do.

Article Problem Exercise

1. Remove any unnecessary articles.
2. Add articles where necessary.

Sentence	Correction
A wheat and a rice are both grain crops.	
The British Columbia is the Canada's most western province.	
You can find the sugar by going to supermarket.	

Sentence	Correction
The computers have revolutionized the world.	
At night, full moon can provide a beautiful light.	
I bought a flower at the florist. I gave a flower to my mother.	
I reached for book beside the vase on night table.	
Some doctors warn against eating the beef because the red meat can be bad for your health.	
I plan to travel to the Thailand, Korea, and People's Republic of China.	

4.7 Faulty Parallel Structure

Explanation
Sentences that list two or more items need to present those items in the same format. In that way, the sentence is both easy to read and understand. Sentences that do not list items in the same format have faulty parallel structure.

> This course requires delivering a presentation, researching a topic not on the course outline, and a 1,500-word essay.

There are three items in this list: (1) delivering a presentation, (2) researching a topic not on the course outlines, and (3) a 1,500-word essay. The first items use the same format. *Delivering* matches *researching*; *a presentation* matches *a topic*. The third item is out of sync. It does not follow the pattern the writer chose to use at the beginning of the list.

Causes
Your faulty parallel structure problem may have one of three causes.

Cause 1. The sentence lists items of the same part of speech but then abandons it.

> The essay requires planning, editing, and then I must extensively rewrite it.

(*Planning* and *editing* are nouns. *I must extensively rewrite it* is a clause).

Cause 2. The sentence mixes phrases with clauses.

> The professor stood behind the desk, under the spotlight, and he was near the blackboard.

(The first item in the list is the prepositional phrase *behind the desk*. The second item, *under the spotlight*, is also a prepositional phrase. The third item, *he was near the blackboard*, is a clause.)

Cause 3. The sentence lists clauses but uses a different structure for each clause.

> She had written an extremely good paper, and the presentation was well designed.

(The first clause, *She had written an extremely good paper*, is active, but the second clause, *the presentation was well designed*, is passive.)

Solution
The solution to faulty parallelism is to take the first item in the list as a measure for all the items. One way to do that is to list the items in a column to see if everything matches.

Original List	Revised List
delivering a presentation	delivering a presentation
researching a topic not on the course outline	researching a topic not on the course outline
a 1,500-word essay	writing a 1,500-word essay

The course requires delivering a presentation, researching a topic not on the course outline, and writing a 1,500-word essay.

Original List	Revised List
revision	planning
editing	editing
I must extensively rewrite it	rewriting

This essay requires planning, editing, and rewriting.

Original List	Revised List
behind the desk	behind the desk
under the spotlight	under the spotlight
he was near the blackboard	near the blackboard

The professor stood behind the desk, under the spotlight, and near the blackboard.

Original List	Revised List
She had written an extremely good paper.	She had written an extremely good paper.
The presentation was well designed.	She had designed an excellent presentation.

She had written an extremely good paper and designed an excellent presentation.

Try it on your own and see how you do.

Faulty Parallel Structure Exercise

1. Underline items that are not parallel.
2. Correct the sentence in the space provided.

Sentence	Correction
Your summer job will require you to answer the phone, take orders, and dealing with customer complaints.	
The new student facility is modern, stylish, and the students find they can get a lot of use out of it.	
Improperly supervised exercise can be painful, tiring, and sometimes can even pose a danger.	
His new apartment is by the subway, close to the mall, and is situated near the harbour.	
She is the best dancer in the group and she can choreograph better than all the rest.	
The driving exam included asking me to parallel park, and highway driving.	
We saw a few movies, went to a couple of ballets, and then there were the concerts.	

Sentence	Correction
I got all my research together and the essay was written.	
My interests include playing football, reading science fiction, and computers.	

Answer Key

4.1 Sentence Fragment Exercise

1. Underline the sentence fragment in each of the examples below.
2. Circle the cause.
3. Correct the fragment in the space provided.

Underline the Fragment	Circle the Cause	Correct the Fragment
1. <u>Ran the marathon race.</u> Training took the better part of a year.	Missing subject	He ran the marathon race.
2. <u>She to relax in the garden.</u> It seemed, though, that she just couldn't find the time.	Missing verb	She wanted to relax in the garden.
3. I have many reasons for wanting to leave. <u>The hot weather during last summer.</u>	Incomplete message	The hot weather during last summer is chief among them.
4. She drank a cup of coffee. <u>While she worked out the problem.</u>	Incomplete message	She drank a cup of coffee while she worked out the problem.
5. I like this novel the best. <u>The only one that has a strong plot line.</u>	Incomplete message	The reason is that it is the only one that has a strong plot line.
6. <u>Doesn't make any sense.</u> I have to take a closer look.	Missing subject	This picture doesn't make any sense.
7. The course involves a lot of work. <u>And the exams are difficult, too.</u>	Incomplete message	The course involves a lot of work and the exams are difficult, too.
8. The college facilities have been updated. <u>A new language lab, an expanded computer centre, and a redecorated student lounge.</u>	Incomplete message	They include a new language lab, an expanded computer centre, and a redecorated student lounge.
9. <u>The textbook difficult reading level.</u> The visuals, however, are useful.	Missing verb	The textbook has a difficult reading level.
10. His peer reviewer went through the essay carefully. <u>Identifying every sentence error and making several suggestions.</u>	Incomplete message	His peer reviewer went through the essay carefully, identifying every sentence error and making several suggestions.

Answer Key 235

4.2 Run-on Sentences Exercise

Correct each of the run-on sentences in two ways.

Run-on	Two Corrections
I had difficulty putting the essay together the group feedback was helpful.	1. I had difficulty putting the essay together. The group feedback was helpful. 2. I had difficulty putting the essay together, but the group feedback was helpful.
The meeting went on for hours, the afternoon appointments had to be rescheduled.	1. Since the meeting went on for hours, the afternoon appointments had to be rescheduled. 2. The meeting went on for hours, so the afternoon appointments had to be rescheduled.
The service was poor the food was overpriced.	1. The service was poor, and the food was overpriced. 2. The service was poor; the food was overpriced.
The report was beautifully written the PowerPoint presentation was well designed.	1. The report was beautifully written, and the PowerPoint presentation was well designed. 2. The report was beautifully written; the PowerPoint presentation was well designed.
Using an outline is a good way to prepare an essay it helps ensure a tight structure.	1. Using an outline is a good way to prepare an essay. It helps ensure a tight structure. 2. Using an outline is a good way to prepare an essay, for it helps ensure a tight structure.
She worked on the project day and night, however she missed the deadline.	1. She worked on the project day and night; however, she missed the deadline. **Hint** "However" is not a coordinating conjunction and so cannot connect a sentence with a comma. It is a transition that requires a semicolon in front and a comma after. 2. She worked on the project day and night, but she missed the deadline.

Run-on	Two Corrections
The environment is changing there is no doubt about that.	1. The environment is changing. There is no doubt about that. 2. The environment is changing; there is no doubt about that.
A cause and effect essay can trace the reasons behind an event it also can predict the effects of an event.	1. A cause and effect essay can trace the reasons behind an event. It also can predict the effects of an event. 2. A cause and effect essay can both trace the reasons behind an event and predict its effects.
The textbook has several positive features the index is not one of them.	1. The textbook has several positive features; the index is not one of them. 2. The textbook has several positive features, but the index is not one of them.
A healthy diet is essential to managing medical problems heart disease and diabetes can be significantly improved if you choose the right foods.	1. A healthy diet is essential to managing medical problems like heart disease and diabetes that can be significantly improved if you choose the right foods. 2. A healthy diet is essential to managing medical problems. Heart disease and diabetes can be significantly improved if you choose the right foods.

4.3 Pronoun Shifts Exercise

1. Underline the pronouns.
2. Correct each of the pronoun shifts.

The student committee made their decision on who should get the contract.	The student committee made its decision on who should get the contract.
Either Judith or Marilyn will present their credentials at the head office tomorrow.	Either Judith or Marilyn will present her credentials at the head office tomorrow.
Every participant in the marathon must register his vital statistics before obtaining his number.	All participants in the marathon must register their vital statistics before obtaining their number.
An operator must not engage the machine before the safety guard is down so that you can avoid the risk of injury.	You must not engage the machine before the safety guard is down so that you can avoid the risk of injury.

The student committee made <u>their</u> decision on who should get the contract.	The student committee made its decision on who should get the contract.
A movie extra has a harder job than it looks. <u>They</u> have to stand around for hours and stick out many tedious retakes.	Movie extras have a harder job than it looks. They have to stand around for hours and stick out many tedious retakes.
Neither the professor nor <u>his</u> students were able to present <u>his</u> answer to the puzzle.	Neither the professor nor his students were able to present their answer to the puzzle. **Hint** When you see the *neither ... nor* pattern, look at the number and gender of the second noun to determine the right pronoun.
When someone wants to lose weight, <u>they</u> often make the mistake of choosing a crash diet.	When people want to lose weight, they often make the mistake of choosing a crash diet.
Anybody who thinks dieting is easy should have <u>their</u> head examined.	People who think dieting is easy should have their head examined.
When he fit the two computer pieces on the desk, <u>it</u> broke. **Hint** In this case, the change of pronoun makes the reader think the desk broke.	When he fit the two computer pieces on the desk, they broke.
The crew had to get <u>their</u> cleaning work done by closing time.	The crew had to get its cleaning work done by closing time.

4.4 Modifier Problems Exercise

1. Underline the modifiers.
2. Correct each of the sentences.

Sentence	Correction
<u>Reaching for the salad</u>, the wine glass tipped over.	Reaching for the salad, I tipped over the wine glass.
Judy looked for her boyfriend <u>dressed in a blue evening gown</u>.	Dressed in a blue evening gown, Judy looked for her boyfriend.
<u>Only</u> I want to eat a hamburger.	I only want to eat a hamburger.
My girlfriend told me <u>today</u> she loves me.	Today, my girlfriend told me she loves me.
I gave a birthday cake to my wife <u>laced with chocolate icing and sprinkles</u>.	I gave a birthday cake laced with chocolate icing and sprinkles to my wife.
<u>Failing the exam again</u>, the professor called him into her office.	Failing the exam again, he was called into the professor's office.
<u>After working out a settlement</u>, the contract was signed by both labour and management.	After working out a settlement, labour and management signed the contract.
The old man drove the car <u>wearing a black toupee</u>.	The old man wearing a black toupee drove the car.
The woman I meet for lunch <u>occasionally</u> picks up the cheque.	The woman I meet for lunch picks up the cheque occasionally.
<u>Only</u> solar power is one alternative to traditional sources.	Solar power is only one alternative to traditional sources.

4.5 Comma Problems Exercise

1. Remove any unnecessary commas.
2. Add commas where necessary.

Sentence	Correction
I need, vegetables fruit and dairy products, for this menu.	I need vegetables, fruit, and dairy products for this menu.
"The cost of the project is prohibitive" said a company representative.	"The cost of the project is prohibitive," said a company representative.
At the end of the day, he wrote his final report.	At the end of the day he wrote his final report.

Sentence	Correction
The world will never forget, June 6, 1944 and all the soldiers who gave their lives.	The world will never forget June 6, 1944, and all the soldiers who gave their lives.
The house, which was renovated, is the one for sale rather than the other one.	The house which was renovated is the one for sale rather than the other one.
Before writing a final draft of an essay it is a good idea to work through the rough draft, with some peer editors.	Before writing a final draft of an essay, it is a good idea to work through the rough draft with some peer editors.
The old, wooden, Chinese box contained, a hidden compartment.	The old wooden Chinese box contained a hidden compartment.
He wrote a thorough thoughtful and fascinating research paper.	He wrote a thorough, thoughtful, and fascinating research paper.
The textbook presents a practical not a theoretical approach to the subject.	The textbook presents a practical, not a theoretical, approach to the subject.
I would rather spend my summers travelling, than taking care, of a pool and garden.	I would rather spend my summers travelling than taking care of a pool and garden.

4.6 Article Problems Exercise

1. Remove any unnecessary articles.
2. Add articles where necessary.

Sentence	Correction
A wheat and a rice are both grain crops.	Wheat and rice are both grain crops.
The British Columbia is the Canada's most western province.	British Columbia is Canada's most western province.
You can find the sugar in supermarket.	You can find sugar in the supermarket.
The computers have revolutionized the world.	Computers have revolutionized the world.
At night, full moon can provide a beautiful light.	At night, a full moon can provide beautiful light.
I bought a flower at the florist. I gave a flower to my mother.	I bought a flower at the florist. I gave the flower to my mother.
I reached for book beside the vase on night table.	I reached for the book beside the vase on the night table.
Some doctors warn against eating the beef because the red meat can be bad for your health.	Some doctors warn against eating beef because red meat can be bad for your health.
I plan to travel to the Thailand, Korea, and People's Republic of China.	I plan to travel to Thailand, Korea, and the People's Republic of China.

4.7 Faulty Parallel Structure Exercise

1. Underline items that are not parallel.
2. Correct the sentence in the space provided.

Sentence	Correction
Your summer job will require you to answer the phone, take orders and <u>dealing with customer complaints</u>.	Your summer job will require you to answer the phone, take orders, and deal with customer complaints.
The new student facility is modern, stylish, and <u>the students find they can get a lot of use out of it</u>.	The new student facility is modern, stylish, and useful.
Improperly supervised exercise can be painful, tiring and <u>sometimes can even pose a danger</u>.	Improperly supervised exercise can be painful, tiring and dangerous.
His new apartment is by the subway, close to the mall and <u>is situated near the harbour</u>.	His new apartment is by the subway, close to the mall, and near the harbour.
She is the best dancer in the group and <u>she can choreograph better than all the rest</u>.	She is the best dancer and choreographer in the group.
The driving exam included asking me to parallel park, and <u>highway driving</u>.	The driving exam included parallel parking, and highway driving.
We saw a few movies, went to a couple of ballets, and <u>then there were the concerts</u>.	We saw a few movies, went to a couple of ballets, and listened to some concerts.
I got all my research together and <u>the essay was written</u>.	I got all my research together and wrote the essay.
My interests include playing football, reading science fiction <u>and computers</u>.	My interests include playing football, reading science fiction, and working on computers.

Closing Notes

This book began with specific strategies for reading and restating textbook material, and then continued with a focus on writing academic essays for different purposes. You reflected on your own work and on the work of your group members in each of these parts. Now that you have completed this book, look back on what you have done. To do that, work on the following tasks individually to reflect on your writing.

Assessing the Assignments — TASK ONE

A useful exercise at the end of a book like this one is to identify what you found easy and what you found more challenging. That will help identify your strengths and weaknesses. If you can clearly name your biggest challenge in academic reading and writing, you will be better able to meet and handle it. Which one of the tasks, reading or essay writing, was easier to manage? Which was most problematic?

1. Collect all the pieces of writing you have done in the various units of this book.
2. Read through them and fill out the following form.

Easiest reading or writing task:

The reason it was easy:

Most difficult reading or writing task:

The reason it was difficult:

Hint

Work on the tasks in the conclusion individually. You can, of course, consult your group members, but it is not necessary for you to do so or to show the work you do in this section to them. Take your time: look at your answers to questions throughout the book in addition to rereading or skimming through some of your essays before giving a response.

One of your first tasks in the introduction to this book was to develop a list of personal objectives from which you put together a goal statement. Go back to these objectives and goal statement now. Reflect on whether you have achieved them.

TASK TWO   Personal Objectives for This Book

Objectives attained:

Objectives partially attained:

Objectives not yet attained:
What needs to be done:

GOAL STATEMENT

❑ Fully achieved

❑ Mostly achieved

❑ Partially achieved

❑ Not achieved

Preparing a Reflection on Your Writing — TASK THREE

Use the work in Tasks One and Two to write a final paper addressed to your professor that analyzes the writing you have done in this course. Use specific examples from your own papers, suggest different ways you might have handled your writing, comment on the feedback that you received, and identify what it is that you want to refine in your academic writing.

This book has depended on working with textbooks from your field of study and applying specific strategies for different purposes. Essential to all of the strategies was a process that involved the input of your classmates and your professor. We took this approach so that you could have the advantage of different perspectives in a method that encouraged you to move beyond your first work. When you are able to accept criticism, reflect honestly on your academic writing, and learn from the work of other academic writers, you will find that your own skills will sharpen and improve. In this way, you will be better equipped to meet the challenges of reading and writing in postsecondary studies.